Markets and Development

T0360959

Markets and Development presents a series of critical contributions focused on the *political* relationship between citizens, civil society, and neoliberal development policy's latest form. The dramatic increase of 'access to finance' investments, newly gender-sensitive approaches to building neoliberal labour markets, the universal promotion of public-private partnerships, and the 'development financing' of extractive industries, have all seen citizens, social movements, and NGOs variously engaged in, and against, neoliberalism like never before. The precise form that this engagement takes is conditioned by both the perceived and real opportunities, and the risks, of an agenda which seeks to intern 'emerging' and 'frontier markets' deep within a concretising world market, with transformative repercussions for both those involved and, notably, for state-society relations.

The contributors to this volume focus on essential aspects of the contemporary neoliberal development agenda and its relationship to and with citizens and civil society, tackling questions related to the roles that various actors within civil society in the underdeveloped world are playing under late capitalism, and how these roles relate to current efforts to establish and extend markets, and market society more broadly, in a neoliberal image. This book was originally published as a special issue of *Globalizations*.

Toby Carroll is Associate Professor and Associate Head in the Department of Asian and International Studies at City University of Hong Kong. His research concentrates on the political economy of development, with a particular geographical focus upon Asia. He has published in journals such as *Journal of Contemporary Asia, Asian Studies Review, Globalizations, Development and Change, Pacific Review* and *Antipode*. He is the author of *Delusions of Development: the World Bank and the post-Washington Consensus in Southeast Asia* (Palgrave) and co-editor (with Darryl Jarvis) of *The Politics of Marketising Asia* (Palgrave, 2014) and *Financialisation and Development in Asia* (Routledge, 2015).

Darryl S.L. Jarvis is Professor of Global Studies, Faculty of Liberal Arts and Social Sciences, at the Hong Kong Institute of Education. His research focuses on international political economy and comparative public policy in Asia. His recent publications include *Financialisation and Development*. Routledge (with Toby Carroll); *The Politics of Marketizing Asia*. Palgrave Macmillan (with Toby Carroll); *ASEAN Industries and the Challenge from China*. Palgrave Macmillan (with Anthony Welch); *Infrastructure Regulation: What Works, Why, and How do we Know? Lessons from Asia and Beyond*, World Scientific (with Ed Araral, M. Ramesh & Wu Xun).

Rethinking Globalizations

Edited by Barry K. Gills,
University of Helsinki, Finland and Kevin Gray, University of Sussex, UK.

This series is designed to break new ground in the literature on globalization and its academic and popular understanding. Rather than perpetuating or simply reacting to the economic understanding of globalization, this series seeks to capture the term and broaden its meaning to encompass a wide range of issues and disciplines and convey a sense of alternative possibilities for the future.

Markets and Development

Civil Society, Citizens and the Politics
of Neoliberalism

Edited by
Toby Carroll and Darryl S.L. Jarvis

Routledge
Taylor & Francis Group

LONDON AND NEW YORK

First published 2016 by Routledge

2 Park Square, Milton Park, Abingdon, Oxfordshire OX14 4RN
711 Third Avenue, New York, NY 10017

Routledge is an imprint of the Taylor & Francis Group, an informa business

First issued in paperback 2017

British Library Cataloguing in Publication Data
A catalogue record for this book is available from the British Library

ISBN 13: 978-1-138-95273-7 (hbk)
ISBN 13: 978-1-138-29970-2 (pbk)

Typeset in Times
by RefineCatch Limited, Bungay, Suffolk

Publisher's Note
The publisher accepts responsibility for any inconsistencies that may have
arisen during the conversion of this book from journal articles to book chapters,
namely the possible inclusion of journal terminology.

Disclaimer
Every effort has been made to contact copyright holders for their permission to
reprint material in this book. The publishers would be grateful to hear from any
copyright holder who is not here acknowledged and will undertake to rectify
any errors or omissions in future editions of this book.

Contents

Citation Information

The chapters in this book were originally published in *Globalizations*, volume 12, issue 3 (June 2015). When citing this material, please use the original page numbering for each article, as follows:

Preface

Markets and Development: Civil Society, Citizens, and the Politics of Neoliberalism
Toby Carroll and Darryl S.L. Jarvis
Globalizations, volume 12, issue 3 (June 2015) pp. 277–280

Chapter 1

The New Politics of Development: Citizens, Civil Society, and the Evolution of Neoliberal Development Policy
Toby Carroll and Darryl S.L. Jarvis
Globalizations, volume 12, issue 3 (June 2015) pp. 281–304

Chapter 2

Finance, Development, and Remittances: Extending the Scale of Accumulation in Migrant Labour Regimes
Hannah Cross
Globalizations, volume 12, issue 3 (June 2015) pp. 305–321

Chapter 3

Neoliberal Modes of Participation in Frontier Settings: Mining, Multilateral Meddling, and Politics in Laos
Pascale Hatcher
Globalizations, volume 12, issue 3 (June 2015) pp. 322–346

Chapter 4

Civil Society and the Gender Politics of Economic Competitiveness in Malaysia
Juanita Elias
Globalizations, volume 12, issue 3 (June 2015) pp. 347–364

Chapter 5

Explaining ASEAN's Engagement of Civil Society in Policy-making: Smoke and Mirrors
Kelly Gerard
Globalizations, volume 12, issue 3 (June 2015) pp. 365–382

Chapter 6

The European Bank for Reconstruction and Development's Gender Action Plan and the Gendered Political Economy of Post-Communist Transition
Stuart Shields and Sara Wallin
Globalizations, volume 12, issue 3 (June 2015) pp. 383–399

Chapter 7

Neoliberalising Cambodia: The Production of Capacity in Southeast Asia
Jonathon Louth
Globalizations, volume 12, issue 3 (June 2015) pp. 400–419

For any permission-related enquiries please visit:
http://www.tandfonline.com/page/help/permissions

Notes on Contributors

Toby Carroll is Associate Professor and Associate Head in the Department of Asian and International Studies at City University of Hong Kong. His research concentrates on the political economy of development, with a particular geographical focus upon Asia. He has published in journals such as *Journal of Contemporary Asia, Asian Studies Review, Globalizations, Development and Change, Pacific Review and Antipode*. He is the author of *Delusions of Development: the World Bank and the post-Washington Consensus in Southeast Asia* (Palgrave) and co-editor (with Darryl Jarvis) of *The Politics of Marketising Asia* (Palgrave, 2014) and *Financialisation and Development in Asia* (Routledge, 2015).

Hannah Cross is Lecturer in the Department of Politics and International Relations at the University of Westminster, London, UK, and an editor of the *Review of African Political Economy*. Her research interests include the political economy of migration and labour regimes, remittances, and financialisation, and more broadly, continuity and change in capitalism in Africa in relation to labour. Her publications include *Migrants, borders and global capitalism: West African labour mobility and EU borders* (Routledge, 2013). She is a member of the 'International Initiative for Promoting Political Economy', and co-ordinator of its Africa working group.

Juanita Elias is Associate Professor in International Political Economy, Department of Politics and International Relations at the University of Warwick, UK. Her work has appeared in journals such as *International Political Sociology, Economy and Society, Third World Quarterly*, and *The Pacific Review*. She is the author of *Fashioning inequality: The multinational firm and gendered employment in a globalising world* (2004), co-editor of *The global political economy of the household in Asia* (2013), and co-author of *International relations: The basics* (2007).

Kelly Gerard is Assistant Professor in International Relations in the School of Social Sciences at the University of Western Australia, Perth, Australia. Her research interests span political economy, social movements, and governance in Southeast Asia. Her work has been published in *The Pacific Review* and *Contemporary Politics*. In 2014, she published *ASEAN's engagement of civil society: Regulating dissent*. She is an Associate Researcher of the Asia Research Centre, Murdoch University, Perth, Australia.

Pascale Hatcher is Associate Professor at the College of International Relations, Ritsumeikan University, Kyoto, Japan. She has published in leading international journals such as *Journal* *of Contemporary Asia*, *Revue Tiers Monde*, and the *Canadian Journal of Development Studies*. Her most recent publication, *Regimes of risk: The World Bank and the transformation of mining in Asia*(2014), investigates the role of the World Bank Group in promoting new mining regimes for resource-rich country clients.

Darryl S.L. Jarvis is Professor of Global Studies, Faculty of Liberal Arts and Social Sciences, at the Hong Kong Institute of Education. His research focuses on international political economy and comparative public policy in Asia. His recent publications include *Financialisation and Development*. Routledge (with Toby Carroll); *The Politics of Marketizing Asia*. Palgrave Macmillan (with Toby Carroll); *ASEAN Industries and the Challenge from China*. Palgrave Macmillan (with Anthony Welch); *Infrastructure Regulation: What Works, Why, and How do we Know? Lessons from Asia and Beyond*, World Scientific (with Ed Araral, M. Ramesh & Wu Xun).

Jonathon Louth is a Visiting Research Fellow at the University of Adelaide, Australia, where he is also an Associate Fellow of the Indo-Pacific Research Governance Centre. His research focuses on intersections between international relations theory, international political economy,and the philosophy of (social) science. This informs his emerging research on Southeast Asia and the politics of wider economic integration across the region (with an emphasis on Cambodia).This has generated work on gender, everyday lives, neoliberal governance, financialisation, constructions of order, and the impact of economic thought upon social structures. He has an edited volume, *Edges of identity: The production of neoliberal subjectivities*, forthcoming in 2015.

Stuart Shields teaches International Political Economy at the University of Manchester, UK. His most recent work has appeared in *Millennium: Journal of International Studies*, *Socialism & Democracy*, *Journal of International Relations and Development*, and *Third World Quarterly*. He is the co-editor of *Critical international political economy: Dialogue, debate and dissensus* (2011), and his book *The international political economy of transition: Neoliberal hegemony and Eastern Central Europe's transformation* (2012) was short-listed for the 2013BISA IPEG annual book prize.

Sara Wallin is a doctoral candidate and a graduate teaching assistant in the Department of Politics at the University of Sheffield, UK. Her Ph.D. project explores gender equality politics and neoliberalismin global governance, with a particular focus on the case of the European Bank for Reconstruction and Development. During her Ph.D., she has also worked as a research assistant on high-profile projects on the new Sustainable Development Goals, gender and austerity, and British Parliament.

PREFACE

Markets and Development: Civil Society, Citizens, and the Politics of Neoliberalism

TOBY CARROLL & DARRYL S.L. JARVIS

Department of Asian and International Studies, City University of Hong Kong; Faculty of Liberal Arts and Social Sciences, Hong Kong Institute of Education

This special issue (SI) of *Globalisations* brings together six contributions focused on the *political* relationship between citizens, civil society, and neoliberal development policy. The dramatic increase of 'access to finance' investments, newly gender-sensitive approaches to building neoliberal labour markets, the universal promotion of public–private partnerships and the 'development financing' of extractive industries see citizens, social movements, and non-governmental organisations (NGOs) engaged in and against neoliberalism in ever more intensive configurations. The precise form of this engagement is conditioned by the perceived and real opportunities and risks of an agenda which seeks to incorporate 'emerging' and 'frontier markets' within a world market, with repercussions for state–society relations, citizens, and civil society.

The six contributions to this SI each focus on different aspects of the contemporary neoliberal development agenda and its relationship to citizens and civil society—the latter simply understood as the sphere between family and the state encompassing associations, social movements, and NGOs. In one form or another, an overarching research question being asked by each of the contributors is what roles various actors are playing within civil society under late capitalism in the underdeveloped world and how these roles relate to current efforts to establish and extend markets—and market society more broadly? Starting from this overarching question, each of the articles analyses specific contexts that explore the contested nature of civil society in relation to the constitution of neoliberalism and the world market more generally.

Taken together, the articles detail the complicated relationship between citizens, civil society, neoliberalism and late capitalism, addressing not only the often contradictory nature of capitalist expansion, marketisation, and the emplacement of market relations as a primary form of social organisation, but also the manifest ways in which citizens and civil society have been both the agential authority helping support this change in some instances and, on the other, the principal agents of resistance. Many of the contributions to this SI, for example, highlight the integration of NGOs into the neoliberal project through the routinising of neoliberal processes of 'participation', transparency and accountability, and the degree to which neoliberalism and market discipline have been 'normalised' as the legitimate means of forging the social reproduction of society.

Equally, as the contributions to this SI also highlight, what is increasingly apparent is the manner in which the managed forms of 'participation' contained in the post-Washington consensus (PWC) have been embraced by states and some regional institutions, often in highly circumscribed terms. This has brought into question the legitimacy of such participatory forms and raised questions about the de-politicisation of inherently socially conflicted processes and of an increasing democratic deficit. Indeed, pivotal questions regarding the nature and form of involvement of non-state actors in the market-building project, not to mention the broader social and political impact of such incorporation (including the emboldening of illiberal forms of politics), raise important and ongoing questions about the management of social conflict, the constitution of social relations and the distribution of economic wealth. It is this lens, in particular, through which many of the contributions in this SI analyse and understand the inherently vexed relationship between markets, neoliberalism, citizens, and civil society.

An important dimension of the analyses in many of the contributions to this SI rests in the resistance of civil society to neoliberalism and the impact that this and certain historical material processes have had on the development of neoliberalism. As the contribution by Carroll and Jarvis suggests, these explain to a significant extent how we arrived at the current juncture of neoliberal development policy and practice—and the possible trajectories going forward. As they argue, the vexed process of forging a world capitalist market in a neoliberal image, which explicitly rests on curtailing some risks (such as those for transnational capital) while extending risks for others (especially those for individuals and workers) (Cammack, 2012), has often been a contradictory one. The highly uneven outcomes of neoliberal 'reform' agendas, for example, both in terms of the completeness of implementation and the material results generated have repeatedly challenged neoliberal postulations about the efficiency of markets. Indeed, this reality has frequently prompted dramatic responses from citizens and civil society, and—somewhat dialectically—been central in forcing an evolution within neoliberal development policy, with much effort expended by international finance institutions and others in order to overcome impediments to policy implementation—often through processes such as the incorporation of specific civil society actors (NGOs, for example) and the state into the policy adjustment process.

Examples of these types of accommodations are numerous. Structural adjustment programmes in sub-Saharan Africa, Eastern Europe, Latin America or Asia (during the 1997–1998 'Asian' crisis), for example, often had immediate negative impact upon large segments of domestic populations, raising vocal responses from activists and some governments who subsequently softened neoliberal structural reform programmes or distorted their implementation (see e.g. Stiglitz, 2002, pp. 17–19; The Structural Adjustment Participatory Review International Network, 2004). More obviously, the response by neoliberalism itself in the form of the 'PWC' which emphasised depoliticised notions of 'participation', bottom-up development, 'social development', and 'ownership' also demonstrated the inherent adaptiveness of the neoliberal agenda in exploring alternative mechanisms of political and ideational transfer as part of a broader response focused on strategies of implementation in an effort to overcome the resistance of citizens and civil society. The World Bank, in particular, forged new models of co-option designed to smooth implementation processes by reaching out to forces within the state and civil society, attracting prominent figures from progressive global NGOs to join its ranks, often through formalised roles in community consultation, good governance agendas, and third-party funding for the monitoring of programme implementation and outcomes.

Despite the best efforts of PWC advocates to incorporate elements within civil society, however, developments in the global political economy (in particular, the global financial and economic crises of the late 2000s, the increasingly inequitable distribution of growth under late capitalism, and the persistence of various forces resistant to neoliberalism) have hardly made the job of legitimising neoliberalism and the building of neoliberal institutions a straight-forward task. Much of the blame for the onset of the most recent series of financial crises, for example, lays at the feet of neoliberal policies (particularly banking deregulation), with movements such as 'Occupy' drawing attention to the contradictions of neoliberal policies that, on the one hand, promoted self-regulation or 'light touch regulation' on the basis of economic efficiency and higher rates of return, but on the other witnessed massive state intervention in order to socialise the risks of the private banking sector. Equally, the application of the Troika's austerity measures in Europe has similarly brought negative attention to the social repercussions of neoliberal policy sets, in much the same way that hostility was directed towards the structural adjustment programmes of the 1980s.

In the underdeveloped/developing world, where local resistance to neoliberal policies has continued, a significant challenge to the PWC's appeal has stemmed from broader transformations in the global political economy. Here, two trends are worth noting. First, the rise of less-than-straightforward (in a neoliberal sense) development stories, such as China and Vietnam, has presented examples of developmental/growth success that do not fit the neoliberal mould, presenting demonstrable evidence of other roads to successful development. Second, new flows of foreign direct investment (FDI) derived from capital clamouring for returns in 'emerging and frontier markets' (coined in terms of 'investment-worthy' groupings of countries such as 'the BRICS' (Brazil, Russia, India, China and South Africa), 'the CIVETS' (Columbia, Indonesia, Vietnam, Egypt, Turkey and South Africa), and 'the Next 11') and the rise of a resource-hungry China have presented some underdeveloped countries with new options that diminish the leverage of 'borrowers of last resort'. If the World Bank and the IMF faced implementation hurdles in building idealised institutional bundles to regulate liberal markets before—in the form of 'vested interests' and vocal activists—this new politics of development has demanded yet further reconsideration of the way in which neoliberal development policy and practice sustains its relevance and influence.

Fortunately for adaptive neoliberals, in an environment where states have been incorporated into the global political economy—in part through Washington consensus processes of liberalising capital accounts and trade—there are strong incentives for them to 'establish enabling environments for capital' and engage in something of an end-of-development scramble for FDI, despite the implications this might have upon restive populations. Indeed, it is within this context that the very latest neoliberal development modalities, variously addressed by contributors to this SI, have taken root. Importantly, for states looking for policy options in the face of ongoing challenges within the disciplinary orbit of global capitalism, not to mention emboldened aspirations for representation on the part of some populations, many of these modalities have proven attractive—often with authoritarian states which have seemingly embraced PWC-esque efforts towards managing the emergent forms of politics.

Finally, a note should be made regarding the geographical focus of this SI. All but two of the articles focus on Asia. The collection originally started out as part of a broader project focused on understanding marketising processes in Asia exclusively. This geographical focus was deliberate. Despite being home to the often vaunted 'developmental state', Asia has increasingly been host to market-oriented agendas from well before the crisis of 1997–1998—when Washington consensus-style structural adjustment was famously applied to countries such as South Korea, Indonesia, and Thailand. For neoliberal development organisations, the region has thus been pivotal as both a site of high-growth 'emerging and frontier markets' and also a policy laboratory in which neoliberal structural adjustment, PWC, and contemporary market-led development agendas have been widely plied. Since the late 1990s, for example, the region has been a 'testing ground' for 'cutting edge' neoliberal development modalities such as the World Bank's Kecamatan Development Program in Indonesia and the KALAHI-CIDDS programme in the Philippines—programmes which drew upon particular readings of civil society and its relationship to good governance and liberal markets. Crucially, Asia has also been an important battleground over neoliberalism, with a well-documented history of struggle by both elite and popular interests (albeit often taking very different forms) against market reform and the structural adjustment reform programmes implemented in the wake of the 1997–1998 Asian financial crises. Indeed, even more importantly, neoliberalism's very legitimacy has also been tested in Asia by both the success of non-neoliberal and or heterodox/unorthodox approaches to development—especially by countries such as Vietnam and China, and historically by countries such as Japan, South Korea, and Taiwan. Asia, in this sense, has historically represented the epicentre of conflicting developmental visions and practices, albeit more recently it has been a region of converging policy measures focused on market-led development initiatives, marketisation, and competitiveness.

This said, the SI has broadened to include two excellent non-Asian-focused contributions, with all of the articles united in their analysis of the latest attempts to build market societies and market citizens in a neoliberal image—attempts which are being replicated around the globe. We hope that readers of *Globalisations* will find this collection of use in disentangling the complicated relationship between citizens, civil society and neoliberalism and encourage readers to seek out the three other SIs and two edited volumes that have been part of this broader research project (Carroll, 2012; Carroll & Jarvis, 2013, 2014a, 2014b, 2015).

Funding

This special issue arose out of a research project titled *New Approaches to Building Markets in Asia* which was launched at the Lee Kuan Yew School of Public Policy, National University of Singapore. The guest editors acknowledge the generous financial assistance of the Singapore Ministry of Education and the award of a Tier 1 Academic Research Fund grant. The grant supported travel, workshop meetings and provided the basis for the inception of several published outcomes (Carroll, 2012; Carroll & Jarvis, 2013, 2014a, 2014b, 2015).

References

Cammack, P. (2012). Risk, social protection and the world market. *Journal of Contemporary Asia, 42*(3), 359–377.

Carroll, T. (2012). Neo-liberal development, risk and marketising Asia. *Journal of Contemporary Asia, 42*(3). doi:10.1080/00472336.2014.907927

Carroll, T., & Jarvis, D. (2013). Market building in Asia: Standards setting, policy diffusion and the globalization of market norms. *Journal of Asian Public Policy, 6*(2), 117–128.

Carroll, T., & Jarvis, D. (2014a). Financialisation and development in Asia. *Asian Studies Review, 38*(4), 533–543.

Carroll, T., & Jarvis, D. (Eds.). (2014b). *The politics of marketising Asia*. Basingstoke: Palgrave.

Carroll, T., & Jarvis, D. (2015). *Finacialisation and development in Asia*. Abingdon: Routledge.

Stiglitz, J. (2002). *Globalisation and its discontents*. Camberwell: Penguin.

The Structural Adjustment Participatory Review International Network. (2004). *Structural adjustment: The SAPRI report*. London: Zed Books.

The New Politics of Development: Citizens, Civil Society, and the Evolution of Neoliberal Development Policy

TOBY CARROLL & DARRYL S.L. JARVIS

Department of Asian and International Studies, City University of Hong Kong, China, SAR; Faculty of Liberal Arts and Social Sciences, The Hong Kong Institute of Education, China, SAR

ABSTRACT   *In this article, we explore the evolution of neoliberal development theory and practice, its manifestations and impact on the political economy of the state, domestic classes, and the material conditions of populations in emerging economies. Specifically, the article focuses on the modes of resistance to the rollout of neoliberal development practice by citizens, civil society, and NGOs, and, in turn, the responses of international financial institutions such as the World Bank—a process that we argue has forced the reinvention and transformation of neoliberal development policy. Furthermore, we attempt to situate the evolution of neoliberal development policy and the changing modes of resistance to it within a theoretical framework that explains emergent class and material interests in the context of the increasing functionality of pro-market agendas to modes of accumulation that benefit discrete elite and class interests but which also generate substantial and ongoing contradictions.*

Introduction

The last 30 years have witnessed a radical transformation in the global political economy with the emergence and consolidation of a truly global set of markets. These include a global trade regime supporting the exchange of goods and services, rule-based regimes supporting foreign investment, investor protections and risk mitigation to capital, and a global financial regime supporting the expansion of international debt, capital, bond, currency and equities markets. Coupled with the emergence of trading, clearance, and settlement platforms facilitating the transmission of trans-border payments and capital transfers, the sense in which current global markets operate within twentieth-century conceptions of time, geography and space have been increasingly displaced, constituting what Cammack describes as the ongoing project of global capitalism (Cammack, 2012, 2014).

This transformation and the emergence of these markets have not occurred by accident. They have been aided, abetted and often coerced by the application of neoliberal policy sets promoted by international financial institutions (IFIs), sectional class and business interests, institutional actors charged with the management and regulation of international rule-based regimes (e.g. the World Trade Organization, the World Intellectual Property Organization, the Bank for International Settlements, the International Maritime Organization, the International Organization for Standardization, and the International Electrotechnical Commission, among others), and various governments whose trade, investment and financial interests rest in enlarging the spatial reach of markets and market relations (Busch, 2014; Scholte, 2005).

In this article, we explore these developments but in relation to their contested nature; specifically, the modes of resistance to the encroaching rollout of neoliberal development policy across various political, economic, and social domains, and to the methods of facilitation and instantiation designed to overcome domestic resistance to the construction of 'enabling environments' for markets. In doing so, the article seeks to contextualise the key dynamics and relationships that are operating in relation to the transformation of neoliberal development policy under late capitalism, with a specific focus on how these have impacted—and been impacted by—citizens and civil society.

The article proceeds in three parts. First, we map the changing contours of the political economy of emerging economies and their evolving relationship to global capitalism over the last several decades. More broadly, we attempt to situate the evolution of this relationship within a theoretical framework that explains emergent class and material interests, and the increasing utilisation of market-based policy prescriptions as part of a process of deepening reciprocity, where specific class interests are reinforced by the extension of market rationality, development policy increasingly defined exclusively in relation to the logic of extending market relations, and the logic of neoliberal development practices increasingly legitimated as *the* singular set of policy options available for sustaining development and material accumulation.

In the second section, we address the relationship between citizens, civil society and neoliberalism specifically, analysing critically the historical and political contexts in which these relationships have evolved and been mutually conditioned—processes which we argue explain the complicated and transformative nature of the neoliberal project. However, we characterise these processes not as *a*political, discrete historical periodisations but as a series of interconnected and fundamentally contested political confrontations (Peck, Theodore, & Brenner, 2012, p. 19). Echoing Antonio Gramsci and other materialist analyses of similar socio-political phenomena (see e.g. Gill, 1997; Soederberg, 2004, pp. 18–19), we point to this relationship involving patterns of coercion, co-option, and consent operating between states, supra-state organisations (such as IFIs) and civil society amid a 'crisis of hegemony' (what Gramsci dubbed an 'organic crisis') for neoliberal organisations and proponents of market agendas. As we argue, neoliberal development policy became increasingly focused on civil society because of its internal contradictions, generating a political imperative to co-opt, coerce, and internalise the agency of civil society and redirect it in ways that supports social reproduction and the legitimisation of neoliberalism.

To highlight our argument, we outline three discernible ideational and practical shifts in neoliberal development policy—(i) the Washington consensus; (ii) the post-Washington consensus

(PWC); and (iii) what we call 'deep marketisation'. As the most recent phase of development practice, deep marketisation is not simply a form of policy evolution representing a progressive trajectory of 'policy learning' and 'refinement', but a fundamental attempt to deepen the 'pathways of market-disciplinary regulatory restructuring' in emerging markets and, at the same time, a form of development practice necessitated by the process of neoliberalisation which is 'crisis-inducing' in terms of the economic outcomes it produces (market failures, regulatory capture, inequality, among others) (Peck et al., 2012, p. 17). Furthermore, we argue that these re-legitimising efforts reflect a functionalist imperative inherent in capitalism to reconfigure social relations in ways that support capital and market exchange relations, with neoliberal development policy at the forefront of engineering social and economic 'fixes' in emerging economies—albeit in ways that often contribute to, or expose deeper contradictions in capitalist exchange relations more generally.

The third and final section of the article reflects on these findings and their theoretical and practical implications for neoliberal development policy, civil society, and the politics of development.

The New Politics of Development: Neoliberalism, Capital, and Class

The consolidation of global capitalism around what Gill (2000) described as 'disciplinary neoliberalism' and Harvey (1990) as the rise of 'flexible accumulation'—with factions of capital able to adapt profitably to a newly borderless (for capital at least) world—has interred states into highly competitive dynamics, subjecting their populations to what is often labelled as 'market discipline' and, subsequently, considerable stress and turmoil. Indeed, the transformations in the global political economy over the last 30 years or so and the rise of truly global markets have effectively torn asunder the selectively permeable membranes that some states were able to establish to control flows of capital and goods, often with a view of maintaining control over their economies, cultivating industrial capacity, or pandering to the concerns of dominant domestic interest groups (Pradella, 2014).

While this process is far from complete, the depth to which such development practices now penetrate emerging economies, especially efforts focused on the ideational acculturation of populations to neoliberal reforms and market rationality, points to an increasingly dissonant set of agendas and interests. As Baker observes, the introduction of neoliberal reform agendas in the case of Latin America, for example, was typically a process of 'top down influences on public opinion', with elites having to 'sell' market reforms to populations whose experiences of the Washington Consensus reforms 'produced material consequences for consumers' welfare by visibly shifting the affordability, availability, and quality of many goods and services' (2009, pp. 14–15). The average Latin American, Baker notes, disapproves of privatisation, not least because 'citizens consume the economic effects of reforms, and they do so in ways that strongly influence their evaluation of market policies' (Baker, 2009, p. 15; see also Connell & Dados, 2014; Saad-Filho, 2012). These same observations apply in the case of consumers of market reforms in Asia, Africa, and elsewhere, where resistance, especially around affordability, access, and equity issues resonate loudly. It explains, as Cammack (2014) notes, the extensive forces being marshalled at the national, regional, and global levels in support of the extension of market relations and which permeate development practice at virtually all levels, operating most intensively across a spate of international and multilateral agencies.

While the politics of 'selling' and instantiating neoliberal development practice and market rationality highlight points of fissure, resistance and opposition, more fundamentally, as we

7

argue, it highlights the inherent tensions and contradictions within neoliberal development practice and the modes of accumulation it supports. Specifically, our broad thesis rests on the argument that under late capitalism two ongoing meta crises—a crisis of accumulation and the persistent, though as yet not terminal, crisis of neoliberalism's legitimacy—have propelled a symbiotic arrangement that sees capital demanding new pools of cheap labour, new markets, and resources in order to sustain profits, which in turn is propelling the furtherance of neoliberalism and market-based policy prescriptions amid an ever-expanding meta-ideological fiat. In essence, this sets in place contradictory processes, with the continuing rollout of regulatory, rule-based, juridical architectures designed to deepen market-based exchange relations undermining existing social relations, often for the worse. This includes the reduction or elimination of social protection systems (including those related to employment and income security), the disruption of traditional domestic exchange relations, and the exposure of local political economies to new levels of vulnerability and risk. The result, we argue, is a deepening of the risk environments for domestic populations who become progressively more exposed to the vagaries of international markets, deepening inequalities and ineffectual responses by state agencies. As we also argue, the contradictions of this mode of accumulation have meant that various re-legitimising efforts have had to be made within development practice—perhaps most prominently in the form of the post-Washington consensus' emphasis upon 'participatory development', 'ownership', consultation and 'social impact assessments', and by corporations operating in developing countries through the adoption of 'community investment programmes', 'social enterprise', 'impact investing', and other activities that might be characterised as 'corporate social responsibility' (CSR).

Importantly, this signifies what we categorise as the emergence of *a new politics of development*—one that is reordering relationships between capital, IFIs, developing states, and class interests within these states. In part, this plays out in the rise of developing state assertiveness in which underdeveloped states have gained increasing relational authority over capital flows into their territories. As market competition for access to developing states intensifies, especially in an era where investment in mature economies has witnessed stagnant growth and fewer opportunities for new growth drivers and revenue streams, the scramble into developing economies has created pools of inward-bound capital—recently boosted by negative real interest rates and quantitative easing of monetary policies in the global North following the global financial crisis which created plumes of 'hot' (often short term) money—mostly injected into developing country bourses and real estate markets. When coupled with the emergence of domestic pools of capital in many developing economies, notably in post-crisis Asia where the adoption of neoliberal monetary and fiscal policies after the 1997 financial crisis depressed domestic consumption and boosted national savings, the historical power relationships between global financial capital, IFIs and developing economies have altered inextricably.

However, the argument is *not* simply one of changing relational sites of power in terms of capital. Indeed, the 'rise of Asia' and other emerging market narratives often overstate the degree to which the spread of market relations and the emergence of global markets of various kinds have changed patterns of capital and wealth distribution. Despite the rapid development of Asian economies over the last 40 years or so, for example, the distribution of global wealth displays a continuing North–South dichotomy. As Shorrocks et al. observe, North America and Europe continue to account for some 68% of total global wealth, with the Asia Pacific (which includes the two most populous nations on earth—India and China, the world's third largest economy Japan, and the Asian tiger economies of Taiwan, Singapore, and South Korea—collectively accounting for only 23% of global wealth (2014, pp. 4,8).[1] Rather than a transformative shift in the world's centre of economic gravity towards the East our thesis resides in observations about the emergence of new circuits of capital which do not disrupt global patterns of wealth distribution so much as create new sources of financial intermediation that instantiate broadly similar distributional patterns (Economist, 2012). It is, as such, an argument situated in the role of financial intermediation and *deep marketisation* which transforms social relations in emerging economies, re-configures local—domestic class structures and realigns their material interests with that of a broader neoliberal set of values premised on deepening engagement with global markets.

The transformative elements of this new politics of development thus rest in the more mundane nexus between domestic classes and material interests; specifically, in the emergence of what might be termed a domestic *neo-entrepreneurial comprador class*—a class whose growth in absolute numbers has exploded over the last few decades with the onset (to varying degrees) of political and economic liberalisation. These two processes have been mutually reinforcing, albeit supported by dis-contiguous, unrelated events.[2]

First, autocratic regimes, whose historical legitimacy was forged off the back of coalitions of anti-colonial nationalist forces and domestic political elites, witnessed a spate of 'strong men' regimes monopolise economic opportunities through state-controlled enterprises, the 'gifting' of economic sectors or industry through informal networks of patronage (crony capitalism), or through formal instruments of the state that were often linked back to corrupt interests. Market development, entrepreneurship, and the emergence of a substantive neo-entrepreneurial comprador class were effectively hindered by the monopolies enjoyed by rentier interests associated with an ultra-elite situated around political 'strong men'. Political liberalisation over the last decade or so, in part a response to the financial crises that swept Asia in 1997 (and elsewhere) and which ravaged the political legitimacy of ruling elites, in part because of the breakdown of nationalist-elite coalitions, has witnessed a de-monopolisation of *absolute* state/elite/crony control over domestic economies, allowing the emergence of a neo-entrepreneurial comprador class who have exploited these opportunities and benefited from the ability to intermediate supply gaps in domestic economies—gaps which themselves reflected the practices of economic monopolisation as elite/sectional interests were protected via closed investment regimes, restrictions on trade mobility through import taxes on inward-bound goods and services, and other licensing requirements.

Second, and at the same time, economic liberalisation which commenced with the transition from import substitution industrialisation to export orientated industrialisation in the early 1970s as IFIs began to advocate the opening up of domestic investment and trade regimes, the dismantling of industry protectionism, capital account liberalisation and currency convertibility, and a reorientation in the role of the state away from direct ownership of the 'commanding heights' of the economy towards 'management' of the regulatory spaces facilitating private sector engagement, created a spate of economic opportunities that were exploited by a newly emerging neo-entrepreneurial comprador class (Lin & Rosenblatt, 2012, p. 187; Yergin & Stanislaw, 2002). The resulting flows of inward investment, the development of new domestic markets associated with deepening financial intermediation (especially in banking but also wealth management, consumer credit and housing loans, insurance, retirement planning, and the development of equity and debt markets), the commercialisation of state assets—notably in the resources sector—along with investment into low value-adding assembly and manufacturing, collectively explain the much touted 'transformation' of emerging economies over the last few decades and the rise of an increasingly affluent neo-entrepreneurial comprador class—a class who have been both the principal agents facilitating the intermediation of capital and its primary beneficiaries (see also Cahill, 2014, p. 16).

Importantly, however, the extent of this 'economic transformation' needs to be contextualised. Indeed, the structural configuration of economies within which neo-entrepreneurial comprador classes operate, their relationship to the state, patrimonial networks, and other class interests in large measure explains the emergent contradictions of the new politics of development and the increasing emphasis on re-legitimising efforts within development practice.[3] Despite their much touted 'economic transformation', for example, emerging economies remain predominantly agrarian and comprise of an employment structure where a substantial proportion of the population continue to be engaged in the cultivation of crops, raising livestock (fish, poultry, pigs, etc.), and forestry. Vietnam offers a good example of this contradictory structural configuration, where agriculture accounts for '22 percent of the GDP, 30 percent of exports and 60 percent of employment' (Bank, 2014b). Similarly, in Southeast Asia's largest economy, Indonesia, three out of five people are employed in the agriculture sector and, as the World Bank notes, the sector continues to provide 'income for the majority of Indonesian households' (Bank, 2014a). Similar observations could be made of the Philippines, Sri Lanka, Cambodia, Burma, Laos, India, indeed of China too—albeit with variance among these economies.

Similarly, in the context of wage labour the dominance of the informal sector in emerging economies suggests a muted form of 'economic transformation'. Informal labour, defined as 'small firms employing fewer than 10 workers, in which taxes and state regulations are either absent, relaxed or systematically evaded' continues to dominate the global South (Barnes, 2012, p. 146). Studies by Park and Cai, for example, suggest that upwards of 50% of China's urban labour is employed in the informal sector, while similar studies suggest that informal labour accounts for 50% of all work in Latin America and over 90% in India (Barnes, 2012, p. 146; Park & Cai, 2011).[4]

The point, of course, is that economic liberalisation and deepening marketisation have not occurred within a broader context of mass industrialisation involving the fracturing of traditional social relations, an absolute disruption to patrimonial networks, the displacement of agrarian production as an important means of accumulation for large segments of populations in the global South—or the transformation of kinship-familial relations as the primary means of social reproduction. Mass proletarianisation emblematic of industrialisation in the global North and which displaced traditional social relations is an incomplete process in the global South; itself a reflection of the uneven patterns of late capitalist development and the uneven penetration of low and medium value-adding manufacturing into emerging economies.[5]

The emergence of neo-entrepreneurial comprador classes thus need to be contextualised amid these realities. On the one hand, unfolding political and economic liberalisation has created enormous economic opportunities—albeit for specific classes. In practical terms, these have included corporatisation of state-owned assets/companies, privatisation (often through public listings or partial flotation) of state companies, new public management outsourcing/contracting practices, including public–private partnerships or concession arrangements (particularly in energy and resources, electricity, water, telecommunications, and transportation—roads, rail, ports, and airports), along with the deregulation of monopolies in the domestic banking and construction sectors, among others. On the other hand, deep marketisation has been mediated through existing patrimonial relations, political clientelism—typically operative within juridical and regulatory systems—and deeply stratified class and elite networks which have sought to protect and enhance their interests. The *intersection* between marketisation and patrimonialism, in other words, has been the principal resource and point of leverage for neo-entrepreneurial comprador classes, with sources of arbitrage realised through navigating these spaces either as intermediaries for foreign and domestic sources of capital or as entrepreneurial investors servicing demand gaps in various sectors of the economy (Budd, 2004). More importantly, they have been able to do so in conditions where deepening inequalities have been exacerbated by large labour surpluses and widespread informal labour practices—coupled with weak regulatory responses to the protection of labour—all of which have boosted returns on capital, suppressed wage costs, and supported massive rates of accumulation which elites and neo-entrepreneurial comprador classes have been able to capture disproportionately.

Rather than disrupting patrimonialism, deep marketisation has in fact extended opportunities for the emboldening of patrimonial politics. The enormous sources of inward-bound foreign capital as a result of declining opportunities in the global North coupled with the huge amount of domestic wealth that has been released from state ownership and control—and in large part captured by private sectional interests, has been a modern-day bonanza that has reinforced the material advantages and influence of patrimonial-class interests. Well-connected and adroitly positioned classes, for example, have seen their wealth expand at unprecedented rates with the fastest growth segment of 'high net worth individuals' (defined as individuals with minimum assets of USD$30 million) occurring precisely in those jurisdictions where patrimonial interests and marketisation have been coextensive (India, China, and Southeast Asia) (see e.g. Shorrocks et al., 2014). Even for orthodox organisations such as the Asian Development Bank (ADB), these contradictions have been difficult to ignore. As the ADB notes, while marketisation has been responsible for unlocking Asia's economic success it also potentially harbours the greatest risk to the region:

> A key message emerging from the analysis is that technological change, globalization, and market-oriented reform—the main drivers of Asia's rapid growth—are the basic forces behind rising inequality in the region. These forces tend to favor owners of capital over labor, highskilled over low-skilled workers, and urban and coastal areas over rural and inland regions.
>
> The impacts of these forces have been compounded by various forms of unequal access to opportunity—to earn income from labor and to build human capital—caused by institutional weaknesses, market distortions, and social exclusion. Working together, these have led to a falling share of labor income in total national income ... and growing spatial inequality. (ADB, 2012, p. 37)

While it is strange to find evidence for a class-based reading of the contradictions and tensions produced by neoliberal development practice in an institution which has been one of its chief architects, the ADB nonetheless highlights the unfolding realities endemic to emerging economies that have experienced rapid marketisation. First, the causality between market reforms and deepening social stratification. Second, the contribution of de-collectivisation (of national-state assets) to growth but which is disproportionately captured by the 'interests of capital'. Third, the role of marketisation in reinforcing unequal spatial contexts of accumulation—deepening rural and urban divides. And fourth, a declining proportion of national income being captured by wage labour.

The new politics of development thus sits between elite/class interests which are increasingly aligned with neoliberal development practices—including market reforms, liberalisation, the diminution of the state within the economy and a deepening engagement with international capital and global markets—and the consequences of these practices which expose growing disparities in wealth and income distribution, the capture of resource transfers by specific private, patrimonial-class interests, and the increasing risks and vulnerabilities that large segments of populations experience as a consequence of these practices.

It is this nexus, we argue, which exposes sites of contestation and resistance to neoliberal development practice and the interests that benefit from it—resistance mediated principally through citizens and civil society actors (including social protest groups, civic associations and a vast array of advocates working either through non-governmental organisations or other forms of mobilisation—awareness campaigns, advocacy, consumer action, and direct representation). As we argue in the next section, proponents of neoliberalism have increasingly focused on citizens and civil society not only as a reactive strategy to protect the legitimacy and hegemony of the neoliberal project, but also importantly to co-opt the resources of civil society as part of a larger series of social and political fixes to the enduring contradictions inherent in neoliberal development practice (see e.g. Mirowski, 2013, p. 63). As we further argue, the interstitial politics of co-option, coercion, and internalisation of citizens and civil society explains the evolution of neoliberal development practice over the last three decades, its current terminus, and the growing contradictions and tensions which suggest yet another crisis in its legitimacy.

Three Decades of Neoliberal Development Policy: Citizens and Civil Society

The evolution of neoliberal development policy has been conditioned to an important extent by its relationship with and response to civil society forces and these, in turn, to the series of ongoing contradictions in late capitalism and neoliberal development practice.[6] In this section, we analyse the processes of co-option, coercion, and internalisation of civil society, focusing in particular on the role of IFIs such as the World Bank Group and the European Bank for Reconstruction and Development (EBRD), as well as various bilateral agencies. These institutions have played central roles in promulgating neoliberal development policy and facilitating its adoption and implementation in various economies in the global South—in the process exposing populations to various reforms designed to build markets and reorder economies in terms of neoliberal capitalism.

As we have noted, however, this process and the politics of implementing neoliberal development agendas cannot be understood in static or singular terms. On the contrary, neoliberal development agendas represent a suite of policy approaches, many of which have been forced to change in response to pressures from civil society and attempts to re-legitimise the broader project represented in neoliberal market capitalism. Understanding the role of citizens and civil society thus not only helps to explain the evolution of neoliberal development policy but equally transformations within civil society and state-society relations through the course of neoliberalism's evolution.

The Washington Consensus

By the early 1970s, the post-war boom which had reaped huge increases in material wealth for the global North had exhausted itself. Growth and profit rates plunged, the exogenous impact of massive increases in energy prices brought about by the formation of the Organization of the Petroleum Exporting Countries, together with declining employment levels amid increasing inflation, witnessed the worst recession in over a generation. Centre-left governments fell to conservative administrations, most notably in the UK and the USA, ushering in the ascendency of neoliberal policy approaches to economic management and, indeed, an ideological revolution in approaches to market rationality and monetarist policy.

These developments were not inconsequential for development policy and the global South. The dominance of the USA within various IFIs, but particularly the World Bank and International Monetary Fund (IMF), also translated into similar ideological shifts in their institutional approaches to development practice. The Bank's 'basic needs' strategy, for example, which referred to a series of agendas centred upon satisfying essential human requirements including infrastructure provision and which had dominated the Bank's lending policies since the early 1970s, increasingly gave way to an entirely new agenda that reflected the pro-market ideology coming out of the global North (Prashad, 2012, p. 65). While initially championed by World Bank President, Robert McNamara (1968–1981), the relatively progressive basic needs agenda was rapidly surpassed by what came to be known as 'structural adjustment' and a fundamental realignment in Bank thinking and lending practices.

Structural adjustment referred to a raft of institutional and other policy reforms applied by the IMF and the World Bank, utilising the leverage of 'conditional lending' to countries suffering from persistent and unsustainable fiscal and debt positions. Rolled out throughout the 1980s in sub-Saharan Africa, Latin America, and Asia, structural adjustment lending was designed to administer shock treatment to economically sick states, balance government revenues with expenditure, return government budgets to surplus, and restructure external debt to ensure non-default. In reality, structural adjustment was predicated on a politics of austerity, the withdrawal or downsizing of government services to reduce expenditures, and the redirection of revenues to service massive external debts that had been accumulated during the 1970s as a result of the circulation of petrodollars and loose monetary policies that had flooded the international system with excess liquidity. Williamson (1990) would subsequently dub this mixture of austerity, fiscal conservatism, and market disciplining policies the 'Washington consensus'—reflecting emergent political and ideological approaches to economic management that from the late 1970s onwards gained wide appeal among orthodox economists, conservative political parties, and electorates in the global North who were reacting to economic stagflation and a global economic slowdown.

As Brenner and Theodore (2002b, p. 26) note, structural adjustment represented the ideological reassertion of the market through a process of what they referred to as 'roll back neoliberalism'. This was designed to get the state out of the way, reduce the 'crowding out' of markets which had been 'distorted' through government meddling and allow market forces 'to work'. In its simplest expression, this was an attack on the state and its involvement in the economy—the ideological repudiation of Keynesian interventionist state models, state capitalism, and social democratic government. Rather, unfettered by the weight of inefficient, bloated, self-serving state bureaucracies and 'big' government, the restoration of price signals throughout economies would restore efficient market clearing, rebalance supply and demand, and allow value and costs to be reflected in exchange relations. Markets, price signals, and rational free agents within markets would self-correct previous distortions, regenerate investment, enhance economic opportunity, and incentivise economic actors.

These ideological values fed directly into structural adjustment programmes and were reflected in conditional lending requirements stipulating the privatisation of state-controlled assets, trade and capital account liberalisation, and the introduction of austerity programmes designed to reduce state spending—particularly in the provision of social protection arrangements and other discretionary social programmes (London, 2014; Mosley, Harrigan, & Toye, 1991; Prashad, 2012, p. 6).

The application of structural adjustment through conditional lending throughout the 1980s, initially in Latin America and sub-Saharan Africa—the principal geographical regions where a series of states required large injections of capital to sustain their economies and banking systems—was far from smooth, however. Indeed, they faced formidable implementation challenges, widespread domestic opposition, and were often accompanied by deepening patterns of crisis, social displacement, and worsening circumstances for marginal populations—issues that were often exacerbated as a result of the fallout from large-scale infrastructure and resettlement projects (Davis, 2004, p. 4). For the Bank, in particular, these problems increasingly focused attention on the social hardships, injustices, and unintended outcomes of structural adjustment practices, with the Bank's policy approaches increasingly seen as harsh, uncompromising, and hurting the most vulnerable. Increasingly, many civil society actors came to see the Bank as the problem, with its practices contributing to economic displacement and favouring the interests of capital and elites at the expense of marginal communities.

However, rather than any rollback of the Washington Consensus, by the end of the 1980s the fall of the Berlin wall and the dissolution of the centrally planned states of the Eastern Bloc provided yet another theatre for the Bank to roll out structural adjustment programmes (see also Shields & Wallin, 2015). Indeed, amid an air of market triumphalism (if not fundamentalism) the Bank's President, Lewis Preston, went so far to claim that the demise of the former centrally planned economies had led to a convergence in development thinking that had 'replaced ideological conflict' (Berger & Beeson, 1998, p. 492). The way forward was singular: dissolve state ownership, build markets, unleash competition, and sit back and observe economic growth deliver material betterment.

The Bank's market triumphalism, however, was premature. Indeed, the experience of 'shock therapy' rolled out throughout the former Eastern Bloc countries, where market forces were instantly unleashed upon environments that previously had heavily curtailed or formally eliminated market systems, actually played an important role in re-igniting ideological debates over development, both within neoliberalism and outside it. In Russia, for example, between 1989 and 1997, rapid marketisation saw gross domestic product nearly halved, while inequality and poverty skyrocketed with the number of people living on US\$4 a day or less increasing from 2 to over 60 million (see e.g. Chang, Weiss, & Fine, 2012, p. 2; Stiglitz, 2001, pp. 128–129; Stiglitz, 2002). For critics and many civil society actors, the experiences of Eastern Europe and Russia were increasingly seen as evidence of the failure—if not the danger—of structural adjustment programmes and of the Bank.

By the end of the 1990s, civil society activism was targeting multilateral developmental organisations and the Washington consensus reforms more broadly. Indeed, they were reaching large and vocal proportions and being expressed through coordinated movements such as the '50 Years is Enough' campaign.[7] From Latin America, to Africa, Asia, and Eastern Europe, neoliberal development practice was mired in a serious crisis of legitimacy and the Bank and IMF, in particular, suffering under the weight of a growing number of critics (see e.g. Mallaby, 2004, pp. 58–64). As an important report on structural adjustment made clear:

> By the mid-1990s, before Seattle, Prague, Washington and other demonstrations in the North against the World Trade Organization (WTO), the World Bank and the IMF, the world had already witnessed almost twenty years of strikes, mobilizations and other forms of popular protest across the countries of the South in reaction to the economic policies of these institutions. (The Structural Adjustment Participatory Review International Network, 2004, pp. 3–4)

By the time of the arrival of the Bank's new President, James Wolfensohn (1995–2005), it was evident that not only was the Bank's reputation in need of renewal, but so too its relations with civil society. More obviously, the Bank's structural adjustment programmes and their outcomes prompted serious questions about the efficacy of such approaches which, even inside the Bank, were leading to calls for an alternative series of policy approaches. Within the academy too, criticism of the failure structural adjustment programmes and of problems associated with their implementation and management, generated debates about appropriate new policy designs, policy sequencing, and of managerial and institutional issues within recipient countries. These approaches crystallised around proponents of new institutional economics (NIE), a loose collection of institutionally focused economists who would provide the intellectual anchor to modified approaches to liberal market reform *and* serve as an important resource to re-legitimise market-led development (Mallaby, 2004, p. 87).

The Post-Washington Consensus

Under Wolfensohn's Presidency the Bank became the lead institution for redesigning neoliberal development policy with a key portion of this renovation centred on addressing implementation challenges and broader issues of legitimacy—issues that had been generated by structural adjustment policies, resistance to their implementation and outright anti-Bank protests. Importantly, the redesign of neoliberal development policy rested on forging a new relationship with civil society, indeed of state-society relations in emerging economies. To this end, the Bank pursued three strategies.

First, it sought to engage civil society, identifying specific NGOs who were, in turn, systemically internalised within the Bank's lending, community engagement, and management processes. The co-option and internalisation of certain civil society groups, often through formal contractual arrangements for service delivery, or through direct employment of specific civil society advocates, tacitly brought into the Bank important resources designed to overcome domestic resistance to reform programmes, the construction of enabling environments supporting market development, and the reform of state institutions and government programmes. Capacity-building initiatives, education and consultation programmes, along with the development of various off-set services designed to 'sell' reforms and make them more palatable by developing receptive domestic constituencies, became a key innovation of the PWC.

Second, fundamentalist free-market positions were set aside with the PWC recognising the role of institutions as important for markets. Drawing upon the work of orthodox liberal economists such as North (1990) and Stiglitz (2002, 1989) (the latter taking up the role of Chief Economist at the Bank under Wolfensohn), markets were now seen as requiring institutions (largely supplied by the state) to support market probity and the functional operation of exchange relations. While the state had previously been under assault as a site of rent-seeking and market distortion, under post-Washington consensus reforms it was welcomed back in—albeit in a very specific way designed to correct market reform failure and re-legitimise the broader orthodox development agenda. When the Asian financial crisis hit in 1997–1998, for example, the orthodox liberal diagnosis that markets had failed due to 'crony capitalism' and weak institutional oversight provided greater impetus to institutionally minded neoliberals such as Joseph Stiglitz, who re-emphasised institution building and institutional quality as central ingredients for effective market operation.

Indicative of this new push, the *World Development Reports*—the Bank's signature thematically oriented annual manual for delineating neoliberal best practice—systematically outlined a functionalist role for the state, where the state would guarantee macro-economic stability, rule of law, and property rights, for example, while also playing host to 'independent' regulatory bodies to oversee 'ideally' privatised utilities and the like (see e.g. World Bank, 1997, 2002a, 2002b, 2004). These institutions—'rules of the game' and market-regulating structures—were, in the language of NIE, necessary to reduce *transaction costs* and *information asymmetries*—jargon for elements that ostensibly made markets less efficient and or prone to failure, with the latter term coming to refer not only to the actual functioning of market systems but indeed their palatability and legitimacy. Indeed, this latter feature was an important political move on the part of the Bank, since it recognised past failures and the difficulty of 'selling' the benefits of liberal markets to populations who had witnessed economic gains accrue disproportionately to specific sectional interests while regulation had simply been set aside to 'let markets work'. In this respect, emphasising institutions as central accompaniments to markets was not simply a technical development—it also reflected the need to set market-led development on a more legitimate footing in the face of previous reform failures—failures that civil society had successfully highlighted through the mobilisation of large international coalitions.

Third, while the internalisation of civil society and specific NGOs into the Bank's reform efforts along with an emphasis on institutions would provide the central pillars of the PWC, its implementation depended ultimately upon the management of state-society relations—particularly in view of past failures, the capture of resources by specific class and elite interests, and the subsequent political fallout. To this end, the PWC would also place emphases on 'participation', 'partnership', and 'ownership', evoking language typically associated with progressive organisations and grassroots movements rather than multilateral institutions advancing *structural adjustment*. This rebranding was captured in Wolfensohn's signature 'Comprehensive Development Framework' and echoed throughout the World Bank and other mainstream development organisations. This was an explicit attempt to grapple with the political economy of reform by both engaging the state and key actors beyond it. Illustrative of this, 'Country Assistance Strategies' (CAS)—the Bank's key operational documents stating the organisation's assessment of a recipient country's position and the policy reform strategies—began to morph into 'Country Partnership Strategies'. Where previously CASs had been written at some distance from the government concerned, now 'best practice' stipulated that these documents were to be drafted not only in consultation with a given country's government but also in 'consultation' with civil society.

While critics were sceptical about the boundaries of participation in these processes—with accusations that these were pre-ordained agendas in search of endorsement, these processes were an important part of the Bank's effort to reach out to amenable NGOs and have them participate as strategic partners in the Bank's agenda (see e.g. Carroll, 2010, Chapter 6). Importantly too, in the face of intense competition for resources and donor constituencies, the Bank's effort to reach out to amenable NGOs was also accompanied by new resource streams in support of its programme of enhancing institutional quality and probity. NGOs could now secure resources as project and programme managers, implementers, monitors, assessors, and 'independent' third party auditors. Indeed, NGOs became a key pillar of the Bank's strategy of institutional reform, mobilising civil society and NGOs to focus on specific institutional measures such as transparency, accountability, and institutional integrity—in other words, the cornerstone of the PWC agenda—'good governance' (see e.g. Lang, 2013, pp. 13–14; Thompson, 2007).

These strategies of co-option and internalisation did not go unnoticed. Indeed, there was significant debate about the role of NGOs, their relationship to orthodox multilateral development organisations, and whether they were being captured and professionalised within a neoliberal development agenda (Routledge, 1997). These mimicked broader debates about the efficacy of neoliberal development agendas amid alternative political and economic approaches and those who now claimed to be effecting 'change from within the system'. James Petras captured the essence of this debate, and of the Bank's role on internalising the political agency of NGOs amid a broader ideological project that sought to marginalise a 'class analysis of imperialism and capitalist exploitation'—and the maintenance of ruling-class interests:

Throughout history ruling classes, representing small minorities, have always depended on the coercive state apparatus and social institutions to defend their power, profits and privileges. . . .

[I]n more recent decades a new social institution emerged that provides the same function of control and ideological mystification—the self-described non-governmental organizations (NGOs). Today there are at least 50,000 NGOs in the Third World receiving over $10 billion in funding from international finance institutions, Euro-US-Japanese governmental agencies and local governments. The managers of the biggest NGOs manage million dollar budgets with salaries and perks that are comparable to CEOs. They jet to international conferences, confer with top corporate and financial directors and make policy decisions that affect—in the great majority of cases adversely—millions of people . . . especially the poor, women and informal sector working people. (Petras, 1999, p. 429)

For Petras, NGOs were now not only playing a key role in distracting attention from understanding the key sources of underdevelopment, but they were also drawing in talented young people from activist organisations and leftist backgrounds with the offer of substantial remuneration:

The egregious effects of structural adjustment policies on wages and salaried workers, peasants and small national business people generates potential national discontent. And that is where the NGOs come into the picture to mystify and deflect that discontent away from direct attacks on the corporate/ banking power structure and profits toward local micro-projects and apolitical 'grass roots' self-exploitation and 'popular education' that avoids class analysis of imperialism and capitalist exploitation.

The NGOs world-wide have become the latest vehicle for upward mobility for the ambitious educated classes: academics, journalists, and professionals have abandoned earlier excursions in the poorly rewarded leftist movements for a lucrative career managing an NGO, bringing with them their organizational and rhetorical skills as well as a certain populist vocabulary. (Petras, 1999, p. 430)

Petras was sketching out trends for which there was considerable empirical evidence. Writing about the World Bank's experience with reaching out to civil society in the early 1980s, the late Gloria Davis (who both worked for the Bank and wrote an important history of the Bank's social development elements) demonstrated the efforts made by the Bank to 'bring NGOs in' as it were (even attracting senior figures from progressive global NGOs):

. . . the NGO-World Bank Committee formed in the early 1980s within the International Relations Department, underwent a series of transformations which helped make the Bank more open and responsive to external concerns and set the stage for the Bank's work on participation. . . . With the growing participation of Northern NGOs, such as OXFAM, and the addition of developing country NGOs representing regional interests, NGOs were soon setting the agenda for the Committee. Specifically they put pressure on the Bank to make greater use of participatory approaches so that external voices could be better heard in the development process. In response, a Bank-wide learning Group on Participatory Development was formed in 1990 . . . When John Clark from OXFAM was hired to head the NGO unit in 1992, the emphasis in poverty reduction and participation was further increased. (Davis, 2004, p. 4)

These formative efforts set in the context of the negative fallout from structural adjustment programmes and the subsequent arrival of Wolfensohn demonstrate a clear and concerted political agenda seeking to internalise civil society and NGOs—a practice that would become mainstream within orthodox development practice. For example, new social and environmental safeguards were rolled out in an attempt to avoid many of the issues that had plagued large-scale infrastructure projects. By the late 1990s, mainstream multilateral projects had incorporated procedures to assess and mitigate risks, with many of these procedures involving NGOs as sources of information and project implementers (see e.g. Hatcher, 2015). In private sector-targeted projects, such as those associated with the World Bank's private sector arm, the International Finance

Corporation (IFC), new attempts to engage and involve communities and other 'stakeholders' became commonplace, with these efforts effectively complementing 'third way' agendas built around public–private partnerships, private finance initiatives, and other modalities focused on engaging the private sector within development practice. Furthermore, these agendas were facilitated by NGOs whose focus on private sector actors and the development of codes of conduct, CSR, and ethical investment agendas, went hand in hand with the social engagement agendas of the Bank (Carroll, 2012a; see also Gerard, 2015).

Much of the promotion of participatory emphases within neoliberal development practice emanated from sections of the World Bank associated with what was described as 'social development'. Not surprisingly, the stature and importance of social development specialists within the Bank advanced significantly during Wolfensohn's presidency, with the rollout of large social development projects. In contrast to the Bank's dominant power group—orthodox economists—social development specialists saw themselves as promoting progressive change from within the Bank and fostering a consultative and inclusive set of processes. Much of this focused on contributing to an otherwise neglected aspect of development practice, the development of 'social capital'. Inspired by the work of Putnam (1992, 2000), among others, social development specialists leveraged off the negative fallout from the Bank's structural adjustment programmes and aligned themselves with Wolfensohn's 'Comprehensive Development Framework'. Social development staff in the Bank's Indonesian country office, for example, set about putting together what would become one of the largest social development projects yet mounted by the Bank—the Kecamatan Development Program (KDP). KDP attempted to build institutions from the bottom-up by instilling particular norms of good governance in undertaking micro-projects at the village level. Consciously working through the sub-district level (a level of government that was seen to be relatively divorced from the corrupt patrimonial politics at the national and provincial levels), funds were to be allocated in a transparent but competitive fashion for projects that were decided upon collectively and mediated through Bank-trained facilitators. The idea was to create demand from below for changes in patterns of governance above, echoing Putnam's assumptions about social capital and social efficiency (Li, 2006, pp. 243–244).

KDP-style programmes were quickly replicated in the Philippines, Afghanistan, and elsewhere. Indeed, in Indonesia this massive social institution-building project was scaled up so quickly (from a multi-village level study to a multi-billion dollar programme) that it ended up impacting every village in the world's fourth most populous country. While controversial within the Bank, the allocation of massive resources to KDP-style projects and their replication in various countries around the world was indicative of the Bank's crisis of legitimacy and, more obviously, of a crisis for orthodox neoliberalism—especially pronounced around the 1997–1998 financial crisis where the World Bank and IMF structural adjustment programmes were popularly denounced for deepening the crisis and plunging millions into poverty (Carroll, 2010, pp. 180–207; Guggenheim, 2006; Li, 2006, pp. 247–269).

While ostensibly 'progressive' in its efforts to enhance social capital and include civil society—especially compared with orthodox structural adjustment programmes—these programmes were nonetheless classically liberal. Broader issues associated with class, state capture, inequality, social justice, or imperialism, for example, were clearly out of bounds. Rather, for authors such as John Harriss and Ben Fine, the interest of neoliberal development practitioners in civil society and social capital suggested a form of *anti-politics* that masked the social conflict inherent in capitalist and, indeed, global capitalist relations (Fine, 2002, p. 204; Harriss, 2002; Li, 2006, p. 244).[8] For critics, 'civil society' was being used almost synonymously as a term to describe an amenable constituency that could be called upon to play a countenancing role within the constitution of market society (see also Louth, 2015). This was equivalent to applying a 'band aid' to fix a larger surgical problem, masking deeper structural causes of underdevelopment and poverty rooted in the legacies of colonialism, the asymmetric distribution of high value adding means of production, the capture of wealth/economic growth by specific domestic constituencies and classes, and the contradictions inherent in capitalist exchange relations more broadly. Indeed, it implied that social conflict could be reduced to forms of stakeholder representation, mediation, and accountability out of which everybody's interests could be addressed—a kind of technocratic-cum-managerial fix that presented itself as 'beyond politics'. Under the PWC, civil society was essentially de-politicised and internalised within the neoliberal project as the 'third sector' (in tandem with the market and state); a resource to be used to build 'enabling environments' and markets and thus expand entrepreneurial activity and economic growth.

While the policy practices of the PWC continue, not least the engagement of civil society and a focus on state-society relations in fostering neoliberal market development, their centrality in neoliberal development practice has been diluted, in part due to the ongoing crisis of accumulation exacerbated by the global financial crisis and renewed efforts to extend market relations into emerging economies. The response has been an aggressive re-emphasis by neoliberal development practice on market building accompanied by a suite of policy instruments that we term 'deep marketisation'—an aggressive pro-private sector agenda that seeks to rapidly extend market exchange and social relations using means that work *on*, *through*, and *around* the state.

Deep Marketisation

Like the Washington consensus and the PWC before it, deep marketisation is a product of the evolution of orthodox development policy (including its unintended outcomes) and the broader machinations of global capitalism. Within the Bank, it represents the re-emergence of orthodox economists as dominant players and the sublimation of civil society, NGOs and social development programmes within core ideational projects focused on market fundamentalism. Indeed, in many ways, deep marketisation signals something of an apotheosis in neoliberal development policy. While structural adjustment remains a reality, as do attempts to 'build institutions for markets', this latest phase of neoliberal development policy reflects important transformations in the global political economy; in particular, shifts in the relational power between underdeveloped countries, IFIs, markets and capital, and between patrimonial and neo-entrepreneurial comprador classes and their capture of rents and resource flows.

Deep marketisation, in this sense, reflects the increasing reciprocity that has emerged between specific class interests, patrimonial relations, and capital flows, with neoliberal development practice positioning itself at the intersection of these interests. In its simplest expression, it is represented by the re-emphasis and refocus on market fundamentalism: an extreme pro-private sector agenda designed to transform the state from being an economic actor (typified in the era of state-led development) into a regulatory state providing the institutional resources necessary for market operation (Jarvis, 2012). Neoliberal development policy is thus substantively focused on creating 'enabling environments' that support market building and which utilise predominantly private capital to fund development.

The policy instruments used to support the construction of enabling environments and market building are numerous. These include the promotion of public–private partnerships and private finance initiatives, (especially in network infrastructure—electricity, water, sanitation, information communications technology, and the transportation sector—as well as extraction industries), national regulatory reviews and 'sunsetting' audits designed to remove outdated or market-unfriendly regulatory regimes (e.g. restrictions on market operation, the movement of goods and services, and related factor inputs—including restrictions on foreign investment and onerous compliance or tax requirements), and the adoption of risk mitigation regimes for capital such as state guarantees in respect of convertibility and profit repatriation, legal structures that limit government opportunism (contract repudiation or government intervention into the market), along with the adoption of non-discrimination clauses in the treatment of foreign capital (see e.g. OECD, 2012).

Equally, the focus on financialisation as a primary policy instrument to marketise previously closed or co-opted spaces and make them available to private capital has re-emphasised the building of enabling environments, regulatory systems and institutions to facilitate financial intermediation and the penetration of private capital into micro, small, medium, and large size enterprise across virtually all sectors of the economy (Carroll, 2015).

Deep marketisation is thus far from simply a process of government 'restructuring' through 'privatisation' and 'selling off' state assets. Rather, it focuses fundamentally on policy instruments designed to realise *commodification* in which capitalist exchange relations dominate in the provision of goods and services, including social protection arrangements (the construction of markets to service individually procured unemployment insurance, pension and retirement plans, health and disability insurance schemes, and education funds, among others). As Karl Polanyi long ago recognised, such market fundamentalism represents the perverse inversion of social needs and social relations to the interests of the economy—an ideological project he termed the construction of 'market society' and the triumph of market rationalism (Carroll & Jarvis, 2013; Polanyi, 1957).

Evidence of this Polanyian paradox is a core feature of deep marketisation and represented in the instrumental logic of market rationalism that operates not only *on* and *through* the state, but increasingly *around* the state. To be sure, capacity-building programmes, particularly those focusing on central bank staff and key government officials, technical assistance projects, and political leverage exerted through conditional lending and structural adjustment, continue to be important tools deployed by the World Bank, IMF, and other IFIs that focus *on* the state or work *through* the state in order to transform its relationship to markets. In the first instance, for example, under the Washington Consensus IFIs concentrated their efforts *on* the state, using programmes to reposition the state and diminish its role in the economy—or what Brenner and Theodore have termed 'roll back' neoliberalism (2002a). In the second instance, the PWC emphasised working *through* the state insofar as it highlighted the importance of transforming and harnessing state institutions to be market supporting—in effect a project of constructing 'regulatory states' (Carroll, 2012b; Jarvis, 2012). In this third constellation of neoliberal development practice (deep marketisation), however, considerable emphasis is placed on working *around* the state with the rise and increasing omnipresence of market instrumentality deployed through exogenous policy instruments—and which, arguably, are proving the most pervasive in extending market discipline. These instruments include projects that allocate capital direct-to-sector (e.g. 'access to finance', including credit, payment, deposit, insurance, and related instruments designed to facilitate financial intermediation), the continuing promotion of private finance initiatives, public–private partnerships, as well as rankings, scorecards, audits, ratings, and third party reputational indices in which countries and sectors are nominally assessed in terms of their attractiveness or risk to capital—and the cost of capital impacted accordingly. In effect, these coerce states, not least through domestic coalitions of pro-private sector interests, pressuring governments and state agencies to conform with international market norms and reduce state practices that increase the cost of capital or deter capital from entering markets (see e.g. Fenby, 2015; Shields & Wallin, 2015).[9]

Importantly, citizens and civil society have been internalised into this process. The *Doing Business* reports, jointly produced by the IFC and the World Bank, for example, the Worldwide Governance Indicators (World Bank), the legion of credit ratings issued quarterly for countries (on government debt instruments such as bonds) (Moody's, Fitch), the FDI Regulatory Restrictiveness Index (OECD), or the Global Competitiveness Report (World Economic Forum), among many others, serve as important signalling mechanisms (especially to capital) which come to form proxy assessments of governance quality, corruption, efficiency, competitiveness, reform, and development.[10] Governments are increasingly judged by citizens and civil society on the basis of these rankings, which are otherwise seen as 'objective' and offering independent and impartial assessment of government performance. De-contextualised from the larger ideational project which these rankings represent, citizens and civil society have become some of their most enthusiastic consumers and an important source of agency for promoting conformity to the market-disciplining measures implicit in such indices.

The irony, of course, is that at one and the same time, neo-entrepreneurial comprador classes, elites, citizens, and civil society are often aligned in terms of the ideational values promoted by such indices, albeit for different ends and material motivations. For citizens, such indices are seen as a means of getting better government, increasing probity and reducing corruption and cronyism; for neo-entrepreneurial comprador classes, these indices become sources for legitimising pro-market agendas, state divestiture of assets, reducing government regulation, getting the state out of the way and creating economic opportunities; for capital and investors, a way of pricing capital, assessing risks and selecting countries and sectors for investment; while for elites adhering to the pro-market agendas implicit in such indices bolsters opportunities for material gains and resource transfers through persistent (though reconfigured) patrimonial relations.

As we have already noted, however, the contradictions inherent in deep marketisation also reveal growing threats to the neoliberal project; deepening wealth and income inequalities, growing spatial inequalities—most obviously between rural and urban classes, and the capture of large resource transfers by elites and neo-entrepreneurial comprador classes. These represent structural impediments to further growth, accumulation and the deepening of capitalist exchange relations; risks that the ADB has identified as looming larger unless corrected through state intervention and public policy designed to curb the capture of economic growth by specific class interests. The problem, of course, is that these very same neoliberal policy fixes have been instrumental in reducing state capacity in emerging economies, particularly the agential power of the state to tax, spend, and redistribute wealth and income (modes of action that were used by states in the past to offset market outcomes). Resurgent state interventionism into the economy, for example, runs the risk of increasing costs to capital or, worse still, of capital strikes, while the alignment of the state with specific elite/neo-entrepreneurial comprador class interests and the increasing material benefits they enjoy through pro-private agendas diminishes the likelihood of more progressive policy measures being adopted. Indeed, even assuming a sympathetic political coalition available to adopt such corrective measures, the incentives to do so are low—not least because of the political risks of policy adoption at odds with the pro-market agendas of various international rankings and indices.

Conclusion

In its wake, deep marketisation promises a continuation of a modern day form of mal-development: economic growth that is inequitably captured, widening social stratification, reducing opportunities and mobility for lower socio-economic groups (especially those in agrarian settings), and a declining proportion of national wealth captured by wage labour. Furthermore, with the internment of emerging economies into global markets, particularly through investment and capital account liberalisation, the state and domestic economic actors are increasingly disciplined by neoliberal market norms. The state's discretionary fiscal spending, for example, is severely curtailed by market norms that favour budget surpluses over deficits and the discontinuation of national debt financing as a policy tool for long-term development—market preferences that serve to limit the role of the state in the economy.

At the same time, increasingly liberalised investment and trade regimes enable capital to transfer from one jurisdiction to another as wage demands increase or cost structures rise. While this is particularly true of low value-adding industries such as the textile, footwear and call centre sectors, equally these same patterns are replicated in the ever-changing location patterns of manufacturing and assembly in the automotive, electronic (IT equipment), white goods, consumer durables (appliances, furniture) and petro-chemicals sectors—as well as in the location patterns of logistics hubs (including entrepôt trade services) and back office treasury, clearing, and settlement services centres. More obviously, these dynamics have been reinforced by processes associated with outsourcing and the downloading of business establishment, compliance, and operational costs to local third party operators, increasing the ease of market withdrawal as 'buyers' of goods/services within international value chains can contract-out to another third party provider in another jurisdiction.

For wage labour and other economic actors (suppliers, service providers, third party vendors, etc.) within national production and supply chains, the result is an enduring disciplining effect upon costs (labour and related input factors) due to threats of downsizing or 'offshoring'. Indeed, the mantra of 'cost containment', the continuous search for 'efficiency gains' and 'higher productivity yields' reinforces the dynamics of competitiveness and the trend towards work intensification—all serving to discipline labour.

After some four decades of resurgent neoliberalism the toll on citizens, civil society, and NGOs is clearly discernible. Phenomena such as 'NGOization', for example, a process whereby 'social movements professionalize, institutionalize, and bureaucratize in vertically structured, policy-outcome-oriented organizations that focus on generating issue-specific and, to some degree, marketable expert knowledge or services' (Lang, 2013, pp. 63–64), have clearly been facilitated by the efforts of IFIs—and indeed the efforts of various states to circumvent reform impediments, respond to reform fallout and other challenges, and deliver and monitor often value-loaded projects and programmes (Carroll, 2010; Jayasuriya, 2001; Jayasuriya & Hewison, 2004; Thompson, 2010). Similarly, deep marketisation and market instrumentality have clearly pervaded civil society and been politically powerful in altitudinal formation, often defining the limits of political discourse and the framing of economic policy options.

Yet processes of internalisation have not been absolute and any notion of the fatality of citizens, civil society, and NGOs would be premature—in the extreme! Rather, this latest phase of neoliberalism needs to be contextualised amid broader developments, where the weakening of organised opposition has been a global phenomenon—in line with the great strides that global capitalism has made in expanding the circuits of capital and market exchange relations. In the case of organised labour, for example, this has been a triple assault: first, in the form of the entrance of massive new pools of cheap labour from the former Eastern Bloc and China; second, in the disciplining influence of capital mobility; and third, through the impact of 'creative destruction' and the utilisation of labour-saving advancements in automation. Each has undoubtedly contributed to the erosion of hard-fought victories won by working classes in many settings while depressing the wages, rights, and benefits of workers in emerging economy contexts. This said, it is precisely these antagonisms that also expose sites of creative tension and potential agency—albeit unevenly geographically distributed.

The combined impact of reduced worker protections, zero hour contracts, the loss of benefits and falling real income coupled with often diminished (organised) worker representation in the global North, for example, have increasingly provided the political axis on which citizens and civil society have been reinvigorated. Large-scale mobilisations have articulated the broad experience of diminishing opportunity, falling wages in the face of the rise of low-paid 'service sector jobs', increasing household 'distress' as a result of declining affordability (particularly for housing, education, health services, etc.), and diminishing access to social and public services with the deepening of market society. Indeed, the creative tensions posed by these experiences amid the increasing concentration of wealth signal emerging pivots on which citizens and civil society are mobilising and coalescing.[11]

These same fundamental tensions in emerging economies, however, present different challenges for citizens, civil society, and NGOs, particularly in contexts of authoritarianism where, given the very nature of the regimes involved, dissent is not tolerated and organisation and mobilisation controlled. Indeed, in light of the spectacular concentrations of wealth accumulation by elites and neo-entrepreneurial comprador classes as a result of deep marketisation and neoliberal development practice, many regimes have reasserted surveillance initiatives and domestic security agendas to minimise the impact of civil society and representation and secure elite control (Rodan, 2012).

As ever, the challenges for citizens, civil society, and NGOs more broadly remain far from contiguous or politically uniform. As Gills and Gray observe, the 'paradox of neoliberal economic globalisation is ... that it both weakens and simultaneously activates the social forces of resistance' (2012, p. 208). Amid the relentless rollout of neoliberal development policy and the inherent contradictions and tensions it generates, these paradoxes will only deepen in the decades ahead.

Acknowledgements

The authors thank Willis Yim for his research assistance in the preparation of this article.

Disclosure Statement

No potential conflict of interest was reported by the authors.

Notes

1   See also the analysis by Lin and Rosenblatt (2012).
2   We use the term neo-entrepreneurial comprador class to capture a specific emergent class that shares many characteristics with what was referred to in the past as a comprador class but which also exudes important differences. The term comprador class was historically applied to those persons in East Asia (Canton and Guangzhou in Southern China, Hong Kong and Macau) and Southeast Asia who acted as intermediaries in the

trade of European goods in local markets or buyers procuring goods for export on behalf of their European employers. In this sense, the term referred to local indigenous managers working in or for European business houses (Bergere, 1989, pp. 38–39). Later, neo-Marxist scholars such as Paul Baran and Paul Sweezy along with scholars such as Harry Magdoff used the notion of a comprador bourgeoisie to symbolise a class of intermediaries who facilitated foreign investment into third-world economies and which precipitated the net extraction of wealth causing underdevelopment (Baran & Sweezy, 1968; Magdoff, 1969). We use the term neo-entrepreneurial comprador class to capture the contemporary dynamics of a class of persons who operate as entrepreneurs and as financial intermediaries both for domestic and international capital. To be sure, this class is broad and stratified, comprising (1) well-connected individuals with access to elites or state officials and able to connect capital (domestic and foreign) with investment opportunities; (2) intermediators assisting elites to capture resource transfers as a result of marketisation as the state commercialises state monopolies through privatisation, equitisation (the conversion of state assets into standalone commercial entities who are then floated on stock markets), or other commercial vehicles (public private partnerships, concessions, etc.); (3) a broader stratum of individuals who have leveraged off supply/demand gaps in domestic economies as a result of liberalisation (new import markets for goods and services previously restricted entry or whose mobility was constrained through closed trade regimes or ISI import taxation policies) or who have identified export opportunities for goods/services associated with trade liberalisation and are leveraging off the comparative advantage of domestic labour costs.

3   We use notions of patrimonialism in the context of Weber's depiction in which systems of exchange are mediated by personal relations, are particularistic in nature, and where the boundaries between public and private interests are blurred in terms of the utilisation of political and bureaucratic resources (Budd, 2004, pp. 1–2).

4   Barnes provides a useful mapping of the different forms of informal wage labour to highlight the hidden spaces within which a large proportion of labour in emerging economies operate. These include (i) waged workers in informal enterprises; (ii) domestic workers; (iii) casual and day labourers; (iv) unregistered or undeclared workers; (v) industrial outworkers or home-workers; (vi) workers hired by a contractor or intermediary; (vii) residual and part-time workers (Barnes, 2012, pp. 152–160).

5   It is important to stress that we are *not* suggesting that these states are simply 'patrimonial states.' In fact, a more accurate depiction of these states would be that they are what Eric Budd describes as 'neopatrimonial' in as much as 'they exhibit patrimonial features while possessing bureaucracies,' many of which display rational-systematic state planning and varying degrees of probity, transparency and accountability (Budd, 2004, p. 2).

6   We define neoliberalism as a set of ideas and policies associated with extending market discipline to state and society (see for example, Brenner, Peck, & Theodore, 2010; Harvey, 2005).

7   The '50 years is enough' organisation describes itself as 'a coalition of over 200 U.S. grassroots, women's, solidarity, faith-based, policy, social—and economic—justice, youth, labor and development organizations dedicated to the … transformation of the World Bank and the International Monetary Fund (IMF). The Network works in solidarity with over 185 international partner organizations in more than 65 countries. Through education and action, the Network is committed to transforming the international financial institutions' policies and practices, to ending the outside imposition of neoliberal economic programs, and to making the development process democratic and accountable. We were founded in 1994, on the occasion of the 50th anniversary of the founding of the World Bank and IMF. We focus on action-oriented economic literacy training, public mobilization, and policy advocacy'. See URL http://orgs.tigweb.org/50-years-is-enough-network

8   The reification of civil society and its agency is contested by Elias who explores the limits of civil society activism, particularly in environments constrained by authoritarian regimes, non-secular state systems and the impact of patriarchy (see Elias, 2015).

9   Implicit in our periodisation of neoliberal development policy is an evolutionary shift in relational power between IFI's and underdeveloped states. This is important since, on the one hand, the specific power configurations between IFIs and underdeveloped states explain the policy approaches of IFIs to the transfer, adoption and implementation of neoliberal policy agendas and, on the other, the subsequent modes of resistance to these policy agendas, including the policy responses of IFI's to implementation problems. As we also suggest, changes in the these power relationships is one of the main forces propelling the evolution of neoliberal development policy, which has been forced periodically to innovate its policy approaches in order to sustain its broader project. These periodisations, as we have noted, fall into three distinct but interrelated phases: (i) The Washington Consensus, (ii) the Post-Washington Consensus, and (iii) deep marketisation. Under the Washington Consensus, neoliberalism worked *on* the state, emblematic of the power of IFIs as primary actors controlling access to capital for underdeveloped states. This specific power configuration allowed IFIs like the World Bank to impose conditional lending, with underdeveloped states forced to accept such terms in the absence of alternative

sources of capital. Obviously, this was a highly asymmetrical power relationship in which 'reforms' were applied from the 'top-down' and from the 'outside-in'—producing sources of domestic opposition with states regularly accused of 'distorting' reform agendas. In response, the PWC worked *on* and *through* the state, in part reflecting the continuing asymmetrical power relationships between IFIs and underdeveloped states but also policy responses by IFIs to proactively counter sectional resistance to structural adjustment reforms within underdeveloped states and overcome implementation obstacles and political opposition. The PWC's suite of policy responses, as we have noted, included the co-option of civil society, engagement strategies with domestic constituencies, consultation and social development initiatives—all designed to achieve 'buy-in' from bureaucracies, institutional actors and civil society. The latest phase of neoliberal development policy, deep marketisation, similarly displays a range of policy innovations designed to overcome domestic resistance and continue reform agendas that support market development. Again, these policy innovations have been prompted by on-going shifts in the relative power between IFIs and emerging economies, in large measure driven by the increasing availability of capital to underdeveloped states. Capital's new found interest in emerging economies, most obviously in the re-branding of 'underdeveloped states' as 'emerging economies', has provided these states with increasing access to capital, displacing the primacy of IFIs as sources of capital and credit. The leverage historically enjoyed by IFIs has thus been substantially reduced, inspiring policy innovations that now focus increasingly on working *around* the state to support the market building agenda of neoliberal development policy.

10   The explosion of rankings and country based indices in the past few decades reveals their utility in effecting changes in specific state practices, policies and behaviours, and of their broader impact on attitudinal formation, perceptions and public opinion. These observations have been exploited by a growing number of agencies and individuals who have adopted ranking indices as a means of promoting specific agendas. Mo Ibrahim, for example, the billionaire African philanthropist who made his fortune in telephony, established the Ibrahim Index of African Governance in 2007 which annually ranks the performance of African states in relation to reform and regulatory practices supporting market development. Similarly, the Heritage Foundation, a conservative US think tank founded in 1973, produces an annual 'Index of Economic Freedom,' ostensibly on how easy it is to do business in one country compared to another. The values underlying the index, as the Heritage Foundation notes on its web page, reflect the organisation's mission statement: 'to promote conservative public policies based on the principles of free enterprise, limited government, individual freedom, traditional American values, and a strong national defense.' (see The Heritage Foundation URL http://www. heritage.org/about

11   In the global North, evidence of the increasing concentration of both income and wealth is not difficult to find. In the United States, for example, between 1981 and 2008, 96% of the growth generated by the economy went to the richest 10% while only 4% went to the remaining 90% of the population (EPI, 2014). Similar studies by Alvaredo, Atkinson, Piketty, and Saez (2013) also demonstrate a marked upward and accelerating trend in inequality which they also attribute to neoliberal policy agendas. Equally, the Organisation for Economic Cooperation (OECD) in a recent study also found that income inequality since the mid-1980s in the United States, United Kingdom, Australia, Canada, Sweden, Finland, Denmark, the Netherlands, Germany, Hungary, Italy, New Zealand, Mexico, Japan and Austria—among others, had also trended upwards—albeit the rate of growth in inequality displaying differences among countries. Only in Greece and Turkey had income inequality declined since the mid-1980s (OECD, 2014).

References

ADB. (2012). *Asian development outlook 2012: Confronting rising inequality in Asia*. Manila: Asian Development Bank.

Alvaredo, F., Atkinson, A. B., Piketty, T., & Saez, E. (2013). The top 1 percent in international and historical perspective. *Journal of Economic Perspectives, 27*(3), 3–20.

Baker, A. (2009). *The market and the masses in Latin America: Policy reform and consumption in liberalizing economies*. Cambridge: Cambridge University Press.

Bank, W. (2014a). *Indonesia-investments*. Retrieved November 18, 2014, from http://www.indonesia-investments.com/culture/economy/general-economic-outline/agriculture/item378

Bank, W. (2014b). *Vietnam: Rural development and agriculture in Vietnam*. Retrieved November 18, 2014, from http://web.worldbank.org/WBSITE/EXTERNAL/COUNTRIES/EASTASIAPACIFICEXT/VIETNAMEXTN/0,,contentMDK:20534368~pagePK:141137~piPK:141127~theSitePK:387565,00.html

Baran, P. A., & Sweezy, P. M. (1968). *Monopoly capital: An essay on the American economic and social order* (1st Modern reader paperback ed.). New York: Monthly Review Press.

Barnes, T. (2012). Marxism and informal labour. *Journal of Australian Political Economy, 70*, 144–166.

Berger, M. T., & Beeson, M. (1998). Lineages of liberalism and miracles of modernization: The World Bank, the East Asian trajectory and the international development debate. *Third World Quarterly, 19*(3), 487–504.

Bergere, M.-C. (1989). *The golden age of the Chinese bourgeoisie 1911–1937*. Cambridge: Cambridge University Press.

Brenner, N., Peck, J., & Theodore, N. (2010). Variegated neoliberalization: Geographies, modalities, pathways. *Global Networks, 10*(2), 182–222. doi:10.1111/j.1471-0374.2009.00277.x

Brenner, N., & Theodore, N. (2002a). Cities and the geographies of "actually existing neoliberalism". In N. Brenner & N. Theodore (Eds.), *Spaces of neoliberalism: Urban restructuring in North America and Western Europe* (pp. 1–32). Oxford: Blackwell.

Brenner, N., & Theodore, N. (2002b). Cities and the geographies of "actually existing neoliberalism". In N. Brenner & N. Theodore (Eds.), *Spaces of neoliberalism* (pp. 1–32). Malden: Blackwell.

Budd, E. N. (2004). *Democratization, development, and the patrimonial state in the age of globalization*. Lanham, MD: Lexington Books.

Busch, L. (2014). Governance in the age of global markets: Challenges, limits, and consequences. *Agriculture and Human Values, 31*(3), 513–523.

Cahill, D. (2014). *The end of laissez-faire? On the durability of embedded neoliberalism*. Cheltenham: Edward Elgar Publishing.

Cammack, P. (2012). Risk, social protection and the world market. *Journal of Contemporary Asia, 42*(3), 359–377.

Cammack, P. (2014). *The UNDP and the end of human development: A critique of the 2013 human development report*. Working Paper 6: Southeast Asia Research Centre, City University of Hong Kong.

Carroll, T. (2010). *Delusions of development: The World Bank and the post-Washington consensus in Southeast Asia*. London: Palgrave-MacMillan.

Carroll, T. (2012a). The cutting edge of accumulation: Neoliberal risk mitigation, the Baku-Tbilisi-Ceyhan pipeline and its impact. *Antipode, 44*(2), 281–302.

Carroll, T. (2012b). Working on, through and around the state: The deep Marketisation of development in the Asia-Pacific. *Journal of Contemporary Asia, 42*(3), 378–404. doi:10.1080/00472336.2012.687628

Carroll, T. (2015).'Access to finance' and the death of development in the Asia-Pacific. *Journal of Contemporary Asia, 45*(1), 139–166. doi:10.1080/00472336.2014.907927

Carroll, T., & Jarvis, D. S. L. (2013). Market building in Asia: Standards setting, policy diffusion, and the globalization of market norms. *Journal of Asian Public Policy, 6*(2), 117–128. doi:10.1080/17516234.2013.834205

Chang, K.-S., Weiss, L., & Fine, B. (2012). Introduction: Neoliberalism and developmental politics in perspective. In K.-S. Chang, L. Weiss, & B. Fine (Eds.), *Developmental politics in transition: The neoliberal era and beyond* (pp. 1–23). Basingstoke: Palgrave.

Connell, R., & Dados, N. (2014). Where in the world does neoliberalism come from? *Theory and Society, 43*(2), 117–138. doi:10.1007/s11186-014-9212-9

Davis, G. (2004). A history of the social development network of the World Bank 1973–2002. *Social Development Papers*. Retrieved August 2, 2011, from http://siteresources.worldbank.org/INTRANETSOCIALDEVELOPMENT/214578-1111735201184/20502396/History+of+SD+in+WB.pdf

Economist. (2012). The world's shifting Centre of gravity. *The Economist*. Retrieved November 17, 2014, from http://www.economist.com/blogs/graphicdetail/2012/06/daily-chart-19

Elias, J. (2015). Civil society and the gender politics of economic competitiveness in Malaysia. *Globalizations*, doi:10.1080/14747731.2015.1016303

EPI. (2014). *Economic policy institute, inequality indicators*. http://www.stateofworkingamerica.org/who-gains/#/?start=1917&end=1918

Fenby, J. (2015). Guest post: A reform scorecard for EM in 2014. *The Financial Times*. www.blogs.ft.com/beyond-brics/2015/01/06/guest-post-a-reform-scorecard-for-em-in-2015/

Fine, B. (2002). The World Bank's speculation on social capital. In J. Pincus & J. Winters (Eds.), *Reinventing the World Bank* (pp. 203–221). Ithaca: Cornell University Press.

Gerard, K. (2015). Explaining ASEAN's engagement of civil society in policymaking: Smoke and mirrors. *Globalizations*, doi:10.1080/14747731.2015.1016304

Gill, S. (1997). *Gramsci, modernity and globalization*. Paper presented at the Gramsci and the Twentieth Century, Sardinia. http://www.internationalgramscisociety.org/resources/online_articles/articles/gill01.shtml

Gill, S. (2000). *The constitution of global capitalism*. Paper presented at the The Capitalist World, Past and Present at the International Studies Association Annual Convention, Los Angeles.

Gills, B. K., & Gray, K. (2012). People power in the era of global crisis: Rebellion, resistance, and liberation. *Third World Quarterly, 33*(2), 205–224. doi:10.1080/01436597.2012.664897

Guggenheim, S. (2006). Crises and contradictions: Understanding the origins of a community development project in Indonesia. In A. Bebbington, M. Woolcock, S. Guggenheim, & E. Olson (Eds.), *The search for empowerment: Social capital as idea and practice at the World Bank* (pp. 111–144). Bloomfield: Kumarian.

Harriss, J. (2002). *Depoliticizing development.* London: Anthem Press.

Harvey, D. (1990). *The condition of postmodernity: An enquiry into the origins of cultural change.* Oxford: Blackwell.

Harvey, D. (2005). *A brief history of neoliberalism* (I. ebrary, Trans.). Oxford: Oxford University Press.

Hatcher, P. (2015). Neoliberal modes of participation in frontier settings: Mining, multilateral meddling and politics in Laos. *Globalizations,* doi:10.1080/14747731.2015.1016305

Jarvis, D. S. L. (2012). The regulatory state in developing countries: Can it exist and do we want it? The case of the Indonesian power sector. *Journal of Contemporary Asia, 42*(3), 464–492.

Jayasuriya, K. (2001). *Governance, post-Washington consensus and the new anti-politics.* Retrieved February 5, 2007, from http://www.cityu.edu.hk/searc/WP2_01_Jayasuriya.pdf#search=%22Governance%2C%20Post-Washington%20Consensus%20and%20the%20New%20Anti-Politics%22

Jayasuriya, K., & Hewison, K. (2004). The antipolitics of good governance from global social policy to a global populism? *Critical Asian Studies, 36*(4), 571–590.

Lang, S. (2013). *NGOs, civil society, and the public sphere.* Cambridge: Cambridge University Press.

Li, T. (2006). *Government through community: The social development program of the World Bank in Indonesia.* Retrieved from http://www.iilj.org/GAL_2006_3_Li.htm

Lin, J. Y., & Rosenblatt, D. (2012). Shifting patterns of economic growth and rethinking development. *Journal of Economic Policy Reform, 15*(3), 171–194. doi:10.1080/17487870.2012.700565

London, J. D. (2014). Welfare regimes in China and Vietnam. *Journal of Contemporary Asia, 44*(1), 84–107.

Louth, J. (2015). Neoliberalising Cambodia: The production of capacity in Southeast Asia. *Globalizations,* doi:10.1080/14747731.2015.1016306

Magdoff, H. (1969). *The age of imperialism; The economics of U.S. foreign policy* (1st Modern reader ed.). New York: Monthly Review Press.

Mallaby, S. (2004). *The world's banker: A story of failed states, financial crises and the wealth and poverty of nations.* New York: Penguin Press.

Mirowski, P. (2013). *Never let a serious crisis go to waste: How neoliberalism survived the financial meltdown.* London: Verso.

Mosley, P., Harrigan, J., & Toye, J. (1991). *Aid and power. The World Bank and policy-based lending, volume 1, analysis and proposals.* London: Routledge.

North, D. C. (1990). *Institutions, institutional change and economic performance.* Cambridge: Cambridge University Press.

OECD. (2012). *Indonesia: Government capacity to assure high quality regulation.* Paris: Author.

OECD. (2014). *Focus on income inequality.* Author. Retrieved December 9, 2014, from http://www.oecd.org/els/soc/Focus-Inequality-and-Growth-2014.pdf

Park, A., & Cai, F. (2011). The informalisation of the Chinese labour market. In S. Kuruvilla, C. K. Lee & M. E. Gallagher (Eds.), *From Iron rice bowl to informalization: Markets, workers, and the state in a changing China* (pp. 17–35). Ithaca, NY: Cornell University Press.

Peck, J., Theodore, N., & Brenner, N. (2012). Neoliberalism, interrupted. In D. Cahill, L. Edwards & F. Stillwell (Eds.), *Neoliberalism: Beyond the free market* (pp. 15–30). Cheltenham: Edward Elgar.

Petras, J. (1999). NGOs: In the service of imperialism. *Journal of Contemporary Asia, 29*(4), 429–440. doi:10.1080/00472339980000221

Polanyi, K. (1957). *The great transformation* (1st Beacon paperback ed.). Boston: Beacon Press.

Pradella, L. (2014). New developmentalism and the origins of methodological nationalism. *Competition and Change, 18*(2), 180–193.

Prashad, V. (2012). *The poorer nations: A possible history of the global South.* London: Verso.

Putnam, R. (1992). *Making democracy work.* Princeton, NJ: Princeton University Press.

Putnam, R. (2000). *Bowling alone: The collapse and revival of American community.* New York: Simon and Schuster.

Rodan, G. (2012). Competing ideologies of political representation in Southeast Asia. *Third World Quarterly, 33*(2), 311–332. doi:10.1080/01436597.2012.666014

Routledge, P. (1997). Resisting and reshaping the modern: Social movements and the development process. In P. J. Taylor, M. J. Watts & R. J. Johnston (Eds.), *Geographies of global change: Remapping the world in the late twentieth century* (pp. 236–279). Oxford: Blackwell.

Saad-Filho, A. (2012). Neoliberalism, democracy and development policy in Brazil. In C. Kyung-Suo, B. Fine, & L. Weiss (Eds.), *Developmental politics in transition: The neoliberal era and beyond* (pp. 117–139). Houndmills: Palgrave Macmillan.

Scholte, J. A. (2005). The sources of neoliberal globalization *Overarching Concerns Programme Paper Number 8* (pp. 38): United Nations Research Institute for Social Development.

Shields, S., & Wallin, S. (2015). Beyond Eastern Europe: The European Bank for Reconstruction and Development's gender action plan and the fourth wave of neoliberalism. *Globalizations*, doi:10.1080/14747731.2015.1016307

Shorrocks, A., Davies, J. B., & Lluberas, R. (2014). *Credit Suisse: Global wealth report 2014.* Zurich: Credit Suisse AG. Retrieved November 17, 2014, from https://publications.credit-suisse.com/tasks/render/file/?fileID=60931FDE-A2D2-F568-B041B58C5EA591A4

Soederberg, S. (2004). *The politics of the new international financial architecture.* London: Zed Books.

Stiglitz, J. (2001). Whither reform?—Ten years of the transition. In H.-J. Chang (Ed.), *Joseph Stiglitz and the World Bank, the rebel within* (pp. 127–171). London: Anthem Press.

Stiglitz, J. (2002). *Globalisation and its discontents.* Camberwell: Penguin.

Stiglitz, J. E. (1989). *The economic role of the state.* Oxford: Wiley-Blackwell.

The Structural Adjustment Participatory Review International Network. (2004). *Structural adjustment: The SAPRI report.* London: Zed Books.

Thompson, M. R. (2007). The dialectic of "good governance" and democracy in Southeast Asia: Globalized discourses in local responses. *Globality Studies Journal*, *10*(4), 1–19.

Thompson, M. R. (2010). Reformism vs populism in the Philippines. *Journal of Democracy*, *21*(4), 154–168.

Williamson, J. (1990). What Washington means by policy reform. In J. Williamson (Ed.), *Latin American adjustment: How much has happened?* (pp. 5–20). Washington, DC: Institute for International Economics.

World Bank. (1997). *The state in a changing world, world development report 1997.* Washington, DC: Oxford University Press.

World Bank. (2002a). *World development report 2002, building institutions for markets.* Washington, DC: Oxford University Press.

World Bank. (2002b). *World development report 2003. Sustainable development in a dynamic world transforming institutions, growth, and quality of life* (O. U. P. World Bank Ed.). New York: Oxford University Press.

World Bank. (2004). *World development report 2005—A better investment climate for everyone.* New York: Oxford University Press.

Yergin, D., & Stanislaw, J. (2002). *The commanding heights: The battle for the world economy.* New York: Simon & Schuster.

Finance, Development, and Remittances: Extending the Scale of Accumulation in Migrant Labour Regimes

HANNAH CROSS

University of Westminster, London, UK

ABSTRACT *The last decade has seen a heightened level of interest in the relationship between remittances and development, driven by the World Bank and other Bretton Woods Institutions. This has materialised in a global agenda to incorporate migrants and their households in commercial banking. The double significance of this policy rests in the financial incorporation of migrants and their households, and in the deepening entrenchment of the historical labour migration dynamic between sending communities and centres of capital. The central role of labour power in the advance of money forms the core of this analysis of a contemporary market-building strategy. This article presents a threefold critique of the global remittance agenda, based on (1) its transformative profit-driven development ideology, (2) its detachment of remittances from the political economy of migrant labour regimes, and (3) its dismissal of existing modes of remitting and uses of the funds.*

1. Introduction

In recent years, various organisations have tackled issues related to the important topic of international remittances. However, few of these reports have been devoted specifically to the 'payment system aspects' of remittances—in effect, the practical realities of actually transferring money. Understanding these payment system aspects is crucial to understanding remittances and to ensuring that remittance services are safe and efficient. (Timothy F. Geithner, Chairman of the Committee on Payment and Settlement Systems and Michael U. Klein, Vice President of the World Bank, Bank for International Settlements and World Bank, 2007, p. iii)

In order for the new transfer providers to compete with the traditional cash-to-cash MTOs [money transfer operators]—many of whom are long established in the UK—Ghana market and work well with the communities—or even to carve out a corner of the market for themselves, the online and prepaid card providers will be reliant on regulatory changes taking place in Ghana and indeed a shift towards greater financial awareness and inclusiveness amongst beneficiaries. (Developing Markets Associates Ltd and Department for International Development [DMA & DfID], 2011, pp. 27–28)

The largest recorded volumes of remittances flow from wealthier to poorer countries and are congruently linked in global policy with development and poverty alleviation (Ammassari, 2006; Bourenane, Bourjij, & Lhériau, 2011; Isaacs, Vargas-Silva, & Hugo, 2012; Ratha, 2007; United States Agency for International Development [USAID], 2012; World Bank, 2013). During the past decade, the World Bank has driven an agenda to manage remittance money transfers so that they are cheaper, more competitive, and foster 'financial inclusion' for migrants and their beneficiaries. This is consolidated in the '5 + 5' objective of the Bank-coordinated G20 Global Remittances Working Group, which is to attain 'a reduction of the global average costs of transferring remittances from the present 10% to 5% in 5 years through enhanced information, transparency, competition and cooperation with partners' (Cirasino & Ratha, 2009, p. 5). This objective is founded on addressing the market-based issue of high transfer costs and inconveniences that are known to affect migrants and their beneficiaries in some circumstances. However, this article will show that the remittance agenda is one of contradictory aims and mission creep into a (market-building as) development strategy, or the 'deep marketisation of development', by which the constitution of the market in its neo-liberal form is aimed directly at the private sphere (Carroll, 2012, p. 356; Carroll & Jarvis, 2015). The double significance of the remittance agenda rests in the societal impact of financially incorporating migrants and their households, and in the deepening entrenchment of the historical labour migration dynamic between sending communities and centres of capital. Therefore, the central role of labour power in the advance of money is at the core of this study of remittances, where it also belongs in broader discussions of financialisation (Fine, 2007, p. 2).

The existing academic literature on remittances and development is often authored by employees of international financial institutions (IFIs) (although not to be attributed to these institutions), appearing in journals such as *World Economy* (Acosta, Calderón, Fajnzyber, & López, 2006), *World Development* (Adams & Page, 2005), *Journal of Development Studies* (Ebeke, 2012), and *Journal of Development Economics* (Giuliano & Ruiz-Arranz, 2009). The findings vary but the authors engage in 'problem-solving' debates around the relationship between remittances, growth, and equality, also considering the technical barriers to their effectiveness. Further studies focus similarly on the technical aspects of remittances and their implications for the promotion of development (Brown, 2006; Rapoport & Docquier, 2005). Departing from the macroeconomic assessment of remittance flows, there is also a body of empirically rich literature that focuses on the dynamics of remitting and offers insight into the transnational connections between sender and receiver (see Findley, Traoré, Ouedraogo, & Diarra, 1995; Lindley, 2007; Mazzucato, 2006; Pieke, Van Hear, & Lindley, 2007 and Magunha, Bailey, & Cliffe, 2009). Further literature considers critically and holistically the relationship between migration, remittances, and development (Bracking, 2003; de Haas, 2005; Skeldon, 2008). Beside Hudson's (2008) thorough study of 'banking the unbanked' and Cross' earlier (2008) examination of the neo-liberal approach to remittances, critical analysis specifically of the global remittance agenda is lacking. This article foregrounds remittance policy within the broader understanding that it is a neo-liberal project of financialisation—the expansion of the frontier of financial accumulation—that aims to construct markets and integrate economies into global capitalist markets (Mader, 2014, p. 605).

Beyond placing the agenda in the context of the global political economy, further questions emerge about the types of continuity and transformation that the financial absorption of remittances aims for and is beginning to achieve. The implications of the agenda are as expansive and profound as other contemporary expressions of global capitalism, such as the major land and agricultural investments that have been covered in depth in this journal (Vol. 10, No. 1) and elsewhere. In working towards a deeper understanding of the remittance agenda, this article presents a threefold critique, based on (1) its transformative profit-driven development ideology, (2) its detachment of remittances from the political economy of migrant labour regimes, and (3) its dismissal of existing modes of remitting and uses of funds.

Because remittance policy is associated with the alleviation of poverty alongside macroeconomic development, this article is primarily concerned with south–north labour migrations. It will acknowledge and highlight some of the complexities of migrant labour, whilst also developing a theoretically and empirically grounded general understanding of migration patterns against which the development capacity of remittances can be understood. The primary aim is not, however, to understand the potential of remittances, but instead to put them in perspective.

Firstly, I will briefly locate remittance policy in the trajectory of late capitalism, showing how remittances are approached as an expanding market that is seen to constitute development. Secondly, this article looks more broadly at the role of capital accumulation in international migration regimes. In understanding the significance of geographically separating the migrant's community from the host economy, this structural approach to migration and remittances brings to bear the limitations of isolating the flow of money from the circumstances of migrating. Thirdly, this article considers the implications of neo-liberal management of remittance flows by looking closely at existing and historical modes of transferring and spending money, drawing particularly on Senegalese household experiences. In speaking to the themes in this Special Issue, it finally reflects briefly on the level and type of engagement that exist between remittance market-building and civil society. Beyond considering the (ir)relevance of the premise and prescriptions of global remittance policy to the livelihoods of migrants, households, and communities, the ethnographic detail in this article also highlights the analytical importance of locating the sending of remittances in the context of the wider displacement of labour. This is to say that remittance senders are—often momentarily—'elevated' into exploitative wage labour as successful members of a much larger group of people who are underemployed, threatened by hunger, and criminalised. These conditions are the sine qua non of migrant labour and consequentially remittances. The continuous role of this dynamic in global capitalism, therefore, undermines the prospects for remittances to be 'harnessed' or 'tapped' to bring wider benefits of development or poverty alleviation, though they are naturally well directed towards these ends.

2. The Remittance Agenda and Market-Building as Development

Research reports mushroomed in the early 2000s that examined remittances as a development strategy. They have been written and commissioned by international development, finance, and policy institutions, including the World Bank (Ratha, 2003), the UK's Department for International Development (DfID) (Addy, Wijkström, & Thouez, 2003), the International Monetary Fund (IMF) (Bouhga-Hagbe, 2004), the Organisation for Economic Cooperation and Development (OECD, 2005), the International Labour Office (ILO) (Ammassari, 2006), and the Migration Policy Institute (Ratha, 2007). Global remittances increased from around US$30 billion annually in the early 1990s to $318 billion in 2007, with three-quarters of this amount directed towards lower-middle-income and low-income developing countries (Vargas-Lundius, Lanly, Villarreal, & Osorio, 2008, p. 14). To developing countries alone, official remittance flows reached an estimated $401 billion in 2012, surpassing the global sum for 2007, and this figure is projected to reach $515 billion in 2015 (World Bank, 2013, p. 1). This dramatic rise of reported emigrant transfers does not entirely correspond with the real aggregated volume of migrants' earnings that are sent home; instead, it is linked with improved measurement and closer scrutiny of remittance flows, reduction of the transfer costs, and depreciation of the US dollar (Ratha, 2007, p. 2). The sum of remittances is likely, therefore, to continue expanding as monitoring improves and as domestic remittance flows and south–south transactions also come to light (Castaldo, Deshingkar, & McKay, 2012). The gains from international migration in the global south consequently represent a growing portion of GDP compared with official development assistance, private debt, and the fluctuating flows of direct foreign investment (Ammassari, 2006, p. 18; World Bank, 2013).

A senior economist at the World Bank (Ratha, 2007) developed the International Remittances Agenda in a report for the Migration Policy Institute. The overall policy recommendation is that the 'development community' should 'make remittance services cheaper and more convenient and indirectly leverage these flows to improve the financial access of migrants, their beneficiaries, and the financial intermediaries in the origin countries' (Ratha, 2007, p. 1). The Agenda promotes the implementation of monitoring, analysis, and projection; retail payment systems; financial access for individuals or households; and the leveraging of remittances for capital market access of financial institutions or countries. Ratha argues that the development community should achieve these ends through deregulation, rather than direct the money towards taxation or specific development uses (Ratha, 2007, p. 12). A move towards the formalisation of remittances through financial services was also promoted in the International Migration Policy Programme, an inter-agency group that includes the UK DfID, the World Bank, the International Labour Organisation, and the International Organisation for Migration. The report argues that macroeconomic environments in developing countries may pose obstacles to remittance transfers, and that by entering the banking system the money becomes more secure, earns interest, and makes fresh money available for business loans (Addy et al., 2003, pp. 14–15).

The new developmentalist approach to remittances therefore focuses on their 'sheer volume, stable growth over time, and anti-cyclical nature' (Addy et al., 2003, p. 3). Recent studies have explored the relationship between remittances and the global financial crisis. A working paper from the IMF concludes that African nations have been cushioned if they receive most of their remittances from the region, but they will gain in the longer run if they send more labour outside Africa (Barajas, Chami, Fullenkamp, & Garg, 2010). The World Bank recognises the instability of labour markets in destination countries and that there are political pressures to reduce the amount of immigration, which might depress remittance flows (Ratha & Silwal, 2012, pp. 2–3). However, a further chapter in a World Bank volume asks whether remittances to sub-Saharan Africa are a source of resilience or vulnerability: it concludes the former because remittances are 'relatively stable' (Naudé & Bezuidenhout, 2012, p. 346). The overarching logic is that remittances are an expanding market, which in global capitalism presents the enormous prospect not only to channel migrants' money through financial intermediaries, but also to incorporate receiving households in international finance.

A parallel logic with similar consequences of bringing remittances into formal channels is found in post-9/11 attempts to monitor and control international flows of money. This led the US government to close down as much as three-quarters of the hawala networks, often serviced by individuals, that transmit value to Pakistan, India, Somalia, Afghanistan, and other countries

(Pieke et al., 2007). *Hawala* networks emerged in the modes of exchange and value transfer that were particular to Muslim merchants and migrant groups in and around the Indian Ocean, prior to the colonial period. This is a complex system that is largely non-interest bearing and based on trust. It is rooted in historical commercial banking operations to finance long-distance trade. The transactions amount to a transfer of debt through agents, using a network of reciprocity that is known for its efficiency and low costs (Ballard, 2005, p. 326). Revealing the cooperative relationship between security and development agendas, the Bank for International Settlements and the World Bank (2007, pp. 23–24) argue that in the prohibitive political context, it is advantageous to require such informal remittance services to conform to financial regulation rather than outlawing them, because it increases competition.

The expansion of the formal financial services industry has been widely understood as necessary for economic growth and poverty reduction. Financial intermediaries supposedly contribute to the development trajectory by influencing and mobilising savings, channelling savings into investment, promoting the mobility of resources, encouraging the expansion of the market economy, and transforming traditional modes of production and the associated social relations into modern forms (Lawrence, 2006, p. 240). However, in transforming 'the composition and functionality of the economy as a productive space', the role of finance in development departs from that of intermediation, instead seeking to restructure economies to the advantage of financial investors (Froud, Johal, & Williams, 2002, p. 120; Mader, 2014, p. 605). This expansive vision for finance is evident in remittance policy: the earlier quoted report on UK–Ghana remittance corridors (DMA & DfID, 2011), for instance, reveals a higher logic that precludes the aim to reduce transaction costs for migrants. The report summarised that the existing remittance corridor was indeed competitively priced and reliable, but it was 'traditional by nature' and the profit margins, as well as the costs, were low, so 'moving forward changes are needed in both the UK and Ghanaian market in order to take advantage of new business models' (DMA & DfID, 2011, p. 2).

To encourage migrants to enter the banking system, 'financial education' is promoted (Ratha, 2007, p. 12). One contribution to this policy emerges in remittance price comparison websites that are variously led by the World Bank Group, development ministries, international banking organisations, and development consultancy firms.[1] On the receiving end, 'financial literacy' is promoted through further public–private partnerships. The International Labour Organisation, for instance, recommends a 'financial education and counselling programme' in Senegal, to be managed in a partnership between NGOs and financial institutions and with involvement from migrant associations. It is directed at remittance recipients and results in 'the conversion from remittance client to bank client through the cross sale of financial products' (Orozco, Burgess, & Massardier, 2010, p. 33).

This set of policies is consistent with the contemporary phase of 'market-building as a development project under late capitalism' (Carroll, 2012, p. 351; Carroll & Jarvis, 2015). This phase succeeds the post-Washington consensus strategy of 'bringing the state back in':

> ... the incomplete constitution of capitalism in a particular image requires energetic 'remedial' attempts to push forms of 'knowledge' (via technical assistance), 'build' particular institutions and foster whole new spheres of private sector activity via risk mitigation and new instruments of financial support (often directly to the private sector). Not simply constrained to state-oriented (pro-market) reform, as in the not-too-distant past, these new efforts—reflecting shifts in the global political economy and a concomitant new politics of development [...]—*work variously on, through and around the state,* with each reform component seemingly referencing and complementing the other. (Carroll, 2012, p. 351)

This amounts to the deepening of neo-liberalism, which retains the post-Washington Consensus preoccupation with fixing 'informationally-based market imperfections' (Fine, 2001, p. 7) but is more likely to localise risk to individuals and communities. The incorporation of migrants' 'idle' money into global development is further explained as a defensive, problem-solving approach to deeper issues of poverty, inequality, and underdevelopment on the part of the IFIs and national development agencies (Hudson, 2008, p. 316). Its benefits to users of financial services are restricted, however, by the relationship between the credit system and capitalist accumulation, in which 'the credit system derives its fundamental design from relations of accumulation but also promotes development of those relations' (Aybar & Lapavitsas, 2001, p. 38). The financial inclusion programme operates within the country's social, political, and historical context, not merely in a world of imperfect information, and in remittance policy it is the less powerful countries that are targeted by virtue of the role of labour migration in their political economies.

3. The Dynamics of Labour Migration

Having outlined the way that neo-liberal global policy frames remittances, the aim is now to show how and why the global remittance agenda needs to be understood more broadly within the historical relationship between labour and capitalism. Labour power has the twofold character of producing value as other commodities do, while it also creates and forms the value of commodities (Marx, 1867/1970, p. 46). As I have discussed elsewhere (Cross, 2013b, pp. 211–212), capitalist economies seek to pay the lowest possible cost for labour. This is achieved by other means than migration, including extending the work time of the national population, inducing large-scale unemployment to push wage rates down, or moving production to less developed regions (not possible for all sectors of the economy) (Harvey, 2003, p. 141). However, what distinguishes migrant labour from other types of cheap labour is that the cost of renewal is externalised to sending economies (Burawoy, 1980). They reproduce, nourish, house, train, and habituate workers, relieving the host country of this cost (Cohen, 1987). Conversely, in the host economy, migrants receive subsistence wages but are excluded from receiving 'indirect wages' in the form of family allowance, pensions, unemployment benefits, sickness cover, and often health care. The separation of the means of renewal from subsistence is possible because imperialism established 'organic relations' between capitalist and 'domestic', or non-capitalist, economies: subsistence agriculture might continue outside of the sphere of production, where the surplus value is created, but by supplying workers, the domestic economy belongs to capitalism's sphere of circulation (Meillassoux, 1981, p. 95). This would lead to temporary and rotating forms of labour migration that simultaneously preserve and exploit the domestic subsistence economy (Meillassoux, 1981, pp. 109–111). This is how capitalism emerges as the dominant, but not the only mode of production. Patterns of migrant labour are the consequence of primitive accumulation, the 'historical process of divorcing the producer from the means of production' so that the social means of subsistence and of production transform to capital and producers become wage labourers (Marx, 1867/1970, pp. 714–715). This separation is 'reproduced on a continually extending scale' (Marx, 1867/1970) and is a coercive process in that workers' 'willingness' to enter labour markets and their supposed freedom to circulate emerges when starvation looms (Fine & Saad-Filho, 2004, p. 81; also Sassen, 1988, p. 33). Migrants have often successfully integrated themselves in the global economy. They have sometimes gained property and means of production, and therefore are no longer motivated to struggle for the lowest possible reward. This indicates why primitive accumulation was not completed, but instead processes of global capitalism reproduce the separation of the producer and his/her means of production in a continuous geographical expansion and the appetite for displaced workers persists (Fine & Saad-Filho, 2004; Marx, 1867/1970, p. 714; Perelman, 1983).

A further dimension of cheapness, beyond the logic of geographical distance, has persisted in forms of 'unfree labour', by which political-legal restrictions are 'specifically intended to restrict the circulation of certain categories of labour-power within the labour market' (Miles, 1987, p. 33). As capitalist economies have industrialised and continued to grow and compete, there has been a consistent role for the most restrictive and cheap forms of commodified labour because historical relations of domination preclude the improvement of wage relations. The varied contributions of slavery, debt bondage, and indentured or contract labour to capitalist production, alongside the 'free' forms, have determined its 'compatibility' with, and the necessity for, unfree forms of wage labour (Cohen, 2006, p. 17; Miles, 1987). European colonial regimes from the sixteenth to the nineteenth centuries brought lasting and divisive social orders and means of resource management to the colonies in the Americas, Asia, and Africa. The expansion of empire was accompanied and fuelled by the Atlantic slave trade, in which producers and slaves were commodified, becoming an *item of exchange* by force. Subsequently, as Europeans settled in the New World, from the early nineteenth to the mid-twentieth centuries, as many as 30 million indentured workers from China and the Indian subcontinent contributed to industrial expansion, replacing slave labour in the Caribbean and also generating wealth in South-East Asian plantations. After the Second World War, labour movements were directed from the colonies to Europe (Castles & Miller, 2003, pp. 51–55; Papastergiadis, 2000, pp. 22–27).

There has been a continuous need for the highly industrialised countries to stabilise new generations of low-cost labour, which are not an incidental product of uneven development, but are also managed to meet the needs of the labour market. Cammack (2008) has described this as a 'universal convergence on competitiveness', by which the OECD, the World Bank, and national development agencies are committed to global labour mobility in support of competitiveness and this produces a 'global proletariat'. In the contemporary era, Mexico and the USA are leading sending and receiving countries, respectively, and broader 'south–north' migration patterns persist among others, including large-scale labour imports in Western Asia's oil-exporting countries. These movements assume restricted and concentrated forms as border policies are selectively enforced (Sassen, 1988, p. 41). They are broadly manageable because in its modern form, unfree labour mobility is the outcome of a contradictory but interconnected system of constraints that develop as the outcome of economic dispossession, illegalisation, border control, labour exploitation, and processes of underdevelopment (Cross, 2013a).

In spite of the advances in transportation and communication that are associated with globalisation's recent history, the increase in migrant stock in relation to population growth has risen merely from 2.2% of the world population in 1970 to 2.7% in 2005 (this latter figure excludes the nationality changes of those who had lived in the former Soviet Union) (United Nations Development Program, 2009, p. 146).

While these statistics are limited by the invisibility and varied timeframes of many forms of migration, they still necessitate consideration of what happens to those who stay, who are economically coerced to migrate but prevented from doing so. In Senegal, clandestine emigration is commonly considered reckless, yet the well-known 'Barça mba Barzakh' ('Barcelona or the afterlife' in Wolof) motto for would-be migrants in Dakar should be taken more literally than as an exuberant desire to enter 'the West'. Here and in neighbouring countries, households faced the loss of land through commodification and a later devaluation of the franc CFA (Communauté Financière Africaine) in the 1980–1990s era of structural adjustment, at which time remittances from Europe grew in significance. Crisis has persisted in the industrial and agricultural sectors, leading to unemployment levels upwards of 40%, reaching 80% in one of Senegal's primary districts of clandestine migration to the Canary Islands (Bouilly, 2008, p. 15). The global food price hikes of 2007–2008 reverberated strongly in migrants' and stayers' explanations of 'illegal' migration.

Furthermore, the financial system was cited as an important cause of dispossession, by which it would not be possible to save money for family welfare expenses with a local wage and consequentially, loans would be taken out that required the mortgaging of houses and other possessions (Cross, 2013b, pp. 206–207). This again alludes to the importance of understanding capitalism as a dynamic process rather than a historical stage, meaning that colonial forms of exchange repeat themselves: it remains that—separated from the means of production—the producer is forced to 'buy back provisions during a time of need at higher prices and on credit' and this 'encourages speculation and the formation of a parasitic social class' (Meillassoux, 1981, p. 31). People can 'make do', but it is emigrants who are able to 'earn a living', while stayers are unable to find stable work and will struggle with the basic necessities. This is not peculiar to impoverished communities in Africa: a detailed study of 'migration fever' in a Guatemalan town reveals an overwhelming number of farms that cannot support a family, creating the necessity for heavy borrowing with land titles and housing as collateral (Stoll, 2013, p. 8). It shows how capitalism not only encourages people to take risks, but also pressures them to do so in the competitive scramble for a better future. When remittances drive further financialisation, the necessity for families to gamble assets, livelihoods, and lives intensifies. This insight reinforces the importance of moving beyond empiricism to understand the passionate declarations of hopeful migrant workers in any part of the world that is subject to development and 'poverty alleviation' strategies (Stoll, 2013, 192). Modern forms of accumulation—the suppression of local forms of production and consumption; imperial appropriation of assets (including natural resources); the monetisation of exchange and taxation; national debt; and the credit system (Harvey, 2003, p. 145)—lead people willingly, even desperately, into an illegal labour market that often rejects them, particularly in times of global recession.

This global historical perspective presents a grounding challenge to the modern tendency to reify the choice and agency of migrant workers out of context, or to view 'mobility' as a cultural phenomenon that is the outcome of advances in globalisation (Cross, 2013a, pp. 11, 14). This is not to be deterministic about migrants' trajectories or to dismiss the successes that follow epic journeys into the unknown, but is instead to draw attention both to the underlying circumstances of the decision to migrate out of low-income economies, and to the reproduction of an unstable livelihood (see Riddell, 1981, pp. 372–373), which often fails.

Fine (2007, p. 4) warns against the use of Marx's theory of unemployment, or the 'reserve army of labour', to interpret contemporary notions of poverty and unemployment in the developing world because Marx suggests that various circumstances modify its workings. This general law, however, offers at the very least a helpful metaphor by which migrant workers are situated in the wider populations from which they originate. The reserve army of labour consists of three components: the 'floating' section of those who are unemployed but likely to be reincorporated in the workforce; the 'latent' section of people who have never been wage labourers but could potentially join the workforce; and finally, the 'Lazarus-like' layer or 'surplus population' for whom particular circumstances prevent the selling of labour power. The extent of the Lazarus layer, alongside the industrial reserve army more generally, rises with the extent of social wealth and corresponds with the level of 'official pauperism', creating the general law of capitalist accumulation (Fine, 2007). What may be taken from this principle for the evaluation of the remittance agenda is firstly that migrant workers who are sending remittances, by some combination of luck, opportunity, access to resources, determination, or other cause, belong to a more fortunate section of a larger population. Secondly, as a result, a meaningful consideration of the relationship between remittances and development must go beyond the benefits for the migrant's beneficiaries and the finance industry, to assess the broader implications of remittances for poverty and inequality.

4. Remittances: Channels, Uses, and Impact

A USAID report (2012, p. 2) considers that remittances have 'untapped potential' to go beyond financial transfers and 'to extend along the whole spectrum of human development'. Similarly, the President of the International Fund for Agricultural Development (Nwanze, 2013) argues that in the $260 billion of remittances to developing countries in Asia, 'the enormous potential returns for society have not been realised'. The global remittance agenda represents a resurgence of the optimism that was attached to migrant transfers in the 1950s and 1960s, during the 'golden age' of migration, when post-war Northern Europe continued to draw on labour from the south and the risks of migrating were comparatively low. However, this resurgence is part and parcel of a financialising approach to development, shifting from the earlier state-centric focus on migrants' investments in enterprise towards a market-building logic (de Haas, 2007, p. 3).

As explained earlier, the primary concern here with the new approach to remittances is the presumption that development and poverty alleviation would be encouraged if migrant workers managed their money better. The funds, now that they are visible to policy-makers, apparently present a blank slate to the International Development community to foster growth through various types of 'financial innovation'. This amounts to a denial of the severity and persistence of underdevelopment and a denigration of households' long-running spending behaviours in this setting (see the following discussion). Characteristic of late capitalism, a singular, narrow, and universal trajectory of development is presumed which denies the existence of alternatives. While critical of the outcome of capitalist globalisation in Africa, Ferguson (2006) also warns against the reactionary approach to a single-minded modernisation. He importantly points out that it is appealing to recognise that there are 'alternative modernities', but 'once we give up the benchmark of a singular modernity, then what does the term mean, analytically? If Cameroonians practicing witchcraft are in fact being "modern" ... then one wonders: What would count as non-modern?' (Ferguson, 2006, p. 31). With this in mind, is incorporation in 'global' (but non-Islamic) finance the necessary route to modernity? Will deregulated remittance flows create a 'win–win' situation for migrants and owners of capital? The suggestion is more that of a zero-sum game, in that the liberalisation of financial markets represents 'the support of financial interests and activities against those of others' (Fine, 2007, p. 11). This section will indeed argue that there are meaningful modern alternatives to financialisation.

The existence of remittances, let alone the way they function, presents a paradoxical challenge to the methodological individualism that underpins the construction of the capitalist political economy. Neoclassical migration theory did not previously recognise them because it was anticipated, for example, by Todaro, that the benefits of labour migration were found in the equalisation of wage levels and consequentially migration would cease once this essential stage of development was fulfilled (see de Haas, 2007, p. 4). Policy has now shifted towards institutionalising the flow of remittances under the acceptance that they are growing. Econometric models have reappeared in migration literature that aim to compute 'motives' for remitting, including altruism ('pure' and 'impure'), insurance against risk, the repayment of loans, exchange of services, and the aspiration to inherit, contributing to debates around the degree of 'altruism' and 'self-interest' or 'selfishness' (of the migrant and/or recipients) (Lucas & Stark, 1985, p. 904; Rapoport & Docquier, 2005, p. 10; Melkonyan & Grigorian, 2012, p. 1037). This approach to remittances ultimately reduces the migrant to a rational egoist whether s/he is judged altruistic or selfish because the modelling is based on individual actions and desires.

A more objective explanation concerning West Africa shows that migrants' efforts are made on behalf of their villages or districts as a reflection of economic considerations such as previous investments in the migrant and the preservation of the community through times of struggle (Potts, 2010, p. 39). Patterns have emerged by which different family members move back and forth between local agriculture, urban wage labour, and overseas jobs, contributing to village social resources. The sending of remittances shows collective action at different stages of the process, by which 'users of a common-pool resource organise themselves to devise and enforce some of their own basic rules' (Orstrom, 2000, p. 148). These actions are frequently channelled through the informal sector, which in sub-Saharan Africa includes moneylenders, who can be traders, landlords, and pawnbrokers, rotating savings and credit associations (ROSCAs, including *susu* in Ghana, *esusu* in Nigeria, *tontines* in Francophone Africa, and *upatu* in Tanzania) and informal arrangements among relatives and friends, often at zero-interest rates (Lawrence, 2006, p. 246).

In Senegal, the *tontine* organised by the Collective of Women for the Fight against Clandestine Emigration, formed by mothers of migrants lost at sea, has provided emergency funds for the reintegration of repatriated migrants and to prevent others from leaving (Bouilly, 2008; Cross, 2013b, p. 207). In Catalonia, there are tontines of up to 70 members, which include Guinean Women of Lleida, Gambian Women in Mataró, Mixed Cameroonians in L'Hospitalet, and Senegalese Women of la Segarra (Sow, 2007, p. 40). The Senegalese Mouride brotherhoods have a history of setting up migration and work networks and facilitating remittance channels (Diouf, 2000; Lawrence, 2006, p. 246). In less fixed networks, West African remittance senders in Barcelona and other towns in Catalonia pool and exchange resources, including food, accommodation, child care, and work permits. This makes it possible to send significant funds to the household out of a low wage. It was explained to me that conditions of life in Europe were unimportant compared to changes to the family home in Africa: spending on water, electricity, and other basic needs is money wasted, while cash and goods sent to Africa are an investment (Cross, 2013a, p. 116; see Tall, 2008, p. 53).

Known as 'aid which reaches its destination', or an 'internationalised informal welfare system' remittances have helped households to overcome crises (Bracking & Sachikonye, 2010, p. 218; Sakho, 2007). A report compiled in Dakar's Université Cheikh Anta Diop found that around 2.5 million Senegalese remit approximately 600 billion CFA (€914.7 million) and this affects almost 70% of households. The majority of this money comes from Europe and the USA, representing a quarter of imports and a third of exports (Cross, 2013c; Sakho, 2007, p. 11). It is estimated that half of the money is sent by formal channels and half informal (Sakho, 2007, pp. 11, 16). There is strong evidence across Senegal's diverse migrant groups that the money has been directed towards development, investment, and saving as much as possible. Remittances have enabled the development of property, building, construction, and artisanal sectors, creating labour demand. Emigrants constitute half of the proprietors in some quarters of Dakar (Grand Dakar and Parcelles Assaines) and contributed to 60% of construction in Kebemer between 2002 and 2007 (Sakho, 2007, p. 12). Transfers from emigrants have covered expenses for health care and education, provided basic household needs, and have allowed families to acquire land and tools for income generation. Fall noted the construction of a 'life shop' in the village of Sédo-Sébé, funded by remittances, where essential goods were available at lower cost and could offset frequent stock market ruptures (2008, p. 207). More broadly, however, remittances are less likely to end patterns of labour migration in rural areas that experience a greater severity of poverty (Diagne & Diané, 2008, p. 13). In rural Sahel zones, 97% of remittance funds are used for household expenses and thus are said to have ameliorated the food crisis (Willem, 2008, p. 295). At the same time, one migrant from the northern region of Podor in Senegal illustrated the critical level of dependence as she explained to me that: 'Many people in the village are eating only the remittances ... they live on the remittances but some don't have anyone to give them money. These people are eating only little' (Cross, 2013c).

There are a number of challenges to the viability of directing remittances towards development. If we put aside the contemporary limitations to migrating overseas and isolate the remittance flows, still a more complex picture emerges than a simple transfer of wealth from north to south, or west to east. Castles and Kosack (1973, pp. 418–420) noted towards the end of the 'golden age of migration' that high levels of remittances from Northern Europe towards the peripheral countries of Southern Europe and North Africa did not alter the balance of payments situation in these latter countries over time. Workers were not leaving in sufficient numbers to alleviate unemployment problems or to raise wages enough to stimulate growth. Ultimately, the 'development aid' was moving from the poorer to the wealthier countries. This phenomenon would be magnified in the contemporary era. This is because Spain among the other peripheral countries had been a 'labour-frontier' country for Europe, distinguishable from many of the 'labour-reserve' countries that contemporary policy is concerned with. As discussed previously, the labour-reserve, unlike the labour-frontier, countries do not engage fully in capitalist relations of production and this restricts movement for workers (Skeldon, 1997, p. 145).

More recently, economic reports on behalf of the IMF and the African Development Bank (AfDB) have found, respectively, that remittances are negatively correlated with GDP growth and that they have a strong impact on increasing inequality. The IMF report noted that 'remittances do not appear to be intended to serve as capital for economic development, but as compensation for poor economic performance' (Chami, Fullenkamp, & Jahjah, 2005, p. 77). In the latter study, it was concluded that 'international remittances have a strong, statistically significant impact on increasing inequality in Africa' (Anyanwu, 2011, p. 19). This was based on data from five eight-year windows between 1960 and 2006. The report argued that this happened because the remitters' households were not poor in the first place. It is also likely that the smaller remitters will move through informal and less detectable channels, to a greater number of households even if the quantities are lower. In this respect, research into the local dynamics of remittances and inequality have also been useful alongside the macroeconomic studies. Bracking (2003, p. 267) related inequality to the phenomenon in which remittance-receiving households undermine the spending power of households that do not receive remittances. Similarly, Bertrand argues that in Senegal, the accumulation of migrants' savings has intensified social relations, reflecting the 'paradox of resource abundance' (cited in Fall, 2008, p. 205; Tall, 2008, p. 52). This problem does not, however, feature significantly in global remittance policy and it is argued in this context that 'countries have to learn to live with these persistent flows' because it is expensive to sterilise their impact (Ratha, 2007, p. 7).

In sum, remittances are an important, often necessary, source of income in receiving households and they move in significant volumes, yet they also are likely to intensify inequalities. This is a persistent problem between sending and receiving economies. It is also widely noted at the local level, especially in low-income countries, although particular instances show that 'domestic' communities that are outside the capitalist sphere of production can find ways to address this issue within the constraints of their economies. The remittance agenda, in aiming to 'enhance' the modes of remitting, is poverty alleviation at its narrowest if it takes its idealised form. It offers at best nothing practical in overcoming local inequalities. The assumption is simply that competing financial institutions will alleviate poverty at the same time as generating profit and that those who are not participating in this path to development lack knowledge. The ideological dimension of the financialisation project prevails, meaning that it presents 'special interests as the exclusive or general interest, or vice-versa, and as inevitable, unavoidable, natural even, TINA', featuring the '8 Cs' of being 'constructed, construed, contested, collective, contradictory, contextual, closed, and chaotic' (Fine, 2007, pp. 11–12). This project of financial incorporation sustains an existing point of tension within labour regimes, which emerges in the continuous and chaotic geographical expansion and deepening of capital, as in low-income regions it is migrant workers' separation from the capitalist economy that brings them to sell labour power in distant labour markets and their incorporation that limits the flow of cheap labour. The role of this turbulent dynamic in capitalist development limits the extent and quality of potential incorporation of the 'labouring poor' (Bush, 2007).

The global remittance agenda has begun to take material form by which it co-opts, or rather 'teaches', parts of civil society as the space of earners of money. If in Africa's postcolonial era, the nation-state was associated positively with modernity, democracy, development, and progress, while society was 'tribal and primordial', then neo-liberal economic and political adjustments reversed these paradigms as 'civil society' became supposedly dynamic and progressive, keeping the venal state in check (Ferguson, 2006, p. 99). As the sphere that is 'sandwiched between the patriarchal family and the universal state' (Hegel/Mamdani, cited in Ferguson 2006, p. 92), civil society provided a means of working around the state in the reforms of the Washington Consensus and beyond. In the era of market-building as development, however, the global remittance agenda aims for transformation directly at the household or individual level. The direct route to communities and individuals is enhanced by the Western expansion of security and control, which provides development finance institutions with a legal mechanism for undermining and controlling parallel channels of money. To dig up the tired critique of Development from the era of structural adjustment, the direction is 'top-down', deploying civil society as a conduit while global change also enables this level of engagement to be bypassed.

5. Conclusion

This article has undoubtedly raised as many questions as answers and it is hoped that the financial incorporation of migrant labourers and their households might be analysed in future from a range of critical perspectives, on different scales, and through close examination of different cases. What is important is that the focus moves away from the way remittances contribute to growth and development, and how good migrants and recipients are at using them, as is the tendency in much IFI-linked academic literature on the subject. Instead, the wider circumstances of sending remittances; the ways that remittance sending illuminates, recreates, and challenges contemporary relations between high- and low-income economies; and the implications and eventual outcomes of 'harnessing' this money in financial markets are all interesting questions. I aim in these final paragraphs to draw out some insights in this direction.

The first claim in this article was that the remittance agenda adopts a profit-driven approach to development. While there are a range of motives in the formulation of neo-liberal policies, it has been demonstrated here that the aim to reduce the transaction costs of remittances for migrants is subordinated to the expansion of financial markets and therefore, they are not harmonious aims. This is the outcome of incorporating financial stakeholders in policy-making and development practice and it is consistent with other analyses of contemporary capitalism. This is to say that development problems are seen as a technical issue concerning information flows and the efficiency of markets, for which financial services surpass their intermediary role and seek to reconstruct economies from their own perspective. Political support allows them to do so at the expense of cheaper and more efficient services and their users. Secondly, this article linked remittance sending with the historical relationship between migrant labour and capitalism. Remittances are the *raison d'être* of labour migration and IFIs understand them in aggregate form as a continuous and growing flow of funds, hence their 'stability'. However, the funds targeted for development originate in labour that has been displaced by modern forms of dispossession, and this is precisely why they are more significant in the poorer countries. Furthermore, if broader development outcomes were to be encouraged, the populations that are coerced into migrating but held back from doing so would also be taken into account. This understanding of the circumstances of labour migration provides the essential bridge between the political narrative of remittances and their potential for development. Thirdly, I showed that the global remittance agenda approaches remittance flows as a *new* opportunity for growth and development. This raises wider questions about development and modernity. It was pointed out here that in the West African case among others, there is a fundamental problem with the incorporation of remittances in capitalist finance because they are built on collective actions. The cooperative social relations that enable remittance money to be gathered, sent, and used, such as zero-interest lending and transferral, or the pooling and exchange of resources, are not to be dismissed as 'traditional', nor is it romanticising to view these processes as practical. They are the rational outcome of a livelihood that would be otherwise unable to reverse the destruction of the household. In this case, the remittance agenda is based on a false problem—that remittances do not contribute enough to development because they are not managed efficiently—and the solution points to another means for capitalism to extract surplus from migrant workers.

Disclosure Statement

No potential conflict of interest was reported by the author.

Note

1   See: http://remittanceprices.worldbank.org (World Bank Group's International Finance Corporation); http://www. enviacentroamerica.org (World Bank, the Center for Latin America Monetary Studies, and the Multilateral Investment Fund of the Inter-American Development Bank); http://www.moneymove.org/English/httpdocs/ services.cfm (Developing Markets Associates Ltd.); http://www.envoidargent.fr (French Development Agency).

References

Acosta, P., Calderón C., Fajnzyber, P., & López, H. (2006). Remittances and development in Latin America. *The World Economy, 29*(7), 957–987.
Adams, R. H., & Page, J. (2005). Do international migration and remittances reduce poverty in developing countries? *World Development, 33*(10), 1645–1669.

Addy, D. N., Wijkström, B., & Thouez, C. (2003). *'Migrant remittances – country of origin experiences'. International conference on migrant remittances: Developmental impact and future prospects.* London: DFID and World Bank.

Ammassari, S. (2006). *Migration management and development policies: Maximising the benefits of international migration in West Africa. No. 72E.* Geneva: International Labour Office.

Anyanwu, J. C. (2011). *International remittances and income inequality in Africa.* Working Paper No. 35. Tunis: African Development Bank Group.

Aybar, S., & Lapavitsas, C. (2001). Financial system design and the post-Washington consensus. In B. Fine, C. Lapavitsas, & J. Pincus (Eds.), *Development policy in the twenty-first century: Beyond the post-Washington consensus* (pp. 28–51). Abingdon: Routledge.

Ballard, R. (2005). Coalitions of reciprocity and the maintenance of financial integrity within informal value transmission systems: The operational dynamics of contemporary *hawala* networks. *Journal of Banking Regulation, 6*(4), 319–352.

Bank for International Settlements and World Bank. (2007). *General principles for international remittance Services.* Committee on payment and settlement systems, Basel. Retrieved July 5, 2013, from http://siteresources.worldbank.org/INTPAYMENTREMMITTANCE/Resources/New_Remittance_Report.pdf

Barajas, A., Chami, R., Fullenkamp, C., & Garg, A. (2010). *The global financial crisis and workers' remittances to Africa: What's the damage?* IMF Working Paper, WP/10/24, International Monetary Fund.

Bouhga-Hagbe, J. (2004). *A theory of workers' remittances with an application to Morocco* (WP/04/194). International Monetary Fund.

Bouilly, E. (2008, March). La couverture médiatique du collectif pour la lutte contre l'immigration clandestine de Thiaroye-sur-Mer (Dakar–Sénégal). Un mise en abîme du discours produit au 'Nord' sur le 'Sud', Terra-Infos.

Bourenane, N., Bourjij, S., & Lhériau, L. (2011). Réduire les coûts des transferts d'argent des migrants et optimiser leur impact sur le développement : Outils et produits financiers pour le Maghreb et la Zone franc. Agence Française de Développement and Epargne sans Frontière. Retrieved July 5, 2013, from http://www.afd.fr/webdav/site/afd/shared/ConferenceESF_BAD_DGT_AFD_2011_Transferts_argent_migrants_rapport_fr.pdf

Bracking, S. (2003). Sending money home: Are remittances always beneficial to those who stay behind? *Journal of International Development, 15*(5), 633–644.

Bracking, S., & Sachikonye, L. (2010). Migrant remittances and household wellbeing in urban Zimbabwe. *International Migration, 48*(5), 203–227.

Brown, S. (2006). Can remittances spur development? A critical Survey. *International Studies Review, 8,* 55–75.

Burawoy, M. (1980). Migrant labour in South Africa and the United States. In T. Nichols (Ed.), *Capital and labour: A Marxist primer* (pp. 138–173). London: Fontana.

Bush, R. (2007). *Poverty and neoliberalism: Persistence and reproduction in the Global South.* London: Pluto Press.

Cammack, P. (2008). *Universal convergence on competitiveness.* Papers in the Politics of Global Competitiveness, No. 10, Institute for Global Studies: University of Manchester.

Carroll, T. (2012). Introduction: Neo-Liberal development policy in Asia beyond the post-Washington consensus. *Journal of Contemporary Asia, 42*(3), 350–358.

Carroll, T., & Jarvis, D. S. L. (2015). The new politics of development: Citizens, civil society and the evolution of Neo-liberal development policy. *Globalizations*, doi:10.1080/14747731.2015.1016301

Castaldo, A., Deshingkar, P., & McKay, A. (2012). *Internal migration, remittances and poverty: Evidence from Ghana and India.* Migrating out of Poverty Research Programme Consortium and DfID (Working Paper 7). University of Sussex.

Castles, S., & Kosack, G. (1973). *Immigrant workers and class structure in Western Europe.* London: Oxford University Press.

Castles, S., & Miller, M. J. (2003). *The age of migration: International population movements in the modern world* (3rd ed.). Basingstoke: Palgrave Macmillan.

Chami, R., Fullenkamp, C., & Jahjah, S. (2005). Are immigrant remittance flows a source of capital for development? *IMF Staff Papers, 52*(1), 55–81.

Cirasino, M., & Ratha, D. (2009, November 9). *The activities of the Global remittances working group.* G8 international Conference on remittances. Rome: World Bank. Retrieved July 3, 2013, from http://siteresources.worldbank.org/FINANCIALSECTOR/Resources/282044-1257537401267/RomeConferenceRemittances.RathaAnd Cirasino.pdf

Cohen, R. (1987). *The new helots: Migrants in the international division of Labour.* Aldershot: Avebury.

Cohen, R. (2006). *Migration and its enemies: Global capital, migrant labour and the Nation-State.* Aldershot: Ashgate.

Cross, H. (2008). Migration, remittances and development in West Africa: The case of Senegal. *Global Development Studies, 5*(3–4), 133–164.

Cross, H. (2013a). *Migrants, borders and global capitalism: West African labour mobility and EU Borders*. Oxon: Routledge.

Cross, H. (2013b). Labour and underdevelopment? Migration, dispossession and accumulation in West Africa and Europe. *Review of African Political Economy, 40*(136), 202–218.

Cross, H. (2013c). Globalisation du marché du travail, frontières et migrations à partir du Sénégal. In M.-C. Diop (Ed.), *Le Sénégal sous Abdoulaye Wade. Le Sopi à l'épreuve du pouvoir* (pp. 729–746). Paris: Karthala.

Developing Markets Associates Ltd and Department for International Development. (2011). *Constraints in the UK to Ghana remittances market*. Retrieved September 14, 2012, from http://www.dfid.gov.uk/Documents/publications1/Constraints-UK-Ghana.pdf

Diagne, Y.S., & Diané, F. (2008). *Impact des transferts des migrants sur la pauvreté au Sénégal*. Document d'Etude No. 7, Direction de la Prévision et des Etudes Economiques. Dakar.

Diouf, M. (2000). The Senegalese Murid trade diaspora and the making of vernacular cosmopolitanism (S. Rendall, trans.). *Public Culture, 12*(3), 679–702.

Ebeke, C. H. (2012). Do remittances lead to a public moral Hazard in developing countries? An Empirical investigation. *The Journal of Development Studies, 48*(8), 1009–1025.

Fall, P. D. (2008). Migration internationale et développement local dans le Nguènar sénégalaise. In M.-C. Diop (Ed.), *Le Sénégal des migrations: Mobilités, identités et societés* (pp. 195–210). Dakar: CREPOS, Karthala and ONU Habitat.

Ferguson, J. (2006). *Global Shadows: Africa in the Neoliberal world order*. Durham: Duke University Press.

Findley, S. Traoré, S., Ouedraogo, D., & Diarra, S. (1995). Emigration from the Sahel. *International Migration, 33*(3–4), 469–507.

Fine, B. (2001). Neither the Washington nor the post-Washington consensus: An introduction. In B. Fine, C. Lapavitsas, & J. Pincus (eds.), *Development policy in the twenty-first century: Beyond the post-Washington consensus* (pp. 28–51). Abingdon: Routledge.

Fine, B. (2007, July 2–7). *Financialisation, Poverty, and Marxist Political Economy', Poverty and Capital Conference*. University of Manchester.

Fine, B., & Saad-Filho, A. (2004). *Marx's Capital* (4th ed.). London: Pluto Press.

Froud, J., Johal, S., & Williams, K. (2002). Financialisation and the coupon Pool. *Capital and Class, 26*(3), 119–151.

Giuliano, P., & Ruiz-Arranz, M. (2009). Remittances, financial development, and growth. *Journal of Development Economics, 90*(1), 144–152.

de Haas, H. (2005). International migration, remittances and development: Myths and facts. *Third World Quarterly, 26*(8), 1269–1284.

de Haas, H. (2007). *Remittances, migration and social development: A conceptual review of the literature* (Social Policy and Development Programme Paper, No. 34). UNRISD.

Harvey, D. (2003). *The new imperialism*. Oxford: Oxford University Press.

Hudson, D. (2008). Developing geographies of financialisation: Banking the poor and remittance securitisation. *Contemporary Politics, 14*(3), 315–33.

Isaacs, L., Vargas-Silva, C., & Hugo, S. (2012). *EU remittances for developing countries, remaining barriers, challenges and recommendations* (EuropeAid/129783/C/SER/multi. European Commission with HTSPE Ltd). EuroTrends.

Lawrence, P. (2006). La liberalización financiera y el desarrollo en el África Subsahariana. In C. Oya & A. Santamaría (Eds.), *Economía Política del Desarrollo en África* (pp. 239–262). Madrid: Akal.

Lindley, A. (2007). *The early morning phonecall: Remittances from a refugee perspective* (Working Paper No. 47). Centre on Migration, Policy and Society, University of Oxford.

Lucas, R. E. B., & Stark, O. (1985). Motivations to remit: Evidence from Botswana. *Journal of Political Economy, 93*(5), 901–918.

Mader, P. (2014). Financialisation through microfinance: Civil society and Market-building in India. *Asian Studies Review, 38*(4), 601–619.

Magunha, F., Bailey, A., & Cliffe, L. (2009). *Remittance strategies of Zimbabweans in Northern England*. Leeds: School of Geography, University of Leeds

Marx, K. (1867/1970). *Capital* (Vol. 1). London: Lawrence and Wishart.

Mazzucato, V. (2006, March 19–21). *Informal insurance arrangements in Ghanaian migrants' transnational networks: The role of reverse remittances and geographic proximity*. Paper presented at the conference Reducing poverty and inequality: how can Africa be included? Centre for the Study of African Economies, University of Oxford.

Meillassoux, C. (1981). *Maidens, meal and money: Capitalism and the domestic community*. Cambridge: Cambridge University Press.

Melkonyan, T. A., & Grigorian, D. A. (2012). Microeconomic implications of remittances in an overlapping generations model with Altruism and a motive to receive inheritance. *The Journal of Development Studies, 48*(8), 1026—1044.

Miles, R. (1987). *Capitalism and unfree labour: Anomaly or necessity?* London: Tavistock Publications.

Naudé, W., & Bezuidenhout, H. (2012). Remittances to sub-Saharan Africa in the wake of a financial crisis: Source of resilience or vulnerability? In I. Sirkeci, J. Cohen, & D. Ratha (Eds), *Migration and remittances during the Global financial crisis and beyond.* Washington, DC: The World Bank.

Nwanze, K. (2013). Harnessing the remittance boom. Project Syndicate, 18 May. Retrieved August 2, 2013, from http://www.project-syndicate.org/commentary/remittances-by-migrant-workers-as-a-development-tool-by-kanayo-f-nwanze

Organisation for Economic Cooperation and Development. (2005). *Migration, remittances and development.* Paris: Author.

Orozco, M., Burgess, E., & Massardier, C. (2010). *Remittance transfers in Senegal: Preliminary findings, lessons, and recommendations on its marketplace and financial access opportunities* (International Migration Paper No. 109). Geneva: International Labour Office.

Orstrom, E. (2000). Collective action and the evolution of social norms. *Journal of Economic Perspectives, 14*(3), 137–158.

Papastergiadis, N. (2000). *The turbulence of migration: Globalization, deterritorialization and hybridity.* Cambridge: Polity Press.

Perelman, M. (1983). *Classical political economy, primitive accumulation and social division of labor.* Totowa, NJ: Allanheid and Rowman.

Pieke, F., Van Hear, N., & Lindley, A. (2007). Beyond control? The mechanisms and dynamics of 'in-formal' remittances between Europe and Africa. *Global Networks, 7*(3), 348–366.

Potts, D. (2010). *Circular migration in Zimbabwe and contemporary Sub-Saharan Africa.* Oxford: James Currey.

Rapoport, H., & Docquier, F. (2005). *The economics of migrants' remittances* (Discussion Paper No. 1531). Institute for the Study of Labour, Bonn, Germany.

Ratha, D. (2003). Workers' remittances: An important and stable source of external development finance. In World Bank, *Global development finance 2003* (pp. 157–176). Washington, DC: The International Bank for Reconstruction and Development/ World Bank.

Ratha, D. (2007). *Policy brief: Leveraging remittances for development.* Washington, DC: Migration Policy Institute.

Ratha, D., & Silwal, A. (2012, April 23). *Remittances flows in 2011 – an update.* Migration and Development Brief, 18.

Riddell, J. B. (1981). Beyond the description of spatial pattern: The process of proletarianization as a factor in population migration in West Africa. *Progress in Human Geography, 5,* 370–392.

Sakho, P. (2007). *Les migrations internationales senegalaises: Potential financier et changement social. Actes du Dîner-Débat. institut de formation et de recherche en population, développement et Santé de la population.* Dakar: Université Cheikh Anta Diop.

Sassen, S. (1988). *The mobility of labor and capital.* Cambridge: Cambridge University Press.

Skeldon, R. (1997). *Migration and development: A global perspective.* Harlow: Longman.

Skeldon, R. (2008). International migration as a tool in development policy: A passing phase? *Population and Development Review, 34*(1), 1–18.

Sow, P. (2007). *Epargne populaire des africains en Catalogne: Types et formes souterraines de practiques financières des immigrants. Grup d'Estudis i de Reflexió sobre Africa, September.* Barcelona: Fondació Jaume Bofill.

Stoll, D. (2013). *El Norte or Bust! How migration fever and microcredit produced a financial crash in a Latin American town.* Lanham, MD: Rowman and Littlefield.

Tall, S.M. (2008). La migration internationale sénégalaise: Des recrutements de main d'oeuvre aux pirogues. In M.-C. Diop (Ed.), *Le Sénégal des migrations: Mobilités, identités et societés* (pp. 37–67). Dakar: CREPOS, Karthala and ONU Habitat.

United Nations Development Program. (2009). *Human development report: Overcoming barriers: Human mobility and development.* New York: Author.

United States Agency for International Development. (2012). *Partnering with USAID: Building alliances for sustainable solutions.* Washington, DC: USAID.

Vargas-Lundius, R., Lanly, G., Villarreal, M., & Osorio, M. (2008). *International migration, remittances and rural development.* FAO and IFAD. Retrieved March 6, 2012, from http://web.ifad.org/pub/remittances/migration.pdf

Willems, R. (2008). Les 'fous de la mer': Les migrants clandestins du Sénégal aux Îles Canaries en 2006. In M.-C. Diop (ed.), *Le Sénégal des migrations: Mobilités, Identités et Societés* (pp. 77–303). Dakar: CREPOS, Karthala and ONU Habitat.

World Bank. (2013, April 19). Migration and Development Brief No. 20, Migration and Remittances Unit, Development Prospects Group. Retrieved July 5, 2013, from http://siteresources.worldbank.org/INTPROSPECTS/Resources/334934–1288990760745/MigrationDevelopmentBrief20.pdf

Neoliberal Modes of Participation in Frontier Settings: Mining, Multilateral Meddling, and Politics in Laos

PASCALE HATCHER

Ritsumeikan University, Kyoto, Japan

ABSTRACT   *After decades promoting highly liberalised mining codes, the World Bank Group has now positioned poverty reduction and environmental sustainability as the fundamental objectives of its involvement in the sector. Within this new approach, local participation occupies a central position, whereby a loosely defined mix of local associations, as well as residents of local communities affected by mining activities, is to have a voice in every stage of a given mining project. Building on the case of Laos, this article investigates both the participatory model promoted by the World Bank and the politics of the model's implementation. The analysis suggests that the involvement of local communities is ensconced within a framework which conceives participatory schemes as a management tool to, first and foremost, circumscribe the risks faced by mining investors. While this represents a clear attempt to mitigate political risk in order to facilitate the larger project of building new liberal markets, it further raises questions linked to the remodelling of political notions of empowerment and representation.*

The abundance of natural resources of Lao People's Democratic Republic (hereafter 'Laos') has, in recent years, become the mantle upon which the Laos government has promised much-needed employment, education, health care, clean water, and infrastructure. Alongside the multiplication of dams rapidly being erected upon its rivers, the aspiring 'battery of Southeast Asia' has also been resolutely eyeing its hitherto largely untapped mining sector for the prospective contributions it can make to burgeoning growth. If for decades Laos was one of the poorest countries in the region, it now boasts steady economic growth and appears determined to shed its 'Least Developed Country' (LDC) status by 2020. Not surprisingly, international organisations who, until recently, were the lifeline of the country, are cheering such fast pace developments vociferously and supporting the clamour over the exploitation of the country's resources.

In this regard, this article investigates the particular role played by the World Bank Group (WBG) in fostering the country's rapidly emerging large-scale mining sector. Of particular interest is the recent addition of a strong social-development narrative attached to multilateral guidelines promoted by the WBG. This novel approach, here referred to as the 'social-development model' (SDM), is a narrative emphasising poverty reduction as a central objective of the Bank's actions within the sector, as well as social and environmental concerns. Within this new approach, and evoking a progressive air that contrasts significantly with issues that have notoriously plagued resource exploitation in the underdeveloped world, local participation is supposed to occupy a centre stage, with a loosely defined mix of local associations, as well as residents of local communities affected by mining activities, to have a voice in each stage of a given mining project. Echoing the WBG's framework, Vientiane has quickly twinned pro-mining investment incentives with a pro-poor and environmentally sustainable narrative, suggesting that the implementation of WBG policy to combat often egregious problems in the mining sector is more than just multilateral wishful thinking. However, as with many situations involving underdeveloped locales and new patterns of growth in countries now frequently described as 'frontier markets', the reality is complicated (see Carroll & Jarvis, 2015). In particular, the promotion of new mining regimes ostensibly designed to tackle problems of the past *and promote growth* has rapidly revealed tensions broadly relating to existing patterns of governance and newly emboldened revenue flows. Moreover, despite the call for increasing levels of participation in mining sector operations in underdeveloped countries, emerging evidence suggests that local people remain disproportionately affected in a negative sense and that the role of organisations within what might be broadly described as 'civil society' is far from a panacea to address this, especially in environments where political participation is traditionally heavily circumscribed.

In this article, the dual provisions of the mining regime promoted by the WBG are viewed as a particular strategy employed by pro-market interests to both contain and manage opposition to mining activities. While the new model stems from serious consideration of the socio-environmental legacy of mining activities and the need for the involvement of local communities, the implementation process of the Laotian mining regime stands as testimony to difficulties in realising idealised liberal regulation in underdeveloped and authoritarian environments. Importantly, the case of mining in Laos serves as a clear example of the larger discussion over civil society's increasingly functionalist role (as demarcated by organisations such as the World Bank) in the broader project of building new liberal markets in Asia (see Carroll & Jarvis, 2014, 2015; Hatcher, 2014). While this represents a clear attempt to mitigate political risk in order to facilitate capital accumulation, it further raises questions linked to the remodelling of political notions of empowerment and representation, and indeed the promotion and implementation of a form of mining governance that is enabling and abetting highly problematic outcomes.

The paper is divided into five parts. The first section describes the role of the WBG in promoting large-scale mining activities, delineating the various incarnations of mining regimes and their travails. The second section presents an overview of mining in Laos and its recent fast pace development, segueing into a third section that describes the influential roles played by the WBG in enabling such development. The fourth section explicitly teases out the numerous components of what I describe as the 'SDM' enshrined within Laos' mining regime. With two of the country's largest natural resource projects in the foreground (Sepon and the Nam Theun II (NT2)), the final section deals with the alarming disparities between the SDM's narrative and experiences on the ground. The analysis focuses on how the involvement of local communities translates into a renewed emphasis on sociopolitical risk management for capital and multilateral institutions rather than an opening of political space, an issue particularly acute in Laos, for people impacted by mining activities and extant patterns of governance.

Growing a Socio-environmental Conscience: The Rise of the SDM

The overarching involvement of the World Bank[1] in the liberalisation and deregulation of the mining sector is of course by no means limited to Laos.[2] The *Extractive Industries Review* (EIR), which was established in 2001 to independently evaluate the WBG's involvement in extractive industries, estimated that under the leadership of the Bank, no less than 100 countries reformed their laws, policies, and institutions during the 1990s (2003b, p. 10). To understand such involvement, the work of Campbell (2004) is instructive. In her extensive analysis of the World Bank's influence over African mining regimes, Campbell catalogued three generations of mining codes, which essentially followed the Bank's evolving guidelines over the better part of the last three decades. The first wave of reform, which was carried out under the umbrella of the structural adjustment programmes of the World Bank and International Monetary Fund (IMF) in the 1980s, saw a dramatic retreat of the state from the sector. Oblivious to the decline in the demand for mineral resources in the 1980s, the Bank's reassessment of the sector led to a new wave in the liberalisation of mining regimes which extended well into the 1990s. However, the turn of the century was not kind to the Bank's historical involvement in large-scale projects. The highly publicised environmental damage and the multiplication of reported cases of human rights abuses linked to Bank-sponsored projects were a painful thorn in the institution's image.[3] While the Bank did acknowledge that a certain degree of regulation was necessary, notably in terms of environmental protection, it is only within the past decade that the ultimate need for the state to play a regulatory role was acknowledged and instantiated in a 'third generation' of mining codes (Campbell, 2004).[4]

The EIR found that while extractive industries can yield benefits for countries, data suggest that developing countries with few natural resources grew two to three times faster than resource-rich countries from 1960 to 2000 (2003b, p. 12). Furthermore, the Review observed that the majority of the 45 countries that did not manage to sustain economic growth during that time also experienced violent conflict and civil strife in the 1990s (2003b, p. 12). As such, the multiplication of socio-environmental problems linked to extractive activities, notwithstanding the ambiguous economic benefits of the industry, led to highly critical literature suggesting that the actual benefits of the mining industry may have been overstated.[5] In acknowledging the impact of mining on development, the WBG itself fell into line with this analysis: 'resource-rich countries are indeed more likely to have problems achieving important development goals', states the Bank in a recent evaluation of its experience in the extractive sector (Operations Evaluation Group, 2005, p. 120).

It is in light of the extent of the social and environmental problems linked to the extractive industry that the then World Bank President, James Wolfensohn, ordered a two-year moratorium in 2001 on the WBG's mining investments and a review of its involvement in the industry. While the EIR, which emerged from this process, did conclude that there was still a role for the Group in the sector, it underlined that such a role should be strictly limited to one of contributing to sustainable development (EIR, 2003b, p. 4).

In its official response to the EIR (in 2004), the Bank declared: 'Our future investments in extractive industries will be selective, with greater focus on the needs of poor people, and a stronger emphasis on good governance and on promoting environmentally and socially sustainable development' (World Bank, 2004, p. iii).[6] While the Bank acknowledged that extractive industries may 'aggravate or cause serious environmental, health, and social problems, including conflict and war' (World Bank, 2005, p. 1), it, however, remains adamant that such negative impacts are not inevitable. Subsequently, wanting to maintain a presence in the sector while attending to the recognised risks, the Bank substituted its conventional policy recommendation framework for one that promoted far stricter socio-environmental standards, notably, participatory mechanisms for local communities. The ensuing birth of what is here referred to as the 'SDM' echoed throughout the mining industry and within regulatory regimes across the Global South and, as discussed further in the following section, to Lao PDR as well.

The SDM is here understood as a narrative emphasising poverty reduction as a central objective of the Bank's actions within the sector, as well as social and environmental concerns. However, beyond its narrative, the SDM should be viewed as a particular management tool to tackle local opposition to mining projects, therefore curtailing investment risks. It is to be emphasised that this shift closely imbricates itself within the wider shift at the Bank under Wolfensohn's presidency, a shift which echoed throughout the international aid architecture.[7] The latter has been studied extensively, mostly under the umbrella of the 'post-Washington Consensus'.[8]

Today, the WBG is the unchallenged global leader in both the design and the promotion of socio-environmental practices in the mining sector. Such influential work appears to be viewed by the Bank as 'neutral' advice that manages to bridge communities' needs not only with corporate profit-driven behaviour, but also with governments' zeal for fast-paced development. In the words of the Bank:

> The impact of mines on local communities has been an area of growing concern and attention, and one that mining companies, NGOs and governments are grappling with. The World Bank has used its *convening power* and *neutral* position to bring together a number of different agencies to pursue discussion in this area, share experiences and enable diverse agencies to work more cooperatively together, with the view to resolving some of the problems affecting this area. The convening of conferences, meetings, analytical research and the dissemination of good practice are among the number of ways in which the Mining Department has been working to gain a better understanding of these issues, develop mechanisms for resolution and propagate good practice. (Our emphasis, World Bank, 2010d)

In line with this self-assigned role, the World Bank has assumed leadership over key socio-environmental mining research. It is illustrative to note that the Bank's Mining Department website lists a wide range of key issues, notably AIDs and Mining; Mine Closure; Mining and Community; Mining and the Environment; Mining and Local Development; and Mining and Poverty Reduction. Crucially, it should also be emphasised that the WBG, most notably the IFC, has been pioneering various global guidelines and safeguards on mining-related issues.[9]

By following the development of Laos' mining regime from the particular perspective of the WBG, this article sheds light on the highly political, formal and informal, multi-front roles played by the institution in the overarching promotion of the SDM as the main strategy for the development of Laos' mining sector. The case is illustrative of how these plural roles are performed by the WBG and how they have alternated from more direct roles such as investor and lander, to more indirect yet crucially influential, meddling roles as sponsoring mining conferences.

The Promises of a Sector: Mining in Laos PDR

Laos' dire social indicators have long positioned the landlocked country as one of Asia's poorest countries. By the end of the 1990s, almost 40% of this LDC's population was still living in poverty (World Bank, 2010b, p. 14) and, as observed by a WBG fact-finding mission, its social indicators were far closer to those of Sub-Saharan Africa than other Asian countries (Boland, Kunanayagam & Walker, 2001, p. i). However, short of the last decade, Laos has radically transformed its economy, resolutely turning to its impressive abundance of natural resources. Notwithstanding its hydropower potential, Laos, somewhat strikingly, is one of Asia's most resource-rich countries, with more than 570 mineral deposits identified so far.

Pressed between Myanmar, Cambodia, Vietnam, and, more importantly, resource-hungry China, Laos has high hopes for the sector. The potential attached to the large-scale development its natural riches have led to the multiplication of social and economic promises. Today's goal is bold: to become a middle-income country by 2020.[10] The World Bank estimates that Laos will require a steady average growth of 7.5% for this to occur (2010b, p. 10). Thanks to the rapid development of the mining and hydropower sectors, the country appears to be well underway on this front—both sectors have contributed 2.5% of the annual 7% growth witnessed by the country in 2007–2009 (World Bank, 2010b, p. 1) and more recently, 8%. According to the World Bank, these figures are expected to persist in the medium and long term (2012–2020), with a predicted growth of 7.5% per year until 2015 (2012, p. 10).

While in the early 1990s mining activities were 'virtually negligible' (United States Geological Survey [USGS], 1994, p. 491), by the end of the same decade the sector was identified as 'one of the most promising long-term growth areas' (USGS, 1999, p. 13.1). Contrary to many of its neighbour countries which have a rich history of industrial mining, Laos' ventures only truly began in 2003, making it one of Asia's 'final frontiers for miners' (CLC Asia, 2009).[11] The country's industrial mining production value has increased nearly a 100-fold observes a World Bank background report, from around US$8 million in 2002 to US$600–700 million in 2007 and 2008 (Larsen, 2010, p. 4). However, it should be noted that these numbers are a poor indication of the potential offered by the country's natural resources as only 10% of the 200 proposed mining and hydro projects are currently in operation (World Bank, 2010b, p. 1). The World Bank projects that the cumulative revenues of the mining sector alone will total $2 billion by 2025 (cited in United Nations [UN], 2010, p. 33).

Since Laos remains highly dependent on foreign aid—and with the country's external debt totalling 54.5% of its gross domestic product (GDP) (International Council on Mining and Metals [ICMM], 2011, p. 59)—the natural resource sectors (mining and power) have become a much-welcomed source of government revenue. The International Council on Mining and Metals (ICMM) notes that the country's foreign debt is significant enough 'to worry the World Bank and the IMF who believe that there is a high risk of debt distress' (2011, p. 17).

Together, the resource sectors account for 20% of the government's total fiscal revenues, as well as most of the country's foreign direct investment (FDI) inflows—about 80% in 2008 (World Bank, 2010b, p. 1, 2010c, p. 7). However, it is the mining sector that now dominates the country's exports with approximately 50% of all exports.

To contextualise the increased prominence of the resource sector in Laos' economy, it is telling to note that while the mining and quarrying sectors only contributed to 1% of the country's GDP in 2001 (Boland, Kunanayagam & Walker, 2001, p. i), they now contribute 18% (Boungnaphalom, 2010).[12] According to the United States Geological Survey (USGS), in 2010 alone, Laos' production of tin, copper concentrate, silver, and gold increased by 46%, 26%, 7.2%, and 0.6%, respectively, compared with that in 2009 (2012, p. 16.1). Crucially, the revenues flowing from royalties and taxes from mining projects now account for the sharp decline in the government's budget deficit—from 7.58% during 1995–2000 to 6.29% during 2000–2006 (Kyophilavong, 2010, p. 75). By 2009, mineral taxes were contributing to 12% of total government revenues (ICMM, 2011, p. 10). Together, the country's two largest mines—Sepon and Phu Kham—make up for over 90% of total national mining production (ICMM, 2011, p. 17). The recent opening of these mines marked 'a new era of scale and efficiency for the Lao mining sector', comments the UN (2010, p. 32).

The Sepon mine is operated by Lane Xang Minerals Limited (LXML),[13] which is controlled by Minerals and Metals Group (90%) and the Lao government (10%).[14] Gold production at Sepon commenced in 2002 and copper production in early 2005. Today, the mine accounts for about 50% of the country's total exports (UN, 2010, p. 36). The government exercised its right to take a 10% share in the mine only in 2009.

Phu Bia Mining Limited, which is controlled by its parent company Australia's PanAust Limited (with a share of 90%[15] and the Lao government receiving the other 10%), operates the Phu Bia gold mine (since 2005) and the adjacent but much larger Phu Kham copper–gold mine (the latter commencing production in 2008). Additionally, not only did Phu Bia Mining Limited start operations at the Ban Houayxai Gold-Silver Operation (about 25 km from Phu Kham) in 2012, but it also announced the discovery of copper and gold ore in the Xieng Khouang province, which is expected to yield six to seven million tonnes of ore ('Phu Bia strikes gold', 2012).[16]

In addition to these flagship mines in Laos, there are several other projects in the works. Explorations of the bauxite deposits in the Bolavens Plateau suggest that the region might contain some of the largest undeveloped bauxite deposits in the world (UN, 2010, p. 34). A greenfield bauxite exploration project covering 484 km was established in 2009, less than 500 km away from the Chinese border[17] and its insatiable appetite for the material. Since 2010, Rio Tinto and Mitsui's Lao Sanxai Minerals Co. Ltd also have a stake in a bauxite project covering 484 km^2 in the Sanxai District.

The World Bank and the Promotion of Large-Scale Mining in Laos

'Today', observe Guttal and Shoemaker, 'the World Bank is the most powerful policy institution in the Lao PDR' (2004, p. 1). Echoing this claim, the Group has been key in advancing Laos' recent 'resource-boom'. As stated by a Bank official in Vientiane, the multilateral organisation has been busy assisting the government not only with its new Mining Law and its implementing regulations, but also with its broader regulatory framework as well (World Bank, personal communication, February 16, 2011). The direct and indirect roles of the multilateral institution in shifting the country's economy towards the exploitation of its natural resources are tackled in this section.

If the country officially remains socialist, Vientiane has been courting foreign investors since the mid-1980s, as it started opening up to the market-oriented economy. The series of reforms that were to be implemented in the decade that followed were crucial to the success of the country's current natural resource boom. In 1986, it introduced the 'New Economic Mechanism (NEM)', which put an end to central planning and opened the economy to trade and investments.[18] In 1989, the World Bank and the IMF stepped in with additional reforms ranging from the expansion of fiscal and monetary reforms, the strengthening of the banking system, and the promotion of private enterprise and foreign investment, to the privatisation or shutting down of non-performing state-owned enterprises (UN, 2010, p. 8). Additionally, the Lao government agreed to maintain a flexible exchange rate, reduce tariffs, and eliminate what were perceived as superfluous trade regulations (UN, 2010, p. 8). In 1991, Vientiane adopted a new constitution which notably formalised the market-oriented economy.

By the end of the 1990s, the Lao government had liberalised the foreign investment law, allowing 100% foreign ownership of enterprises. According to the USGS, by the end of the same decade, the country's foreign investment policies were 'the most "investor-friendly" in the region' (1997, p. 1). Today, the country is officially a full member of the World Trade Organization (since 2 February 2013), and although in practice this appears to be disputed, the 2009 Law on Investment Promotion vows to give equal treatment and incentives to foreign and local investors alike.

Building on these shifts in the 1990s, the government started to turn its attention towards large-scale mining. The ensuing 1997 Mining Law[19] and its Implementing Decree, which were approved in October 2002, triggered a substantial expansion of the sector. Noticeably, the fiscal regime remains quite open, as issues such as tax rates and royalties are to be negotiated in each of the Mineral Exploration and Production Agreements. Despite such a lack of clearly defined rates, the Department of Geology and Mines (2006) affirmed that the negotiation norm appeared to be around 20–35% for privileged income tax rates with a 10% tax levy on dividend and retained earnings, while royalty rates would vary from 3% to 5%.[20]

It is illustrative to note that Sepon benefited from generous subsidies right from the start. For the first two years, Australia's Oxiana Resources (together with Rio Tinto, which held a 20% interest), as the original owner of the mine, was to be exempt from corporate taxes and their employees exempt from income taxes. For the subsequent two years, corporate taxes were to be paid but only at half the usual rate. Furthermore, there were no taxes or restraints on the repatriation of money from the project and the government waived duties on imported equipment. While the Lao government was to receive 2.5% of the value of the ore mined, this was only applied after Oxiana had subtracted the costs of selling, transport, smelting, refining, and other treatment costs (World Rainforest Movement, 2004, p. 86).

According to the Department of Geology and Mineral Resources, as of 2012 there were 290 projects in the country, with 107 prospecting, 125 exploration, and 58 mining projects (Phommakaysone, 2012). There are an estimated 150 mining companies operating in Laos, including companies from China (representing 56.5% of all mining companies), Vietnam, Thailand, Australia, Korea, Canada, Germany, India, Japan, the UK, and Russia (Boungnaphalom, 2010). Such a presence of FDI, states the USGS, is 'largely owing to the Laos government's aggressive efforts to promote mining investment and to strengthen its management and regulation of the mining sector under the framework of the Mining Law of 1997 and the Investment Law' (2008, p. 16.1).

Despite a notable increase in mining investments, the industry, in partnership with the World Bank, quickly started lobbying for a revision of the Mining Law. Of concern in the Laotian case, however, was the failure to meet the clarity requirements expected from a 'modern' regime. In addition to a considerable confusion over terms such as the transfer of mining rights (Article 39) and the expiration of mining licences (Article 34), the provisions for the taxation and duties were seen as a cause for alarm within the investor community.[21] Furthermore, while in practice the country did permit 100% FDI, Article 21 allowed the state to compel foreign investors to accept its participation in their mining venture. For Thompson, this 'introduces a conflict of interest given that it is the government which regulates the sector' (2010, p. 8).

In a World Bank commissioned report, the 1997 Mining Law was seen as positioning Laos at 'a competitive disadvantage compared with its neighbours' (2006, p. 23). The Bank proceeded to argue for a 'timely review' of the country's laws and regulations on mining, thus giving Laos the opportunity 'to become the leader in mining legislation reform in competitive agenda in line with international standards' (World Bank, 2006, pp. 23–26).

Additionally, it is important to recognise that the WBG was also busy assisting the country in a wide range of reforms. Between 2001 and 2004, the Bank's lending to the country averaged US$32 million per year, during which it provided lending for the Agriculture Development and Road Maintenance projects; a Poverty Reduction Fund, a Financial Management Adjustment Credit along with a Financial Management Capacity Building Credit; Sustainable Forestry and Land Titling projects; and Second Education and Second Road Maintenance projects. This lending included a Poverty Report, a Country Economic Memorandum, Banking and Financial Sector Report, Production Forestry Policy, Public Expenditure Review and Country Financial Accountability Assessment, a Poverty and Environment Nexus Report, Economic Monitors, a Country Procurement Assessment Report, a support to both the Interim Poverty Reduction Strategy Papers (PRSP) and full PRSP, as well as a Mining Sector Note (International Development Association [IDA], 2005, p. 16).

The point to be made here is that beyond the direct role that the WBG was playing at the time as a credit provider was its overarching role in the structural reform of the country's liberalisation, whether macroeconomics, banking, agriculture, education, or the judiciary. As such, the Group's influence is reflected in its ability to catalyse risk investments not only in countries such as Laos, but also in the entire donor community. Guttal and Shoemaker (2004) are worth citing:

> All bilateral donors and the [Asian Development Bank] align their respective aid, lending and technical assistance programmes with World Bank-IMF determined development and macroeconomic frameworks. The National Poverty Eradication Programme (NPEP), which will serve as the country's national development plan, faithfully follows the World Bank-IMF template [...]. The policy matrix that is at the heart of the NPEP includes far-ranging reforms in all economic and social sectors, from trade and investment to agriculture, education and health. (p. 2)

In December 2008, Laos adopted a new Mining Law,[22] which was notably the product of the World Bank's Seventh Poverty Reduction Support Program (May 2011–February 2012).[23] In line with the SDM, the Program included the development of complementary regulations which promoted standards and detailed regulations for environmental protection.[24]

The 2008 mining code provides that foreign investors wishing to engage in activities such as the prospecting, exploration, exploitation, or processing of mineral resources have to negotiate an agreement with the government, as the specific terms are not addressed in the new Law.[25] Prospecting licences are granted for an initial 2 years (renewable for an additional year), exploration licences for 3 years (renewable for an additional 2 years), and mining licences for a maximum initial term of 20 years (renewable for up to 5 years, upon approval from the Ministry of Energy and Mines).[26] The new Law grants participation rights to the government, which are to be negotiated between the two parties. In addition to the general tax laws applicable to mining investments, such as the profit tax, income tax, value-added tax, import/export duties, and stamp duties, the specific tax and fiscal provisions, as well as any exemptions, are to be negotiated with the government.

Moreover, perhaps tellingly, the thirst for legal clarity and enticing provisions for foreign investors is now the subject of a Bank Technical Assistance Project.[27] Approved in 2010, the latter aims to develop the country's capacity in the mining and hydropower sectors, with US$2.31 million specifically allocated to the development of the mining sector. The Project is resolutely geared towards enticing FDI:

> Clear laws and regulations for the mining sector, along with internationally competitive taxation, are key to developing the sector. While the Government has made considerable progress in these areas, including adoption of a new Minerals Law in December 2008, the legislative and regulatory framework needs to be completed. (World Bank, n.d.)

It should be noted that along with the World Bank, the IFC—the Bank's private sector arm—has also been assisting the government to 'harness the country's natural resources as a significant driver of economic growth, while ensuring the protection of communities and the environment' (2013). In addition to exploring investment opportunities in hydropower systems, forestry, and agribusiness, the IFC has been providing technical assistance for the new mineral law, the drafting of the country's enterprise law, and the preparation of the new unified investment law (World Bank, 2008, p. 38). The Unified Law on Investment Promotion tackles investment risks by offering 'a clear and predictable' regime and creating 'a level playing field for domestic and foreign investors' (IFC, 2012). The IFC also provided financing to the *Lao Business Forum*, which is, according to the Bank, 'an effective mechanism for enabling the private sector to raise their concerns to [the government of Laos]' (World Bank, 2008, p. 38).[28] The funding notably provided the Forum with a secretariat to support its operations and to revise the Mining Law.

In the following section, the rise of this socio-environmental narrative, which is solidly enshrined within the Laotian new mining regime, is assessed in relation to the overall model promoted by the WBG in the mining sectors of its country client. Particular attention will be given to the SDM's emphasis on local community development and participation, which is to play a key role in each step of the development of mining projects.

By the Book: Community Development and Environmental Protection in Laos

In line with the SDM, Laos's new mining regime has been tightly knitted with a strong social-development narrative. The very development of the mining sector is here expected to be twinned not only to the country's national economic interests but also to the need to protect the environment and ensure community development. Laos' regulatory framework therefore 'incorporates many environmental and social safeguard policy measures consistent with international standards', boasts a World Bank background report (Gibson & Rex, 2010, p. 1). Laos' 2005 Country Assistance Strategy states that the World Bank's assistance to the hydropower, mining, and forestry sectors is to increase resources and capacities to promote environmental conservation, involve local communities in natural resources management, and strengthen the application of social and environmental safeguards in development projects (IDA, 2005, p. 24). The Bank has further been involved in building the government's capacity to 'ensure that mining operations respect the relevant national and international standards with regard to environmental protection and management', and it further funded a review of the country's environmental legislation and practices as they pertain to the mining sector (IDA, 2005,

p. 25). The UN concludes that: 'In terms of laws and regulations on environmental protection and management, the Lao People's Democratic Republic is not wanting' (2010, p. 35).

In addition to the provisions embedded in the new Mining Law, which notably require a feasibility study and an environmental impact assessment (EIA), the country's legal framework boasts several provisions to ensure environmental protection and sustainable development. Both the Environment Protection Law (1999)[29] and the Regulation on Environmental Protection and Management (2000) are grounded in the concepts of sustainable development and public involvement.

The country's regulatory framework further ensures that project-affected people are compensated and assisted to improve or maintain livelihoods, incomes, and living standards (Decree 192 and Regulation 2432 and supporting Guidelines for Compensation and Resettlement). Decree 112 on the Regulation for Environmental Impact Assessment (2010) also requires impact assessments and the protection of affected people, including grievance procedures and information disclosure requirements.[30] The legal framework also states that the broader pursuit of economic growth shall be steered by social objectives. The Law on the Promotion of Foreign Investment (2004) promotes foreign investments, which are expected to contribute to improving living conditions and the overall development of the country (Art. 1). Boungnaphalom, the country's Director of the Environment and Mining Inspection Division (Department of Mines, Ministry of Energy and Mines), notes that today investors have to comply with a framework that assures a balance between mining and socio-economic development activities, as well as natural resources conservation and environmental protection; remedies any negative impacts that occur during mining and after mine closure; and provides community development (2010).

Crucially, in agreement with the SDM, local communities occupy a centre stage within the socio-environmental dimensions of Laos' new regulatory mining regime. Local actors are indeed positioned to be key beneficiaries of the booming sector, which is to bring employment and infrastructure (roads and electricity) to isolated regions, provide funds for the building of schools and hospitals, and have a long-lasting spillover effect by generating new business for agriculture, livestock farming, and retail trade (Kyophilvong, 2010, p. 76). Ultimately, mining activities are to nurse 'community development', which can be defined as:

> [...] the process of increasing the strength and effectiveness of communities, improving peoples' quality of life, and enabling people to participate in decision making to achieve greater long-term control over their lives. Sustainable community development programs are those that contribute to the long-term strengthening of community viability. (Energy Sector Management Assistance Programme, the World Bank, & International Council on Mining and Metals, 2005, p. 7)

The Bank's 2010 Technical Assistance Project directly addresses the need 'to promote models for corporate social responsibility, and risk mitigation and community benefit-sharing approaches' (World Bank, n.d.). The country's new Minerals Law requires investors to study and recommend a strategy for the sharing of fiscal benefits related to the mine operation and that they contribute to Community Development Funds, which are allocated a substantial portion of the government's revenues from mining (UN, 2010, p. 33). These funds are to be designed and administered in close partnership between companies, the government, and communities. The latter are to be closely involved within each phase of a mining project. The basic principles of benefit sharing include the following:

- Participatory planning, gaining public acceptance and community participation;
- Recognising the importance of providing opportunities to improve livelihoods and living standards;

- Recognising affected people as beneficiaries of the project;
- Equitable revenue sharing;
- Environmental protection and development; and
- Sustainable community development. (Gibson & Rex, 2010, p. 14)

If, under the overarching guidance of the World Bank, Laos' unfolding mining regime has been tightly knitted with a strong social-development narrative and participatory mechanisms, the issue of meeting the social, environmental, and economic promises attached to the sudden and fast-paced development of the natural resources sectors raises several questions, as argued in the following section.

The Technocratic Management of Socio-environmental Risks: The Cases of Sepon and NT2

All branches of the WBG have repeatedly stated that it is in light of the particularly heightened risks that mining activities represent for local communities and the environment that they should be involved in the industry. This narrative was closely repeated in Laos, notably for two of the country's largest natural resource projects. The World Bank was involved both in the Minerals and Metals Group Sepon (Sepon) mine and the NT2 hydroelectricity project. Both have repeatedly been cited as 'best practice' cases, especially in terms of their strong participatory requirements and socio-environmental safeguards.

Located in Savannakhet Province, which is in the south-central region of the country, Sepon is an open-pit gold and copper mine.[31] It was also the country's very first large-scale mine.[32] While Oxiana, the owner of the mine at the time, later obtained its own financing, it had initially requested the IFC's involvement in the project—the latter approved a US$30 million loan in February 2002.

There is no doubt that the IFC's involvement contributed to the extensive socio-environmental impact assessments which took place in the initial phase of the project[33] which, like most mining projects, was classified as 'Category A' by the IFC, which means that the project is expected to have adverse impacts that may be sensitive, irreversible, and diverse. In its *Asia and Pacific regional workshop: Testimonials and consultation report*, the EIR (2003a) noted: 'The positive aspects of IFC participation were greater stakeholder participation, formal documentation of the consultation process, a widely-accepted assessment framework (i.e. WBG safeguard policies), expert advice and increased stakeholder confidence in Oxiana' (p. 30). However, there were sizeable disparities between the IFC's socio-environmental narrative and its actual implementation on the ground.

The country's 2004 PRSP states that 'the Government will ensure that development of the mining activities are conducted in an environmentally and socially sustainable manner, while making a significant contribution to economic development at all levels of society' (International Monetary Fund [IMF], 2004, p. 105). The report further states that in this spirit, the government, in partnership with private sector interests, will work with the communities involved to ensure a full understanding of the impacts; a climate of trust and cooperation; guidelines for development and operation of the mine; resettlement and compensation for any loss of assets and earnings; and assistance programmes centred on asset creation and human capital formation, all of which 'principles are being applied to the Oxiana Gold Mine and will apply to all future mining activities' (IMF, 2004, p. 105).

Among the international non-governmental organisation (NGO) critics of the Oxiana mine at the time,[34] Aid Watch observed 'a serious number of anomalies and shortcomings' in the application of the Environmental and Social Impact Assessment of the project, adding that: 'In many cases there has not been sufficient in-depth study and analysis, and mitigation planning often has been superficial, alluding to further studies and further elaboration of details later' (cited in EIR, 2003a, p. 31).

Furthermore, the participatory process leading to the project, which was advertised as resulting from the presence of the IFC, appears to have been limited to an *information* dissemination process: 'One limitation of the ESIA [Environmental and Social Impact Assessment] was the consultation process of Oxiana, which mainly consisted of providing information and not having discussions', concludes the EIR (2003a, p. 31).

Another key example of an existing disparity between the participatory narrative embedded within the SDM and the implementation on the ground is the case of NT2. While the hydroelectricity sector in itself extends beyond the theme of this article, NT2 nonetheless warrants a few words, as it received the World Bank's endorsement and has today become a best-practice flagship project.[35] Furthermore, the fast-paced development of hydropower has positioned itself as a significant purveyor of government revenues, which are, in fact, projected to eventually surpass the mining industry.[36] According to the UN, investments in this sector alone are expected to raise around US$2 billion in revenues over a 25-year period (2010, p. iii).

NT2's dam, watershed, and reservoir are located in central Laos, among one of the most biologically diverse forests in the world (Goldman, 2005, p. 194). Strikingly, NT2, which began operations in April 2010, is the country's largest dam—and the project that has attracted the most foreign investments to date.[37] Built at a cost of US$1.3 billion, it was funded in part by the ADB and the World Bank.[38]

The World Bank has been involved in NT2 since the mid-1980s, when it financed a feasibility study for the project (see Lawrence, 2009, p. 83), and later in several other ways: helping the Lao government to appoint and finance a panel of experts to advise on the handling of social and environmental issues related to the project, providing legal experts to negotiate financing arrangements, and requiring project developers to carry out technical, social, environmental, economic, and resettlement studies that have been instrumental in project preparation (Guttal & Shoemaker, 2004, p. 1). More specifically, the IFC was initially expected to provide loans for Lao government equity project; Multilateral Investment Guarantee Agency (MIGA) investment guarantees; and IDA concessional loans for the macroeconomic assessment and the alternative study. The Bank's Environment Department was also involved (Hirsch, 2002, p. 162).

Crucially, the involvement of the Bank in the project was to ensure that, in addition to local participation by communities and civil society, the dam would be 'green'. Goldman's work (2005) is worth citing in this regard:

> Associated with the dam, and reflecting the Bank's new concern with environmentally sustainable development, is a state-of-the-art suite of linked projects that includes investment for a Forest Conservation and Management Project, Wildlife and Protected Areas Management Project, indigenous peoples' extractive reserves, irrigated and modernized agriculture with experimental farms, electricity and new roads, megafauna and tree plantations, and new housing settlements. (2005, p. 157)

As it was the case during the initial phase of Sepon, the very presence of the Bank was seen as bringing emphasis on participation and environmental protection. In fact, the 2005 Country Assistance Strategy boasts that NT2 is 'an example of an area-based, sustainable natural resource development program that contributes to growth, social outcomes, capacity development, and stronger partnerships' (IDA, 2005, p. ii).

However, while the project *did* bring an additional emphasis on public consultation, environmental protection, and disclosure processes (EIR, 2003a, p. 30),[39] the superficiality of the endeavour has been emphasised by critics. In an analysis of the participatory process linked to NT2, Guttal and Shoemaker (2004) observe that the project had actually failed to meet the Bank's own standards, notably with regard to indigenous groups—most of the people to be resettled or affected by the project are part of indigenous communities. The authors further added that: '[...] consent for the project is neither free, nor prior, nor informed' (Guttal & Shoemaker, 2004, p. 3). This resonates with the organisation International Rivers' own conclusions:

> Provisions of the [Concession Agreement] and of World Bank and [Asian Development Bank] policies, particularly regarding resettlement and information disclosure, have been violated. But despite numerous monitoring missions, the [Multilateral Development Banks] have not taken strong enough stances—including withholding loan and grant disbursements—to correct Nam Theun 2's problems and minimize negative impacts on affected people. (Lawrence, 2008, p. 45)

This is an issue that speaks directly to the overarching role of the WBG in strengthening a project's legitimacy on the one hand, and enticing international investors on the other. The Group's involvement indeed has a dual impact: on the legitimacy front, it promises beyond industry socio-environmental standards, while on the investment front, it reassures potential investors in terms of political risk. 'From the start', argues Guttal and Shoemaker, 'it was apparent that the private sector would be unwilling to support a project of this size [NT2] in Laos without the involvement of the World Bank' (2004, p. 1). Lawrence further observes that by 2003:

> Given the size of the investment and the risks of operating in Laos, commercial banks were unlikely to fund the project without guarantees from the World Bank. The potential financiers also primarily relied on the World Bank to lead the economic, social and environmental due diligence for NT2. (2009, p. 85)[40]

A common misunderstanding about the overarching significance of the SDM is linked to the novelties that it actually brings forth. Facets of what I describe as the SDM are always promoted as a complement to the relentless push for the expansion of large-scale mining markets. Framed in such a light, the profound contradictions embedded in the participatory process mandated by the WBG in Laos are understandable.[41] Participation is here also an instrument for the World Bank to justify its own presence in such a controversial project. As Guttal and Shoemaker note:

> As the public participation process unfolded, it soon became apparent that its overall goal was not to foster genuine participation of project affected communities as described in the [World Commission on Dams]'s final Report and Recommendations, but rather to 'jump through the hoops' of appearing to conduct public consultation in order for the World Bank to have sufficient political cover to proceed with the controversial decision to support the project. (2004, p. 3)

The issue of particular importance with the case of Laos is the fact that the country's 'civil society' remains firmly nestled in the arms of a one-party regime built not around open space for political participation and freedom of association, but rather its official mass organisations, such as the Lao Women's Union, the Lao People's Revolutionary Youth Union, the Lao Patriotic Front for Reconstruction, and the Lao Federation of Trade Unions (ADB, 2011, p. 1).

Kunze (2010) observes that in addition to being sparse, civil society organisations lack capacity:

[...] some assessments indicate there are only about 15 to 20 associations capable of operating with any impact, whether they are school-parent associations or farmers associations. Most Lao citizens are unaware that such associations exist at all, much less what role they can or do play.

Crucially, less than a decade ago, Laos simply had 'no political, cultural, historical, or institutional structures' for liberal participatory processes such as those built into the SDM (Guttal & Shoemaker, 2004, p. 3). Countenancing this, Kunze (2010) bluntly concludes that civil society in Laos may be one of the most limited in the world.

While forming an organisation or an association is technically legal,[42] the number of Laotian 'non-governmental' organisations remains particularly small. The government did initiate reforms to facilitate the creation of associational life with the November 2009 implementation of the Decree on Associations. However, no laws currently exist to carry out the constitutional provisions with respect to the establishment of national NGOs and, therefore, there are currently no such organisations recognised by the government (ADB, 2011, p. 2). It should be noted that the government has gradually embraced and encouraged the work of international NGOs in the country. Crucially, this openness to outsiders has remained conditional upon such organisations strictly refraining from political activities. As such, the number of organisations and associations that are genuinely independent and dedicated to human rights or advocacy is seriously limited, if not completely inexistent.

Quite tellingly, the ADB further observes that the government has recently questioned the activities of some international NGOs, specifically their criticism of large foreign investment and infrastructure development projects (2011, p. 2). Yet the Bank remains undeterred. A senior Bank official remains positive, arguing that since 'Laos society is a consensual oriented society', it makes 'political sense' for the government to be genuinely committed to socio-environmental issues, thus 'the substantial institutional reforms that are aimed at trying to better the situation' (World Bank, personal communication, February 2011).

The Bank's 'can do' attitude in Laos is startling, especially in light of its active promotion of the natural resources sectors. In addition to a highly restricted local civil society and an international NGO presence which is expected to remain apolitical, in Laos all media (print, radio, and television) are firmly controlled by the state. Despite a constitutional guarantee of freedom of press, the Lao People's Revolutionary Party keeps a tight control over all print and broadcast news and, as such, press freedom remains highly restricted (Freedom House, 2012).[43] Freedom House (2012) observes that despite the adoption of a new press law in 2008, few changes had been registered:

> Under the criminal code, individuals may be jailed for up to one year for reporting news that 'weakens the state' or importing a publication that is 'contrary to national culture.' Defamation and misinformation are criminal offenses, carrying lengthy prison terms and even the possibility of execution. However, due to high levels of official censorship and self-censorship, legal cases against media personnel are extremely rare.

The Southeast Asian Press Alliance (2013) argues that while foreign investment in the country has successfully boosted the country's GDP, the multiplication of projects has taken place without public transparency and accountability:

> Being state-owned or controlled, they [the media] were prohibited from doing investigative reports on growing problems involving land dispute and the controversial hydropower projects. [...] Land disputes, especially those involving foreign investment with the consent of the authorities, is a taboo topic for the media.

Setting aside the thorny issue of political space in Laos, the alarming signs which indicate the capacity of the government to monitor, regulate, and implement the socio-environmental dimensions of the new regime are seriously lacking. The UN observes that: 'Environmental governance [...] remains weak. There have been reports of mining companies not conducting effective environmental controls, with no proper environmental mitigation activities and lacking in longer-term rehabilitation and reclamation programme' (2010, p. 35).

Sepon and Phu Bia have both already experienced environmental incidents. In 2009, an acidic water spill killed fish that had migrated into the operation's on-site containment ponds, although no water from these ponds was reported to have been released into the external river system (ICMM, 2011, p. 20). In 2005, Phu Bia experienced a chemical spill in the Nam Mo River (ICMM, 2011, p. 21). Villagers living in the vicinity of the site have reported health issues linked to the spill, as well as dead fish downstream of the river.

In a 2012 survey conducted in two villages (Ban Nammo and Ban Namyone) located in proximity of the Phu Bia gold and copper mine, Marley-Zagar assessed the villagers' attitudes towards mining.[44] While opinions remain polarised, the survey flagged key issues pertaining to health, land ownership, and livelihood. A total of 43.5% of villagers complained of allergies, headaches, diarrhoea, dizziness, heart issues, and tiredness, which they believed were induced by mining activities. In terms of property, 29% of respondents thought mining had degraded their land and 56% felt they were affected by land concessions. Moreover, villagers argued that their household had witnessed a decline in terms of livelihood due to river degradation (67%) and forest degradation (44%) (Marley-Zagar, 2012, pp. 8–9).[45]

Another issue arose from the compensation schemes in place. While 61% of the villagers interviewed had received aid or compensation as a result of the mining activity in their area, 67% of the respondents 'felt that the compensation received was insufficient for their needs'. Furthermore, it appears that compensation was not evenly allocated between the different ethnic groups: while 87% of the Hmong respondents had received compensation, only 27% of Thai Dam tribe had received any aid (Marley-Zagar, 2012, p. 9).

The World Bank office in Vientiane observes that Laos is a low-income country and, when compared to its Asian neighbours, still has little in the way of legal frameworks (World Bank, personal communication, February 2011). The failure to adequately enforce environmental standards echoes concerns in relation to the requirements for the implementation of meaningful social impact assessments (SIAs) to take place. Notably, as early as 2001, this problem was highlighted by a WBG fact-finding mission: 'specific work on SIA regulations and guidelines within the mining sector is at a very preliminary stage' (Boland, Kunanayagam, & Walker, 2001, p. iii). As is the case for the other countries studied in this contribution, Laos appears to overwhelmingly rely on the industry to supply monitoring reports, upon which the social and environmental impacts are assessed (Marley-Zagar, 2012).

Interestingly, a recent World Bank background paper observes that while the laws and regulations in Laos encourage the protection and sustainable use of natural resources, 'some gaps, especially in implementation and enforcement capacity, remain' (2010a, p. 2). The report identifies alarming deficiencies:

- Despite the economic wealth generated by natural resource projects, sustainable financing for environmental protection is still inadequate. Foreign assistance has been the main source of financing for natural resource management so far;
- Overlapping mandates and a lack of coordination among the agencies involved in natural resource use and management and among the central, provincial, and district levels of government;

- Financial, capacity, and human resources constraints in environmental management, planning, and the monitoring of the environmental and social impact assessments have become the binding constraints to implementing existing legislation, as well as to responding to emergency situations;
- The legislation does not specify types of penalties for breaking the law;
- The responsibility for mitigating damage at the local level is not clearly defined and not included in the project design;
- A lack of public access to information on environmental effects and on proposed and ongoing mitigation measures exacerbates the negative impact. (World Bank, 2010a, pp. 2–3)

If a consensus does exist on the part of all donors regarding the urgency of allowing the regulation process to catch up with the fast expansion of the natural resources sector, progress remains slow. The Bank further notes that while the Lao government is keen on developing a solid framework, 'there is a gap between what [it is] intending to implement and what is being implemented on the ground' (personal communication, February 2011).

In addition to the German aid agency, which has recently stepped in with a technical support project to tackle the sustainable development of the mining industry,[46] the IFC is currently assisting the Ministry of Natural Resources and Environment (MONRE) to strengthen key water and hydropower-related laws, policies, and regulations, as well as providing training to government staff in order to ensure 'that authorities have the skills necessary to implement and monitor compliance with new laws and regulations' (2013).

Beyond the technocratic assessment of the government's capacity to implement the socio-environmental safeguards attached to the fast expansion of the natural resources sectors, there does exist a puzzling dislocation between the relentless encouragement on the part of the WBG for Laos to capitalise on its abundance of natural resources while wholeheartedly acknowledging that the government's capacity to monitor, evaluate, and implement the socio-environmental safeguards for Category A projects are not in place. This further resonates with a deep conflict of interest within the current monitoring structure of the Department of Geology and the Department of Mines, the two government agencies that oversee Laos' Mining Law. On the one hand, these government agencies are mandated with having to inspect and monitor mining activities and, on the other, to 'assist in the negotiation of mining contracts and in mineral exploration and mining licensing activities, promote investment in the mining sector, maintain geologic databases, and provide mineral exploration support and data analysis studies' (USGS, 2010, p. 16.1).

The dislocation between the sustainable-development narrative embedded in the government's mining policy and its pursuit of further investments in the sector is also illustrated by the forestry sector. The government is planning to increase the total land area of forest from the current 41.2% to 70% by 2020 (Schönweger, Heinimann, Epprecht, Lu, & Thalongseng-chanh, 2012, p. 67). However, the country has actually witnessed deforestation and forest degradation, some of which can be linked to mining activities. In fact, while a substantial area of the country has been labelled as 'forest area' (64% of the country's total land), 29% of this land is currently the object of land investment, of which mining covers 51% (Schönweger et al., 2012, p. 67). However, as observed by Schönweger et al.:

> While regulations and stipulations for the distinct management of each category of forest land is [sic] typically expected to determine investment trends in such areas, their enforcement remains inconsistent, leaving room for wide debate around the impacts of large-scale land investments and their potential to undermine national objectives in forest management. (2012, p. 67)

It is to be emphasised that empowered by the country's new Mining Law, potential mining investors have been assailing Laos:[47] 'the number of land deals has skyrocketed in recent years, increasing fifty fold from 2000 to 2009' observe Schönweger et al. (2012, p. 9). In the sector of mining in particular, the authors report 564 currently ongoing projects in the country, constituting 21% of total land projects—approximately half of the total area under investment in Laos (2012, p. 40). In fact, 10% of the total land area of the country has already been granted to investors for development (Schönweger et al., 2012, p. 75).

Ironically, the scale of the current mining rush is now making the Bank voice great caution, warning that the government's capacity has not yet coped with the challenges posed by such rapid expansion. A Bank officer further explains:

> the process through which [Laos exploits its natural resources] and the pace through which it is done is really beginning to have a big influence on the ultimate outcomes. Doing it so quickly, with limited capacity, may mean that the outcomes are not as good as [the Lao government] would like them to be [...]. (personal communication, February 2011)

Complementing this perspective, the Bank's *Lao PDR development report: Natural resource management for sustainable development* conveys the institution's uneasiness with the fast pace of the sector's development and the country's lack of capacity, notably with regard to the implementation and enforcement of existing socio-environmental regulations (World Bank, 2010b, p. 1).

Aviva Imhof, the campaign director of the NGO International Rivers, argues that the World Bank is not prioritising capacity: 'if you want to build capacity, start small!' (personal communication, August 2011). Referring to the NT2 experience, which was the very first natural resources project involving the World Bank in the country, Imhof further observes that: 'They began with the biggest project: three provinces, 120,000 people affected; far bigger than the Lao government could handle.' She bluntly concludes: 'It's not a government that lacks capacity, it's a government that doesn't care' (Imhof, personal communication, August 2011).

It is further telling to note that Laos ranked 151 out of 180 countries on the Corruption Perceptions Index of Transparency International (2009).[48] The organisation highlights a distinct increase in the country's corruption index over time, an increase that appears to match the expansion of the natural resources sectors. Crucially, a United Nations Development Programme (2011) paper on illicit financial flows, here defined as flows involving the 'cross-border transfer of the proceeds of corruption, trade in contraband goods, criminal activities and tax evasion', concludes that between 1990 and 2008, Laos would have lost over US$6 billion in such flows.

There nevertheless exists a certain hypocrisy in simultaneously promoting strong socio-environmental standards as well as the active liberalisation of the sector to foreign investors and then suggesting that any failures in the model should be blamed on the lack of a government's capacity. The World Bank's Vientiane office argues: 'We are not engaged in reviewing individual projects, we basically provide the government with the tools and they are supposed to then use these tools' (personal communication, February 2011).

The Bank appears undeterred by the need to develop the country's hydropower, mining, forestry, and agricultural potential, although it now suggests that the process should involve 'world-class sponsors and financial institutions to partner' with such projects, which are being seen as tokens of implementation of 'best practice environmental and social standards' (World Bank, 2012, p. 19).

In fact, despite the multiplication of concerns over the socio-environmental impacts of NT2, the Bank wants to build on the 'success' of the dam project which it believes 'demonstrated the country's ability to adhere to the rigorous environmental and social safeguards demanded by high quality sponsors' (World Bank, 2012, p. 19). Building on such 'success', IFC has been offering new grants and policy assistance—to the tune of US$2.4 million—to the Lao MONRE to support further hydropower development across the country (Boh, 2013).

In June of 2012,[49] Vientiane announced its decision to ban new mining projects (as well as eucalyptus and rubber projects) until 2015 on grounds of environmental and community disruption concerns. As stated by Schönweger et al., the moratorium 'provides an opportunity to reconsider sustainable alternatives to the current pace and approaches of attracting capital through large-scale investment in land, and to examine and address negative impacts accrued already' (2012, p. 77). While welcomed by civil society groups, it appears that the freeze will not extend to the projects that have already been given the green light to conduct economic feasibility studies ('Economist backs', 2012). It is important to add that this is not the first time the government has decided to impose a moratorium. Previously, in May 2007,[50] Vientiane had announced that it would stop granting any new land concession exceeding 100 ha for industrial trees, perennial plants, and mining purposes. The reasons for the decision resonate with today's moratorium: to give the government time to review its policies and to address previous shortcomings in its management. Notably, during the 2007–2009 moratorium, new agreements were nonetheless issued[51] and problematic concessions were unrevoked (Baird, 2008, p. 324).

The fast expansion of the mining sector, in conjunction with other usage of land for export commodities, does bring forth the issue that of the 6 million people living in Laos, 75% are engaged in subsistence agriculture, a sector that also contributes to more than half of the country's annual GDP (Head, 2012). As such, the mining sector has been encroaching on the country's main employment sector while increasingly funnelling its economy towards a problematic enclave sector which now characterises mining. Schönweger et al. conclude that:

> Investment in land, particularly large-scale foreign direct investment, has been championed as an effective development tool by a number of actors. Such a vast expansion of land investment has brought significant transformations in national landscapes. These transformations, in turn, engender drastic socioeconomic and environmental changes, affect food security and traditional livelihoods and could ultimately pose challenges to national sovereignty. (2012, p. 75)

The case of Sepon is illustrative of this point. On its website, the company highlights a 2011 ICMM report which boasts the 'long-lasting and positive impact' of the mine (MMG, 2013). The report, entitled *Utilizing mining and mineral resources to foster the sustainable development of the Lao PDR*, makes the point that in just nine years of operation average incomes at Sepon have increased sevenfold, while in 2010 alone, Sepon has contributed US$412,044 to its Social Development Trust Fund (MMG, 2013). Furthermore, in 2010, the mine employed 2300 people through direct employment, 1600 workers by means of indirect employment, and 9750 others via induced employment, while contributing approximately US$6.5 million for employee training. While these numbers appear substantial, the total number of the people relying on Sepon and Phu Bia combined comprise a little over 1% of the country's total workforce (ICMM, 2011, p. 26). Moreover, the ICMM observes that while the physical footprint of Sepon is expected to expand and take over more of the land currently used by villagers, 'it is probable that employment opportunities will not increase proportionally with the operation's footprint' (2011, p. 30).

Crucially, it is to be emphasised that mining activities are taking place in some of the country's poorest regions. Schönweger et al. estimate that 50% of villages affected by mining activities have a poverty incidence higher than the national average (2012, p. 62).

In such light, the moratorium may offer a much-needed pause for perspective for Vientiane, allowing a reconsideration of the urgent need to diversify its economy away from the simple exploitation of natural resources. As such, the Ministry of Planning and Investment is advocating the development of agribusiness, the mining processing industry, education, health, and tourism, although the low education standards and the largely unskilled workforce remain a challenge ('Economist backs', 2012). The question will be to establish whether Vientiane really intends to resist the contradictory push for the development of its mining resources and its stated policy of diversification. On this note, the development of the massive bauxite reserves in the Bolavens Plateau will be instructive given its location on some of the country's most fertile lands. In prioritising bauxite, the government could compromise not only the touristic activities in the region but also, more importantly, the prime coffee plantations which occupy the plateau. Approximately half of these plantations and the livelihood of its farmers are now threatened by the proposed mining (Marley-Zagar, 2012).

The recent moratorium now taking place in Laos may fall short of challenging the neoliberal norms embedded in the country's mining regime. Superficial changes in policies which only seek to tame the more extreme forms of deregulation may prove insufficient to address the medium- to long-term consequences of the current race for the country's mineral resources.

Conclusion

Building on the case of Laos, this article has analysed the recent emphasis on socio-environmental safeguards promoted by the WBG and the political underpinning of their implementation. In particular, I have drawn attention to the magnitude of the influence of the World Bank and its promotion of what I describe as the SDM, arguing that the liberal assumptions regarding the role of civil society organisations and safeguard mechanisms in the promotion of mining activities face a challenging environment in the form of Laos' political landscape, characterised by a one-party regime, illiberal approaches to dissenting voices, clear conflicts of interest in regulatory bodies, and institutional capacity deficits.

In light of these clear obstacles to the implementation of the socio-environmental safeguards embedded in Laos' mining regime, the analysis has suggested that the involvement of local communities is actually rooted within a framework which, first and foremost, conceives of participatory schemes as a management tool to circumscribe the risks faced by mining investors. As such, the SDM should not be read as a novel attempt to empower local stakeholders politically. Rather, participatory schemes and civil society engagement here serve to mitigate the negative impact of mining activities on the ground, while also offering a depoliticised path to vent, in a limited sense, local opposition.

Ultimately, this may bring the debate to another level. Rodrik observed that 'every politician knows the clamour for controls and restrictions overcome markets when markets produce outcomes that are not endowed with popular legitimacy' (cited in Ahrens, 2004, p. 11).

Acknowledgements

The author is grateful for the comments provided by Toby Carroll and Tim Hilger on earlier versions of this paper, as well as the anonymous reviewers of the journal *Globalizations*.

Disclosure Statement

No potential conflict of interest was reported by the author.

Notes

1 Hereafter, the International Bank for Reconstruction and Development and the International Development Association (IDA) are referred to as 'the World Bank' or 'the Bank'.

2 For a comparative analysis between Laos, the Philippines, and Papua New Guinea, see Hatcher (2012).

3 On the specific roles of the International Financial Corporation (IFC) and MIGA in the industry, notably see Hatcher (2010).

4 See Hatcher (2004) for an analysis of the Malian mining sector as an example of third-generation mining code implementation.

5 Today, mining is understood to be one of the most environmentally disruptive activities that can be undertaken as business (Bebbington, Hinojosa, Humphreys Bebbington, Burneo, & Warnaars, 2008, p. 893) and the concept of the 'resource curse' is widely acknowledged by all stakeholders in the industry. The term refers to when an abundance of natural resources creates political and economic distortions which increase the likelihood that countries will experience negative development outcomes (Rosser, 2006, p. 7). Also see Auty (1993) and Sachs and Warner (1995).

6 For a thorough analysis of the EIR and the World Bank response, see Campbell (2009).

7 It is to be noted that this greater emphasis on the environmental and social consequences of mining activities is part of a greater shift within the Bank as a whole. While the specifics of the changes carried out within the Bank amidst the Wolfensohn presidency (1995–2005) are beyond the range of this contribution, it should be noted that the period marked an all-encompassing shift within the Bank's narrative. From its austere emphasis on the blind pursuit of economic growth, which characterised the 1980s and the better part of the 1990s, the Bank in the last decade embraced a more 'comprehensive' way of doing business. 'Our dream is a world free of poverty', Wolfensohn declared, and in so doing, he committed the institution, at least discursively, to addressing the social aspects of poverty and to forging closer partnerships with other actors in development, including those within civil society (on the topic, see Hatcher 2006).

8 There exists a rich critical political-economy literature on the topic. See notably Cammack (2003), Carroll (2010), Fine, Lapavitsas, and Pincus (2001), Gill (1995), and Soederberg (2004). Soederberg (2004) refers to the *New International Financial Architecture*, a class-based strategy that forces the Global South to accede to the neo-liberal rules of free market mobility. Cammack (2003) points towards the 'completion of the world market', while Gill refers to the 'political project of attempting to make transnational liberal, and if possible liberal democratic capitalism, the sole model of future development' (1995, p. 8).

9 Such as the Resettlement and Indigenous Peoples; effective public consultation and disclosure (1998); HIV/AIDS's guide for the Mining Sector (2004); and Sustainability in Emerging Markets (2002). *World Bank OP 4.01 Environmental Assessment* (1999); *World Bank OP 4.12 Involuntary Resettlement* (2002); *World Bank OP 4.10 Indigenous Peoples* (2005); *World Bank OP 4.11 Physical and Cultural Resources* (2006); *IFC Policy on Social and Environment Sustainability* (2006); *IFC Performance Standards on Social and Environmental Sustainability* (2006); *IFC Guidance Notes: Performance Standards on Social and Environmental Sustainability* (2007); *IFC Health, Safety and Environment Guidelines* (General—2007 and Mining—2007).

10 As stated in the Lao 'National Socio-Economic Development Plan'.

11 As of 2009, only 50% of the country area had been geologically mapped (1/200,000).

12 As of 2009.

13 Lane Xang means 'one million elephants' in Laotian.

14 Sepon was established by Rio Tinto in 1999, and it was then bought by Australia's Oxiana one year later, although Rio Tinto kept a 20% share. Minerals and Metals Group was formed in June 2009—when China Minmetals Non-ferrous Co., Ltd acquired key assets of OZ Minerals. The latter was itself formed in July 2008, when Oxiana merged with Zinifex Ltd. Listed on the Hong Kong Stock Exchange, Minerals and Metals Group Limited is primarily controlled by shareholder China Minmetals Corporation (with 71.72%) and by public shareholders (with the remaining 28.28%). From an operational standpoint, Sepon is run by the Australians since Minerals and Metals Group was created through the purchase of Australia-based OZ Minerals by Minmetals Resources in 2009.

15 Via its subsidiary Pan Mekong Exploration Pty Limited.

16 According to 'Phu Bia Strikes Gold' (2012), the company launched a pre-feasibility study in June 2012 and production could start in late 2015.

17 The project is run by Ord River Resources and China Nonferrous Metal Industry's Foreign Engineering and Construction Company (NFC) (managed by Sino Australian Resources—SARCO).

18 The NEM further allowed for farmers to own land and freely sell crops, for the elimination of almost all government-fixed prices, and for a higher degree of management independence from state-owned enterprises. The latter also lost their monopoly status along with most subsidies (UN, 2010, p. 8). The NEM was expanded throughout the following decade.

19 Law No 04/97/NA on Mining (12 April 1997). Implemented by Decree in 2002.

20 Examples of royalty rates for different minerals: iron 3%; copper 4%; lead 3%; zinc 3%; tin 3%; gold 5%, silver 4%; platinum 5%; sapphire 5%; ruby 5%; emerald 5%; potash 3%; and gypsum 3% (Department of Geology and Mines, 2006). Additional fees apply such as rental fees which range from US$0.5 to US$1 per ha/year for general surveys and exploration, and from US$3 to US$12 per ha/year for preparatory mining (Feasibility and Construction Phase). In terms of import and re-export facilities, foreign investors shall pay an import duty on equipment, means of production, spare parts, and other materials used at a maximum rate 1% of the imported value (Department of Geology and Mines, 2006).

21 For example, the 1997 Mining Law allowed royalty rates to fluctuate between 2% and 5% of sales depending on mineral commodities.

22 The Law was made publically available only in late 2009.

23 Approved in May 2011 (and ended in 2012), the Project (P122847) committed US$10 million.

24 See World Bank, Technical Assistance Project P122847.

25 The terms of the new Mining Law do not retroactively affect licences and agreements that were effective prior to the new Law.

26 There is no automatic right under the Mineral Law, allowing an investor who holds an exploration licence to exploit mineral resources if a commercially viable deposit is discovered in the exploration area.

27 World Bank Technical Assistance Project for Capacity Development in Hydropower and Mining Sector (P109736).

28 For example, the Lao Business Forum held in June 2008 drew nearly 300 participants from business, government, and donor representatives (World Bank, 2008, p. 38).

29 More specifically, the Environmental Protection Law notably requires EIAs and the protection of natural resources, biodiversity, and cultural and historic sites.

30 For further details, see Gibson and Rex (2010, p. 16).

31 As of 30 June 2011, it had the following reserves: 0.7 million tonnes of copper, 0.9 million ounces of silver, and 0.2 million ounces of gold (Minerals and Metals Group [MMG], 2013).

32 It started gold production in January 2003.

33 The EIR observes that:

> In addition to the 5 volume Environmental and Social Impact Analysis, 16 targeted studies were commissioned, a Public Consultation and Disclosure Plan; a Resettlement Action Plan; and a Community/Indigenous Peoples Development Plan were submitted) and meetings were conducted with the government, communities, and NGOs. (2003a, p. 29)

34 On the topic, notably see EIR (2003a) and World Rainforest Movement (2004).

35 The Board of Directors of the World Bank (US$270 million) and the Asian Development Bank (ADB) (US$107 million) approved loans and guarantees for the project in 2005.

36 The majority (95%) of the generated power has so far been earmarked for Thailand, and the remaining 5% for local consumption (USGS, 2012, p. 16.1).

37 For a thorough analysis of the case of NT2, notably see Goldman (2005), Hirsch (2002), and Lawrence (2009).

38 NT2 is owned by Lao Holding State Enterprise (25%), Electricity Generating Public Company Limited (25%), Electricité de France International (35%), and Italian–Thai Development Public Company Limited (15%).

39 There were, after all, over 200 consultations and workshops conducted for the people both in the preparatory work and during the implementation process.

40 NT2 was expected to be financed with a 30% equity from the shareholders and 70% international loans and guarantees from the World Bank, the ADB, the European Investment Bank, the Agence Francaise de Developpement, export credit agencies, and commercial banks (Lawrence, 2009, p. 85).

41 For a thorough analysis of the diverse participatory and assessment processes which took place during the early phase of NT2, see Hirsch (2002).

42 As stated in Article 44 of the country's 1991 Constitution (revised in 2003): 'Lao citizens have the right and freedom of speech, press and assembly, and have the right to set up associations and to stage demonstrations which are not contrary to the laws'.

43 Media personnel are appointed mostly from within the Party and all publications must be approved by the Ministry of Information and Culture (Freedom House, 2012).

44 There were a total of 85 residents interviewed for the survey, with a variety of age groups, genders, occupations, and ethnic groups. Only villagers who had been affected by mining operations were selected for the survey, so that their opinions on the mining industry could be assessed (Marley-Zagar, 2012, p. 8).

45 Other anecdotal incidents were reported such as the one in Palay village (Borikhamxay province) in 2012, when approximately 100 villagers were reported to have become ill after inhaling the vapours of a chemical spilled from a truck on its way from a mine site in Vientiane Province (Marley-Zagar, 2012).

46 The five-year project will run in partnership with the Department of Mines, in order to aid capacity building with regard to formulating regulations, supervising, and inspecting mining projects (Marley-Zagar, 2012).

47 See World Bank (2010b).

48 The Index is a measurement tool of perceptions of public sector corruption.

49 Government of Laos, 'Notification PM/13', 6 November 2012.

50 The moratorium was briefly lifted in April 2009 and rapidly reinstated in July of that year.

51 For example, Amanta Resources Ltd would have been granted rights over a concession located in Luang Namtha province, while Shandong Sun Paper Co. Ltd. would have been granted a concession for a eucalyptus plantation in Savannakhet province.

References

Ahrens, J. (2004). *Toward a post-Washington consensus: The importance of governance structures in less developed countries and economies in transition.* Department of Economics, University of Göttingen. Retrieved July 10, 2009, from http://www.sigov.si/zmar/apublic/jiidt/ iib0400/08-ahren.pdf

Asian Development Bank. (2011). *Overview of civil society.* ADB Civil Society Briefs. Author. Retrieved January 6, 2012, from http://beta.adb.org/publications/civil-society-briefs-lao-peoples-democratic-republic

Auty, R. (1993). *Sustaining development in the mineral economies: The resource curse thesis.* London: Routledge.

Baird, I. G. (2008). Laos. In K. Wessendorf (Ed.), *The Indigenous world 2008* (pp. 319–327). Copenhagen: International Work Group for Indigenous Affairs.

Bebbington, A., Hinojosa, L., Humphreys Bebbington, D., Burneo, M. L., & Warnaars, X. (2008). Contention and ambiguity: Mining and the possibilities of development. *Development and Change, 39*(6), 887–914.

Boh, M. (2013, April 12). A dam too far in Laos. *Asia Times Online.* Retrieved November 9, 2013, from http://www.atimes.com/atimes/Southeast_Asia/SEA-01-120413.html

Boland, N., Kunanayagam, R., & Walker, A. (2001). *Lao PDR mining sector: Social and environmental sustainability* (Report of the World Bank Group Fact-Finding Mission). World Bank Group Mining Department.

Boungnaphalom, E. (2010, May 23–27). *Mineral development in Lao PDR.* International conference on mining staking a claim for Cambodia, Phnom Penh.

Cammack, P. (2003). The governance of global capitalism: A new materialist perspective. *Historical Materialism, 11*(2), 37–59.

Campbell, B. (Ed.). (2004). *Regulating mining in Africa: For whose benefit?* (Discussion Paper No. 26). Groupe de recherche sur les activités minières en Afrique (GRAMA). Uppsala: Nordiska Afrikainstitutet.

Campbell, B. (Ed.). (2009). *Mining in Africa: Regulation and development.* Groupe de recherche sur les activités minières en Afrique (GRAMA). New York, NY: Pluto Press.

Carroll, T. (2010). *Delusions of development: The World Bank and the post-Washington consensus in Southeast Asia.* Basingstoke: Palgrave-MacMillan.

Carroll, T., & Jarvis, D. (2014). *The politics of marketising Asia.* Basingstoke: Palgrave.

Carroll, T., & Jarvis, D. S. L. (2015). The new politics of development: Citizens, civil society and the evolution of neoliberal development policy. *Globalizations,* doi:10.1080/14747731.2015.1016301

CLC Asia. (2009). *Political risk and regulatory overview in Laos for natural resource companies.* Author. Retrieved January 2011, from http://www.clc-asia.com/analysis/political-risk-and-regulatory-overview-in-laos-for-natural-resource-companies/

Department of Geology and Mines. (2006, June). *Mining law and related regulations in Lao PDR.* Mining conference at Lao Plaza Hotel, Vientiane.

Economist backs mining investment freeze in Laos. (2012). *Vientiane Times. Business Desk, Asia News.* Retrieved June 1, 2013, from http://www.asianewsnet.net/news-30480.html

Energy Sector Management Assistance Programme, the World Bank and International Council on Mining and Metals. (2005). *Community development toolkit.* Washington, DC: World Bank and ESMAP.

Extractive Industries Review. (2003a). *Asia and Pacific regional workshop: Testimonials and consultation report*. Washington, DC: World Bank Group. Retrieved February 19, 2015, from http://documents.worldbank.org/curated/en/2013/04/18874150/extractive-industries-review-eir-asia-pacific-regional-workshop-testimonials-consultation-report

Extractive Industries Review. (2003b). *Striking a better balance: The final report of the extractive industries review* (Vol. 1). Jakarta: World Bank Group and Extractive Industries.

Fine, B., Lapavitsas, C., & Pincus, J. (Eds.). (2001). *Development policy in the twenty-first century: Beyond the post-Washington consensus*. London: Routledge.

Freedom House. (2012). *Freedom of the press 2012: Laos*. Retrieved June 1, 2013, from http://www.freedomhouse.org/report/freedom-press/2012/laos

Gibson, D., & Rex, H. C. (2010). *Social impact mitigation from hydropower and mining in Lao PDR: Examining potential for benefit-sharing approaches* (Background paper for Lao PDR development report 2010). Washington, DC: World Bank.

Gill, S. (1995). Globalisation, market civilisation, and disciplinary neoliberalism. *Millennium: Journal of International Studies*, 24(3), 399–423.

Goldman, M. (2005). *Imperial nature: The World Bank and struggles for social justice in the age of globalization*. New Haven, CT: Yale University Press.

Guttal, S., & Shoemaker, B. (2004). *Manipulating consent: The World Bank's public consultation and acceptance process for the Nam Theun 2 hydroelectric project*. Retrieved February 19, 2015, from http://www.internationalrivers.org/files/attached-files/manipulating0904.pdf

Hatcher, P. (2004). Mali: Rewriting the mining code or redefining the role of the state? In B. Campbell (Ed.), *Regulating mining in Africa: For whose benefit?* (No. 26, pp. 39–52). Uppsala: Nordiska Afrikainstitute.

Hatcher, P. (2006). Partnership and the international aid reform: Challenging citizenship and political representation. In D. Stone & C. Wright (Eds.), *The World Bank and governance: A decade of reform and reaction* (pp. 189–206). New York, NY: Routledge.

Hatcher, P. (2010). The politics of the curse: The international finance corporation & the Multilateral Investment Guarantee Agency in risk countries. *Ritsumeikan International Affairs*, *10*, 57–84.

Hatcher, P. (2012). Taming the risks in Asia: The World Bank group and new mining regimes. *Journal of Contemporary Asia*, *42*(3), 427–446.

Hatcher, P. (2014). *Regimes of risk: The World Bank and the transformation of mining in Asia*. London: Palgrave-Macmillan.

Head, J. (2012, October). Laos gets set to join the World Trade Organization. *BBC News*. Retrieved June 1, 2013, from http://www.bbc.co.uk/news/business-20078312

Hirsch, P. (2002). Global norms, local compliance and the human rights-environment nexus: A case study of the Nam Theun II dam in Laos. In L. Zarsky (Ed.), *Human rights and the environment: Conflicts and norms in a globalizing world* (pp. 147–171). New York, NY: Routledge.

International Council on Mining and Metals. (2011). *Utilizing mining and mineral resources to foster the sustainable development of the Lao PDR*. London: Author.

International Development Association. (2005). *Country assistance strategy for the Lao People's Democratic Republic* (Report No. 31758-LA). Southeast Asia Country Unit.

International Financial Corporation. (2012). *International best practices help Lao PDR build new investment regime*. Retrieved January 6, 2012, from http://www.ifc.org/ifcext/mekongpsdf.nsf/Content/Feature24

International Financial Corporation. (2013). *Improvement of policies and regulations for the hydropower sector in Lao PDR*. Retrieved June 1, 2013, from http://www1.ifc.org/wps/wcm/connect/region__ext_content/regions/east+asia+and+the+pacific/countries/improvement+of+policies+and+regulations+for+the+hydropower+sector+in+lao+pdr

International Monetary Fund. (2004). *Lao People's Democratic Republic: Poverty reduction strategy paper* (IMF Country Report No. 04/393). Washington, DC: Author.

Kunze, G. (2010). New decree opens way for civil society in Laos. In *Asia: Weekly insight and features from Asia*. The Asia Foundation. Retrieved January 6, 2012, from http://asiafoundation.org/in-asia/2010/06/02/new-decree-opens-way-for-civil-society-in-laos/

Kyophilavong, P. (2010). *Mining sector in Laos*. Institute of Developing Economies. Retrieved February 14, 2012, from http://www.ide.go.jp/English/Publish/Download/Brc/pdf/02_ch3.pdf

Larsen, M. (2010). *Economic assessment of the future of the Lao mining sector* (Background paper for Lao PDR Development Report 2010). Washington, DC: World Bank.

Lawrence, S. (Ed.). (2008). *Power surge: The impacts of rapid dam development in Laos*. Berkeley, CA: International Rivers.

Lawrence, S. (2009). The Nam Theun 2 controversy and its lessons for Laos. In F. Molle, T. Foran, & M. Käkönen (Eds.), *Contested waterscapes in the Mekong Region: Hydropower, livelihoods and governance* (pp. 81–111). London: Earthscan.

Marley-Zagar, E. (2012, June). *The mining industry: Laos can't live with it, can't live without it*. I-Light. Retrieved June 1, 2013, from http://www.indochinaresearch.com/newsletter/june2012/going_further.html

Minerals and Metals Group. (2013). *Sepon*. Retrieved June 1, 2013, from http://www.mmg.com/en/Our-Operations/Mining-operations/Sepon.aspx

Operations Evaluation Group. (2005). IFC's experience. In A. Liebenthal, R. Michelitsch, & E. Tarazona (Eds.), *Extractive industries and sustainable development: An evaluation of World Bank Group experience* (Annex D, pp. 113–171). Washington, DC: World Bank.

Phommakaysone, K. (2012). *The geology and mineral resources of Lao PDR*. Department of Geology and Mineral Resources, Ministry of Natural Resources and Environment. Retrieved June 1, 2013, from http://mric.jogmec.go.jp/kouenkai_index/2012/briefing_120316_3.pdf

Phu Bia strikes gold in Phonsavan. (2012). *Vientiane Times*. Retrieved June 1, 2013, from http://www.worklivelaos.com/phubia-strikes-gold-in-phonsavan/

Rosser, A. (2006). *The political economy of the resource curse: A literature survey* (IDS Working Paper No. 268). Institute of Development Studies.

Sachs, D. J., & Warner, A. M. (1995). *Natural resource abundance and economic growth* (Working Paper Series, No. 5398). National Bureau of Economic Research.

Schönweger, O., Heinimann, A., Epprecht, M., Lu, J., & Thalongsengchanh, P. (2012). *Concessions and leases in the Lao PDR: Taking stock of land investments*. Bern: Centre for Development and Environment (CDE), University of Bern and Vientiane: Geographica Bernensia.

Soederberg, S. (2004). *The politics of the new financial architecture*. London: Zed Books.

Southeast Asian Press Alliance. (2013). *Stifling media and civil society in Laos*. Retrieved June 1, 2013, from http://www.seapabkk.org/seapa-reports/press-freedom-on-southeast-asian-countries/100747-stifling-media-and-civil-society-in-laos.html

Thompson, R. (2010, May 26–27). *Regional and international country experiences lessons learned*. Paper presented at the international conference on mining staking a claim for Cambodia, Phnom Penh.

Transparency International. (2009). *Corruption Perceptions Index 2008*. Retrieved February 2, 2011, from http://www.transparency.org/

United Nations. (2010). *An investment guide to the Lao People's Democratic Republic: Opportunities and conditions*. Geneva: Author.

United Nations Development Programme. (2011). *Illicit financial flows from the least developed countries: 1990–2008*. Retrieved June 1, 2013, from http://content.undp.org/go/cmsservice/download/publication

United States Geological Survey. (1994). *The mineral industry of Laos*. U.S. Geological Survey—Minerals Information.

United States Geological Survey. (1997). *The mineral industry of Laos*. U.S. Geological Survey—Minerals Information.

United States Geological Survey. (1999). *The mineral industry of Laos*. U.S. Geological Survey—Minerals Information.

United States Geological Survey. (2008). *The mineral industry of Laos*. U.S. Geological Survey—Minerals Information.

United States Geological Survey. (2010). *The mineral industry of Laos*. U.S. Geological Survey—Minerals Information. Retrieved May 2, 2014, from http://minerals.usgs.gov/minerals/pubs/country/2010/myb3-2010-la.pdf

United States Geological Survey. (2012). *The mineral industry of Laos*. U.S. Geological Survey—Minerals Information. Retrieved May 2, 2014, from http://minerals.usgs.gov/minerals/pubs/country/2011/myb3-2011-la.pdf

World Bank. (2004). *Striking a better balance: The World Bank Group and extractive industries: The final report of the extractive industries review World Bank Group management response*. Washington, DC: Author.

World Bank. (2005). *Extractive industries and sustainable development: An evaluation of World Bank Group experience*. Washington, DC: Author.

World Bank. (2006). *Final report for international competitiveness element and downstream potential of mining industry: Sector plan for sustainable development of the mining sector in the Lao PDR*. Washington, DC: Author.

World Bank. (2008). *Lao PDR economic monitor*. Vientiane: World Bank Office.

World Bank. (2010a). *An environmental perspective on hydropower and mining development in the Lao PDR* (Background paper for the Lao PDR Development Report 2010: Natural Resource Management for Sustainable Development). Washington, DC: Author.

World Bank. (2010b). *Lao PDR development report: Natural resource management for sustainable development-hydropower and mining* (Report No. 59005-LA). Washington, DC: Author.

World Bank. (2010c). *Lao PDR recent economic developments: Mid-year update* (Issue No. 15). Vientiane: World Bank Office.

World Bank. (2010d). *Mining & communities*. Oil, Gas, Mining Unit. World Bank. Retrieved February 2, 2011, from http://go.worldbank.org/R6ZD7IYYD0

World Bank. (2012). *Country partnership strategy for Lao Peoples Democratic Republic for the period FY 12-FY16* (Report No. 66692-LA). Lao PDR Country Management Unit.

World Bank. (n.d.). *TA for capacity development in hydropower and mining sector* (Technical Assistance Project P109736). Retrieved July 10, 2013, from http://www.worldbank.org/projects/P109736/ta-capacity-development-hydropower-mining-sector?lang=en

World Rainforest Movement. (2004). *Mining social and environmental impacts*. Montevideo: World Rainforest Movement.

Civil Society and the Gender Politics of Economic Competitiveness in Malaysia

JUANITA ELIAS

Department of Politics and International Relations, University of Warwick, Coventry, UK

ABSTRACT *Malaysian government planning and policy-making have increasingly come to recognise the role of women and the household in the promotion of a number of strategies aimed at enhancing economic competitiveness. Government planning documents emphasise the need to boost women's labour market participation, increase women's levels of entrepreneurship, and the need to strengthen and support the family unit—developments that can be understood in terms of a market-building agenda in which women's labour and the household are viewed as untapped resources in the struggle to maintain international competitiveness. This article explores an important dimension of this policy turn: the role of civil society in both promoting and resisting this market-building agenda. The paper focuses in particular on two case studies: religious non-governmental organisations involved in implementing 'family strengthening' programmes and civil society engagements with the issue of women's representation on corporate boards.*

Introduction

In Malaysia, government policies and programmes have increasingly identified the contribution of women and the family to state development projects aimed at enhancing national economic competitiveness. This policy turn has entailed emphasising *both* the need to increase the productive capacity of women as workers and entrepreneurs in the market economy, and their socially reproductive roles as wives, mothers, and unpaid carers in the household (Elias, 2009, 2011). In this context, women are viewed as playing important roles as productive market actors driving economic success and as custodians of those traditional family and religious values that remain centrally important in securing consent for an increasingly neoliberal state-led modernisation agenda. This paper focuses on an important, albeit generally underexplored aspect of this market-building agenda—the role of civil society actors in legitimating state practices that act to (re)produce new market subjectivities that have become central to state-led processes of neoliberal market-building.

By focusing on two specific policy issues (family strengthening programmes and policies aimed at increasing women's representation on corporate boards through an unofficial 'quota'), I aim to demonstrate that certain civil society actors have acted to promote state gender policies that are framed by the desire to build competitive economic growth. Nonetheless, attempts to incorporate gender issues into development policy through a focus on increasing women's engagement in the productive economy exist in uneasy alliance with a more traditionalist focus on women's roles as wives and mothers. Thus, not only women, but the family itself (as a site for the (re)production of good market-citizens) are seen as drivers of competitive economic growth. These gender- and household-focused policy initiatives generate tensions within both state and society over the appropriate role and position of women in Malaysian society—tensions that invariably intersect with other social cleavages centred on ethnicity, class, and religion that permeate Malaysia's political economy. A focus on civil society provides an important lens through which to observe these tensions. Whilst much writing on civil society in Southeast Asia has tended to focus on the limited spaces for activism within authoritarian political structures (Aspinall & Weiss, 2012), the approach adopted here is to point to the complicity of civil society actors in state development projects. The article thus shares many of the concerns found in more Gramscian-inspired understanding of civil society in Southeast Asia, in which civil society is shown to systematically sustain and support authoritarian rule and capitalist developmentalism (Hedman, 2006; Hilley, 2001; Nair, 2007a; Ramasamy, 2004; Sim, 2006) as well as those writings that emphasise the ability of state and international actors to push and condition civil society actors into more 'amenable' spaces of engagement (Carroll & Jarvis, 2015; Gerard, 2015; Rodan & Hughes, 2012). Of particular inspiration to the arguments developed in this paper is the work of Garry Rodan and Caroline Hughes on social accountability activism in Southeast Asia that points to the salience within civil society of liberal and moral agendas that serve to support existing power hierarchies and the effective sidelining (and co-option) of more democratic voices. In the empirical discussion provided in this paper what is shown is that state gender and competitiveness agendas come to be aligned with (a) 'moral' actors in the guise of religious organisations engaged in state-sanctioned marriage and family programmes and (b) a 'liberal' (market feminist) agenda organised around the interests of elite women in promoting women's representation on corporate boards. Little space is left in this context for those actors more critical of those state policies that align women and the household with competitive economic growth.

Taking the first example, that of civil society engagements with family policy, an important component of Malaysia's drive for economic competitiveness are attempts to reconcile economic 'modernisation' with the increased Islamicisation of state and society. Within this context Malay Muslim women come to play important symbolic roles in debates over the appropriate role and position of women in society—with the image of the modern Malay woman presented in relation not only to her engagement in the productive economy, but in terms of her commitments to traditional family roles and personal religious piety. Hence religious non-governmental organisations (NGOs) engage in family-strengthening programmes that act to particular 'traditionalist' understandings of gender roles within the family (albeit a traditionalism that is mediated by the realities of women's increased economic roles outside of the home). Civil society engagement with state family policy agendas is thus shown to support the uneasy and complex ways in which religion has been linked to state modernisation projects as well as the reconfigurations of class and ethnic relations that have taken shape in Malaysia since the launching of the country's New Economic Policy[1] in 1970 (Hadiz & Teik, 2011). The second example, of women's representation on corporate boards, is a case in which a more 'progressive' agenda broadly supported by the feminist-oriented activist women's movement has gained traction in policy-making circles. However, this issue needs to be related to how the Malaysian state has sought consistently to curtail and constrain the spaces and opportunities for engagement with an activist civil society (Nair, 2007a). Despite the existence of a vibrant activist women's movement in Malaysia, the corporate boards issue gained support mainly because of the involvement of civil society actors representing the corporate sector—thus pointing to the fact that the pursuit of women's empowerment agendas is most successful when it engages the support of powerful and influential (corporate and neoliberal compatible) interests within both the state and civil society.

Whilst the analysis presented in this article seeks to contribute to extant studies of the limits of civil society activism in capitalist and authoritarian Southeast Asia (Gerard, 2015; Hedman, 2006; Hilley, 2001; Nair, 2007a; Ramasamy, 2004; Rodan & Hughes, 2012; Sim, 2006), it should also be noted that a central theoretical assumption guiding my analysis is that a materialist feminist analysis also provides important insights into understanding the dynamics of state–civil society relations, in particular by enabling a focus on how transformations in state–civil society relations reproduce and are produced by broader transformations in patterns of productive–socially reproductive relations (Bakker & Gill, 2003; Shields & Wallin, 2015). Thus the concept of social relations of reproduction is employed in the feminist political economy sense to refer to the kinds of deeply feminised household and care-related activities (or 'the fleshy, messy and indeterminate stuff of everyday life' (Katz, 2001, p. 711)) so central to the functioning of the productive economy. In this analysis the state is identified as central to the ordering of localised gender regimes based on specific productive–reproductive configurations (Connell, 1990), how these regimes exist alongside structures of race, ethnicity, and class (Hall, 1986), and how they are being transformed through engagements with a transnational disciplinary neoliberalism (Bakker & Gill, 2003). Furthermore, this 'embedded' (Rai, 2002) understanding of the state has implications for how state–civil society interactions are viewed. Howell (2005), for example, notes the permeability of the boundaries that exist between the thoroughly gendered terrains of state, market, civil society, and the household.[2] In the analysis that follows, the permeability of these boundaries are explored—drawing attention, in particular, to the relationship between civil society actors and tensions that are generated within the state itself over the issue of how best to incorporate women into national development planning (i.e. as productive workers/entrepreneurs, as socially reproductive wives/mothers, or as both).

This paper is structured in three main sections. The first of these briefly outlines the way in which gender issues in Malaysia have been framed in terms of a need to build national economic competitiveness. Part two moves on to examine how notions of national economic competitiveness are linked to a broader moral agenda concerning the role of the family and points to the role that NGOs and an Islamicised civil society more generally have played in terms of the implementation of this agenda. By emphasising the role of religious organisations in delivering state programmes associated with the need to strengthen the family as an important component of economic development, I draw attention to the very culturally specific modes through which processes related to the widening and deepening of the market economy take place. The third part of the paper then turns to look at the configuration of civil society and state interests that have coalesced around the issue of women's representation on corporate boards. I begin this discussion with a look at the politics of the Malaysian women's movement and its embrace of 'market feminism'. The government's promotion of the issue of women's representation on corporate boards can be represented as a market feminist success story. However, it is a success story in which the voices of powerful corporate-linked interests predominate and the message of feminism has been subordinated to the market. The research draws upon interviews undertaken with state officials and civil society groups over the course of three research trips to Malaysia (in 2010, 2011 and 2012). The research also draws upon analysis of relevant publically available government documents (in particular economic planning documents) and analysis of a range of secondary source materials such as news media and NGO-linked websites.

Mobilising Women to Serve the Competitiveness Agenda

In order to understand the way in which a global policy consensus concerning women's role in maintaining economic competitiveness has taken root in Malaysia, it is important to first point out that the desire to maintain and enhance the country's competitiveness by building a knowledge-based economy has long been a hallmark of Malaysian economic policy-making (Elias, 2009, 2011). This focus was initially set out in former Prime Minister's Mahathir Mohammed's 'Vision 2020' (attaining developed country status by 2020) (Mahathir, 1993). It has been reconfirmed in the current Tenth Malaysia Plan (2011–2015) and other political-economic policy instruments such as the Economic Transformation Programme (ETP) focused on the broad economic trajectory of the nation (particularly in terms of enhancing national economic competitiveness and the achievement of Vision 2020) that have been developed under the current prime ministership of Najib Tun Razak and overseen by the Performance Management and Delivery Unit (Pemandu) established in 2009. A consensus on the need to promote economic competitiveness invariably reflects the significance that political leaders in the Asian region attach to this concept (especially in relation to national competitiveness benchmarking practices such as the World Economic Forum's Competitiveness Index (Lall, 2001, p. 1502)).

More substantially, the pursuit of economic competitiveness by states in the Asian region can be linked to wider shifts in configurations of power and productive relations in ways that 'prioritize private interests over social ones' in forms of 'new constitutional governance' (Bakker & Gill, 2008, p. 29) or what Cammack (2006) terms a global politics of competitiveness (see also Carroll, 2012; Carroll & Jarvis, 2015). In this perspective, the pursuit of national economic competitiveness reflects implicit assumptions concerning the need for the poor to engage, as productive actors, in the market economy in ways that consistently privilege the interests of capital over labour and serve to widen the reach of the market economy into traditionally 'non-market' spaces such as the household (Elias & Gunawardana, 2013; Nevins & Peluso, 2009).

A notable emphasis in Malaysian government policy documents and pronouncements on the knowledge economy is a deeply instrumentalist focus on women's role in sustaining national competitiveness through their participation in the productive economy. For example, in the Tenth Malaysia Plan the claim is made that 'it is essential that women are given the right opportunities, environment and mindset so that they can participate and contribute in the various fields of national development' (Malaysia, 2010, p. 180). Such claims can be related more broadly to the emphasis in the Tenth Plan on the role of 'human capital' and 'talent' or, more specifically, knowledgeable and innovative citizens with a 'first-class mentality' (Malaysia, 2010, p. 46) in raising productivity and competitiveness. Despite the dominance of female employment in the economically important export manufacturing sectors of the economy, the overall female labour force participation rate in Malaysia has remained low. This is of concern to policy-makers—for example, in the Tenth Plan, attention is drawn to the fact that although the country's female labour force participation rate rose from 44.7% in 1995 to 45.7% in 2008 to 46.4% in 2009 (a figure that can be contrasted with a male labour force participation rate of around 80%[3]). The desire to increase women's labour force participation has frequently been presented as a way of lessening the economy's dependence on migrant labour and concerns are raised over the fact that many highly skilled and educated women leave the workforce once they start to have children (Loh-Ludher, 2009). In the Tenth Plan, the issue of increasing women's labour force participation is discussed in terms of increasing the opportunities for women to work through better provision of childcare services in the community and the need to further expand the already highly visible group of women 'decision-makers' in the public sector to 30% (Malaysia, 2010).

Under the ETP, a Human Capital Strategic Reform Initiative Lab was established and made recommendations regarding the need to 'leverage on women's talent to increase productivity' that included expanding childcare provision (Pemandu, 2011, p. 235).[4] This recognition of how women's socially reproductive roles serve to constrain their engagement in the productive economy is also manifested in policies that seek to build markets within the household itself via microenterprise development (Malaysia, 2010, p. 178). Whereas there is a recognition that (middle-class, urban) women's labour force participation in the knowledge economy depends on making available flexible work arrangements and childcare services, microenterprise is conceptualised as fostering 'inclusive socio-economic development' (Malaysia, 2010, p. 139) by drawing marginalised women into the market economy and, because most microenterprises are home-based, enabling them to combine paid work with their socially reproductive responsibilities. Both strategies depend, nonetheless, on a conceptualisation of women's labour as an unproductive resource whose capacities can be better utilised in the country's pursuit of economic competitiveness.

The rhetorical commitment of the Malaysian state to increasing women's labour force participation is, in practice, significantly constrained by a failure to support women's socially reproductive roles. For example, commitments to increasing the availability of childcare for the under-4s have depended largely on (deeply unsuccessful) inducements to the private sector to establish workplace crèches (Elias, 2011). Women's labour market participation is supported by a patchwork of privatised socially reproductive arrangements such as the employment of migrant domestic workers, childcare services where they are available—frequently in centres that are unregistered and fail to meet adequate government standards such as staff–child ratios and health and safety standards, as well as an increased reliance on informal and extended family support networks. The 'intensification of exploitation' is thus accompanied by a 'depletion through social reproduction' (Rai, Hoskyns, & Thomas, 2014, p. 88) that government policies have sought to address via policies of 'family strengthening' (see below) rather than through efforts to better address society's socially reproductive welfare needs.

Furthermore, as well as being rather patchy in terms of policy outcomes, the gender and competitiveness agenda is also racked by tensions and inconsistencies, even within the state. For example, it is observable that institutions and departments associated with planning for and delivering large-scale development plans such as the country's New Economic Model launched in 2010 have tended to view increases in women's labour force participation and entrepreneurialism as an important policy goal. But, at the same time, competing sets of state institutions associated with the Islamicisation of the state,[5] including The Department of Islamic Development (JAKIM) and the Islamic courts have tended to emphasise a moral vision of family life in which women take primary responsibility for social reproduction (in particular, the raising of morally responsible and suitably Islamic Malaysian citizens). As will be shown in this paper, the gender politics of economic competitiveness in Malaysia comprises two core strands—increasing women's productivity as market actors and emphasising women's reproductive responsibilities as mothers to the next generation of market-engaged, yet pious, Malaysian citizens. In what follows, I look first at how thoroughly nationalistic and religiously infused moral agendas concerning the family have been tied to understandings of economic competitiveness, before turning to explore the role of civil society actors in supporting and implementing this policy turn.

Family Policy and the Moral Imperative of Development

Policies aimed at bolstering women's productive economic activities need to be situated alongside the long-standing policy emphasis on women's socially reproductive roles—both in terms of population policies (efforts to increase the birth rate—Thambiah, 2010) and in relation to perceptions regarding the central role that women perform in strengthening the family—perceptions that invariably intersect with deeply nationalistic and racialised agendas especially within the Malay community. The family, and the household more generally, comes to be presented as a key site for the (re)production of economically productive and suitably nationalistic and loyal Malaysians. As Prime Minister Najib argued at the launch of the Tenth Plan:

> As the saying goes, the hand that rocks the cradle rules the world. The status of women in society is a good indicator of a progressive and dynamic country. Women are the cornerstone of happy families and the essence of a successful nation. (2010, p. 46)

Women's increased labour force participation is presented in government planning documents as an economic necessity but concerns have been raised that women will neglect their role in the social reproduction of labour (fears that are compounded by the increased reliance on foreign domestic workers). Claiming that '[f]amilies are the cornerstone of a healthy, dynamic and productive nation' (Malaysia, 2010, p. 186), the Tenth Plan highlights the need for '[p]rogrammes that instil character building and family values' that will focus on 'strengthening marriage and promoting equitable sharing of resources, responsibilities and tasks' (Malaysia, 2010, p. 187). These include schemes such as the National Population and Family Development Board (LPPKN)-run pre-marriage guidance programme SMARTSTART (which is tailored to suit the particular religious needs of different ethnic groups) and the Parenting@work programme designed to support young parents. In his forward to the SMARTSTART book (distributed to all course participants), former prime minister Abdullah Badawi overtly links these programmes to national economic success, embracing a modernisation script in which morally upstanding and economically engaged citizens are nurtured within (and not constrained by) family settings in which commitments to 'tradition' and religious values are maintained. Hence:

> The marriage institution is the core to the forming of a family in Malaysia. The strengthening of the family from the early stages of its formation can provide a strong and solid foundation for the development of human capital among the younger generation. Human capital is critical to the well-balanced development of the nation. To enhance the current stage of our country's modernization and the progress that we have achieved, we need to empower and develop human capital that has a first class mentality with a heart for progress. These individuals could then safeguard and manage the great developments that our country has achieved through good leadership and management. (Abdullah, 2006, p. 3)

In what follows I look at the context within which the LPPKN's work on strengthening the family has emerged before turning to consider the nature of the agency's engagement with

NGOs. The LPPKN is an agency that is housed within the Ministry of Women, Family and Community Development. The agency presents the work that it does in terms of the gender-neutral language of shared and equitable parenting. Indeed, the agency's work in this area is noted in the Malaysian government's appearance at a 2006 Convention on the Elimination of All Forms of Discrimination against Women (CEDAW) meeting at the UN in New York (CEDAW, 2006). But, despite these rhetorical commitments to gender equality within the family, LPPKN's work reflects a deeply conservative agenda that needs to be situated within the wider Islamicisation of state and society in Malaysia (Stivens, 2006). Much of the work that LPPKN is involved in is presented in terms of ideas concerning the moral threat(s) posed by the emergence of new family forms that have arisen in the wake of economic development and urbanisation. The following quotation from a former LPPKN Director General provides an example of how these concerns are expressed:

> The most likely family scenario in the coming decades is small nuclear families with high levels of economic activity of both husbands and wives. This is clearly a very different family from the traditional Malaysian family, and care will need to be taken to ensure that family values are not sacrificed at the altar of economic gains, both at the national and individual levels. (Fatimah, 2007, p. 184)

It should be noted, however, that the image of Malaysia as transitioning in a straightforward manner towards small nuclear families belies the extent to which a greater plurality of family forms exists in Malaysia. Not least of which is the significance of single headed (usually female) households which experience disproportionately high levels of poverty (Evans, 2011). But such a story does not fit within a moral agenda that presents the heteronormative family unit as a transitioning yet essential component of development success.

Commitments to the family and family values are operationalised in order to present economic development as possessing a moral dimension. For example, Mahathir's Vision 2020 speech included nine 'strategic challenges' of which the fourth was 'to establish a fully moral and ethical society whose citizens are strong in religious and spiritual values and imbued with the highest ethical standards' (Mahathir, 1993). A seventh challenge was that

> of establishing a fully caring society and a caring culture, a social system in which society will come before self, in which the welfare of the people will revolve not around the state or the individual but around a strong and resilient family system. (Mahathir, 1993)

thus exposing the way in which moral commitments to family values also serve an important political-economic agenda in which welfare state provisioning is to be kept at very minimal levels.

Civil Society Engagements with State Family-Policy Agendas: The SMARTSTART Programme

The conceptualisation of the strong/traditional family as being threatened by forces of modernisation and secularisation continues to inform LPPKN's work. Thus the LPPKN chairman stated provocatively in 2010 that 'the family is under attack' and the deputy LPPKN director general suggested that 'in developing the future human capital needs of our country, we start from the family. But if that very basis is weak, what will happen to the community and country?' (Koshy, 2010). In recent years, issues of declining family values continually re-emerge in the form of various moral panics around issues such as juvenile delinquency, rising divorce rates, the role of migrant domestic workers in raising children, the rise of 'commuter families' (families in which both parents have to travel long distances to work), and teen pregnancy/abandoning of babies by unwed mothers.[6] For the religious organisations engaged with LPPKN programmes, it is precisely these moral issues that need to be addressed through family strengthening activities. Programmes such as SMARTSTART place significant emphasis on the importance of religious values in maintaining healthy and harmonious marriages and family life and faith-based organisations dominate in the delivery of the programme. The SMARTSTART book reiterates the aforementioned concerns about how 'modern' living challenges traditional family values. Hence: 'We live in a touch "n" go era. People want to be free to move about, change jobs, change beliefs even … But marriage is meant to be permanent' (LPPKN, 2006, p. 9). Religious values are presented as central to addressing this problem:

> Families are breaking down and children are leaving the traditional values we grew up with. One of the most important things we can do to preserve our marriages is to follow the guidance of our religious teachings about the home. Whether you are Muslim, Buddhist, Hindu or Christian, if you follow the values taught, it will help foster a much happier home. (LPPKN, 2006, p. 15)

There are numerous religious NGOs that are involved in administering the SMARTSTART programme. These include Christian groups such as Focus on the Family (a US-linked, right-wing Christian organisation) and Calvary Life Ministries (who also runs programmes for people who wish to 'recover' from 'same gender attraction'). Islamic groups administering the programme include ABIM (the Islamic youth movement established in the 1980s), Wanita ISMA (the women's wing of a nationwide Islamic social affairs organisation *Ikatan Muslimin Malaysia* (ISMA)), the Sarawak-based Islamic Information Centre, and Pusat Islam UTHM (based in the southern state of Johore).[7] Although it was not possible to gain access to many of the groups engaged in administering this programme, interviews conducted at Wanita ISMA provide some interesting insights.[8] Whilst ISMA is an Islamic organisation that has taken an increasingly prominent role in Malaysian politics (mirroring the rise of other right-wing Islamic populist Malay organisations such as the rather more influential Perkasa faction that has played an agenda setting role in recent Malaysian political history[9]), Wanita ISMA focuses mainly on educational and family issues. These activities include religious educational programmes for members' children, already existing counselling programmes for married couples, a family conference (held in 2011), and a women's conference (in 2010) in which speakers sought to emphasise the importance of religious values in strengthening families.

Wanita ISMA thus saw the SMARTSTART programme as fitting well within its existing family-focused activities The organisation adopts an approach to social issues in which the fostering of religious values and moral codes within families is viewed as central to the prevention of wider social ills. The emphasis is on personal piety and religious devotion rather than broader structural and political change (thus the 'solution' to the problem of abandoned babies lies in better religious education and observance amongst the young). Issues surrounding the rise in divorce amongst the Malay population are viewed as an important area of concern that can be addressed through better adherence to religious teachings (in the manner suggested in the SMARTSTART book quoted above). Thus the SMARTSTART programme (which it has been offering for the last two years in four different states) was generally offered by this organisation to already married couples—those in the two- to five-year 'danger zone' for divorce.[10] The organisation echoes LPPKN's conception of the family as a form of two-parent nuclear family facing the challenges of modern society in its work. Thus family educational programmes are strongly focused on the role of responsible fatherhood (the father as leader of the household strongly involved in the practical and religious upbringing of children). Family programmes are viewed as supporting particular forms of tolerant, family-focused responsible masculinity understood in terms of 'service to our country, ourselves and our religion also'.[11] Women are viewed as assuming responsibility for the day-to-day management of the household—a perspective that was viewed by the interviewees as in line with Islamic teachings on the family.

Whilst the values of the religious organisations involved in SMARTSTART stem from traditionalist religious sources, it should be noted that many of these religious organisations and NGOs are themselves frequently a product of Malaysia's political-economic transformation Hadiz & Teik, 2011). Islamic groups in particular should not in any sense be regarded as autonomous civil society actors given the extent to which Islam has come to be institutionalised within the practices of the Malaysian state (and the overt role played by JAKIM in incorporating Islamic groups into elite sanctioned appropriate Islamic practice—Hoffstaedter, 2011, p. 72). Whilst we need to be attendant to the fact that there exist multiple and conflicting forms of Islamic women's movements, what is interesting to note is the way in which across the spectrum of organisations involved in Islamic issues, women are viewed as playing important roles in the arenas of the workplace, social activism the household and religious practice (Maznah, 2004). This is not to deny the fact that processes of Islamiciation in Malaysia have had rather contradictory consequences—on the one hand propelling a number of women into significant political roles and on the other hand sanctioning the reinterpretation of Islamic family law and practice in highly gender-discriminatory ways. Within Wanita ISMA, a vision of family life and domestic arrangements was put forward that sought to present Islamic teachings on the family in terms of the realities of family life amongst the urban Malay middle classes. Importantly, women are not viewed solely as housewives/stay at home mothers but modern Islamic motherhood is conceptualised in terms of how women seek to find a balance between their working and their domestic lives. Hence 'besides the fact that we are busy with our careers and our activism and so on, we don't want to leave our children behind'.[12] This in large part stems from the highly educated, middle-class and professional status of these women activists many of whom are able to employ foreign domestic workers to support their multiple roles as activists, workers, entrepreneurs, and students as well as their family responsibilities. The social activism that Islamic women at Wanita ISMA engage in should not be conceptualised as feminism (indeed, they view feminist agendas as morally corrupt), rather, this is a form of activism that seeks to reconcile changes in the economic status of women outside of the home with commitments to religious and family values.[13] This, then, is a 'new' traditionalism thoroughly compatible with constructions of women as good market citizens engaged in both the productive economy and the social reproduction of a generation of morally upstanding and economically engaged Malaysians, and supported by the expansion of the market for (a racialised underclass) of migrant domestic workers.

Market Feminism and the Malaysian Women's Movement

As the previous discussion reveals, the existence of 'traditionalist' discourses concerning how families are 'under threat' and the need to bolster family values is employed by civil society groups in ways that seek to reconcile more conservative values with women's widespread engagement in the productive economy. These processes of reconciliation can be related to the way in which government gender and development policy-making has been framed around ideas of gender equality being attained through market-based freedoms. Thus the kinds of arguments and issues that many more feminist-oriented women's movements have advocated for have gained greater mass appeal *not* because of processes of political mobilisation within the women's movement, but because '[t]he message of feminism can also be subjected to the logic of the free market' (Ng, Maznah, & Hui, 2006, p. 38). Furthermore, 'freedom engendered by the market—and one complemented by a mass-consumer culture—works to depoliticise many of the issues related to reforms and reinforce political apathy in society' (Ng et al., 2006, p. 38). In what follows I seek to illustrate these concerns by drawing upon the example of civil society involvement in campaigns for women's representation on corporate boards. I initially contextualise this issue by focusing on the broad patterns of women's politically engaged and more feminist-oriented activism in Malaysia, before turning to explore the intersections between market feminism and corporate gender initiatives.

Women's civil society activism in Malaysia not only has a very long history but is also made up of a plethora of different organisations with competing political ideologies. There is no space in this paper to provide a comprehensive overview of the Malaysian women's movement although commentators have pointed to the divide that exists between organisations that position themselves more as social service providers and those avowedly feminist and activist-oriented groups that adopt a more antagonistic position against the state (Ng et al., 2006). One way of illustrating this divide is to point to the two main umbrella/coalitional groupings within the Malaysian women's movement—the National Council of Women's Organisations (the official umbrella body for women's NGOs) and the JAG (Joint Action Group for Gender Equality) coalition of activist women's NGOs (made up of the NGOs Empower, All Women's Action Society (AWAM), Women's Centre for Change (WCC) Sisters in Islam (SIS), and Women's Aid Organisation). An important characteristic of the second group is their adoption of transnational feminist framing strategies—witnessed most obviously in terms of an engagement with the CEDAW process and the language of women's rights, especially in relation to the issue of violence against women. JAG members have also been involved in campaigns to protect the rights of migrant domestic workers, the group Empower has been strongly involved in campaigning on issues relating to women's political and economic empowerment,[14] and the well-known Muslim feminist group SIS has campaigned on issues relating to the rise of socially conservative Islamic agendas in areas such as family law (Nair, 2007b).[15] The politically active women's movement in Malaysia also includes other groups such as the Penang-based 3G's (Good Governance and Gender Equality Society) that has pursued issues relating to gender mainstreaming and women's empowerment and organisations such as the pro-migrant worker group Tenaganita who, although not exclusively focused on women's issues, have spearheaded numerous campaigns around the issue of migrant domestic worker employment in Malaysia.

Nonetheless, activist women's groups in Malaysia have all too frequently adopted a form of feminism that is deeply uncritical of state gender policies framed in terms of the linkages between women's economic empowerment and broader national economic goals such as boosting competitiveness. In part, this lack of criticism stems from the (correct) perception that government policies designed to enhance the status of women are continually hindered by both a lack of commitment to gender mainstreaming processes within the state and more traditionalist social forces (both inside and outside of the state). Thus, women's groups have been critical of the way in which gender policy machineries such as the cabinet level committee on gender equality have been downgraded, core feminist concerns such as the need for anti-sexual harassment legislation has been persistently sidelined (Ho, 2011), and the ways in which an increasingly politicised Islam has been employed to undermine Muslim women's legal rights and to shore up patriarchal privileges. Thus, any government policy that is seen as pro-women is regarded in a positive light.

Another important consideration is that the dominance of a market feminist perspective reflects wider global shifts in feminism whereby an instrumentalist 'business-case' approach to gender equality has become the dominant global discourse through which gender equality claims are articulated. The problem is that the logic of such a perspective is to present gender equality claims as only valid if they fit within market logic. One of the features of market feminism is that it results in agendas that serve more the interests of economically powerful and elite groups of women rather than the interests of those further down the economic scale. Whilst I would not want to suggest that there are intrinsic problems with policies aiming to increase women's labour market participation and the representation of women in decision-making roles, these policies need to be subjected to greater scrutiny. For example, questions need to be asked about the extent to which these strategies rest upon the continued expansion of the market for migrant domestic workers in light of continued inadequacies in childcare provision and continuing assumptions about women's domestic responsibilities (Jones, 2012, pp. 267–268).

Feminist or Corporate Success Story? Women's Representation on Corporate Boards

I now turn to explore the recent 'success story' of the decision to implement a gender quota on the boards of publically listed Malaysian companies. This is an important issue because it actually represents one of the few examples of government success on a flagship/high-profile gender and development strategy. The then Minister for Women, Family and Community Development announced in 2011 that the government would be putting in place a 'quota' of 30% female representation on corporate boards by 2016. The quota was in fact more like a target since companies would not be penalised for failure to comply with the policy. Nonetheless, in July 2011 the head of the Malaysian Securities Commission, Zarinah Anwar, launched its *Corporate Governance Blueprint 2011* which stated that Bursa Malaysia listed companies will be required to disclose in their annual report policies and targets for women's representation on the board (Securities Commission Malaysia, 2011, p. 36; Tee & Lee, 2011). The target was compared with the target of 30% of women in decision-making roles that had been announced for the public sector in the Ninth Malaysia Plan and was attained during the Tenth Plan period. The policy target of 30% women's representation on corporate boards would be complemented by the development of a register of potential female corporate directors and training for potential directors. This training, it was hoped, would also function to highlight to senior business women the need for them to act as mentors and champions for women in their workplace. The aim of such policies then is not only to enable more women to break through the corporate glass ceiling, but also to lead to a shift in those gendered boardroom cultures or 'old boys' networks' that have persistently excluded women.[16] More generally, this policy needs to be understood within the context of efforts to increase women's labour force participation. Concerns have been raised that the existence of lack of adequate opportunities for women in highly paying jobs is a major factor in the decision by many educated women to leave the labour force, the 30% target for women on corporate boards is thus perceived as sending an important signal regarding the need for the corporate sector to increase opportunities for women in senior positions (Pemandu, 2011, p. 235).

In a radio interview, following the announcement, a UNDP (United Nations Development Programme) Malaysia official engaged in gender and development work argued that the 'quota' reflected the government taking seriously the voices of women and of activist women in particular who had advocated on this issue (YouTube/undpmalaysia, 2011). But who exactly were the civil society actors who were involved in pushing for and developing this policy issue? Interestingly, it appears that women's NGOs played a rather minimal role—

politically engaged women's groups had certainly raised issues relating to women's empowerment and the lack of women's representation in corporate decision-making, but the policy came about because of a particular alignment of powerful corporate and state feminist interests. One of the most important players in pushing this issue has been the Non-Aligned Movement Institute for Women's Empowerment (NIEW) an agency that falls within the Ministry for Women Family and Community Development, established in 2006 and currently headed by Rafiah Salim, the former Vice Chancellor of the University of Malaya. NIEW acts as a think tank pushing gender-related research and policy ideas. These efforts were supported by other prominent women including the head of the central bank (Bank Negara) and the head of the Securities Commission. Rafiah's credibility as a key proponent (or policy entrepreneur) of this issue was enhanced not only by her very close ties to many of the key corporate bodies involved in this issue (.e.g. before heading NIEW Rafiah was the head of the Bank Negara funded International Centre for Leadership and Governance (Iclif) which promotes corporate governance through senior executive training) but also by the fact that she herself sits on several corporate boards and has experience of senior executive management during a stint as the director of Human Resources at one of Malaysia's largest private sector banks, Maybank.

Several actors more clearly associated with civil society have played an important role in promoting this issue—these groups are associated with the corporate sector rather than being from the women's movement. They included The Malaysian Minority Shareholders Watchdog Group (whose female CEO has played a prominent role in championing the issue[17]), the Malaysian Alliance of Corporate Directors, the National Association of Women Entrepreneurs of Malaysia and prominent Malaysian business women (Tee & Lee, 2011; 'Your 10 questions with Rita Benoy Bushon', 2011). What can be observed, then, is how a particular political opportunity structure enabled the emergence of the gender representation on corporate board policy. Given this configuration of interests, the issue of women's representation on corporate boards tends to be presented as a 'business case' linked to the view that the presence of women on boards improves profitability and has a positive impact on corporate governance. Thus women's presence undermines 'groupthink', and decreases a propensity towards unnecessary risk-taking.[18] It is an agenda that also, it might be noted, sits very well alongside the strong emphasis on corporate governance reform that has accompanied the institutionalist turn in neo-liberal development policy-making since the Asian crisis.

Within a country such as Malaysia where activist women's groups are consistently criticised for engagement in political issues, and are largely excluded from involvement in policies that impact on women (especially in areas such as women's rights in Islam), the corporate board policy represented a rare success. One of the few critical commentaries on the issue came from a representative of the Penang-based 3Gs network who argued on his blog that '[b]y forcing the private sector to adopt 30% women quota without first addressing the problems in existing Government policy and structure, the Prime Minister is privatizing the Government's duty towards gender equality!' (Sim, 2011). Elsewhere, the women's group Empower pointed out that government efforts focused on training and preparing women to sit on boards needed to be set against the lack of government support for low-income earners such as women in the informal sector. Commenting on the issue of women's representation on corporate boards in its *2010/11 Malaysian women human rights report* Empower suggested that 'the ministry [of Women, Family and Community Development] should focus more attention on women's participation in the informal sectors and those working in low wage. Low-skill industries as this group tends to be less visible but more needy' (Chin binti Abdullah, 2012, p. 57).

The issues of women's representation in politics and gendered structures of poverty are certainly much more challenging issues than women's representation on corporate boards. Many activist women's groups have consistently sought to highlight these more complex issues. For example, a Women's Candidacy Initiative (WCI) emerged out of the *reformasi* movement at the 1999 general election and at the 2008 election the WCI ran the 'Mak Bedah' campaign to promote women's issues[19] and women's groups have since the 1990s presented their demands around a Women's Agenda for Change that incorporates commitments to improving the socio-economic status of all Malaysian women. Similarly, in 2012, a women-focused clean government campaign, *Wanita Suara Perubahan*, was formed by the NGO Empower and led protests in March of that year not only around issues of corruption and government accountability, but also focusing on issues such as the need for a living wage, the impacts of privatisation, and violence against women.[20] But such initiatives need to be set within the wider realities of both the state's limited engagements with activist women's groups and the global corporatisation of gender issues—the increased voice of the private sector in issues of gender equality. On a global scale we can point to the plethora of corporate-led gender initiatives such as the WEF's global gender gap reports, the Global Compact gender empowerment principle's and Nike's discovery of the 'girl effect' (Prügl & True, 2014; Roberts, 2014). In the Malaysian context, we need to be attendant to the way in which a corporatised gender agenda has taken shape in ways that clearly privilege the experiences and concerns of elite women. The success of the women on corporate boards agenda was a result of (a) the existence of a powerful and tight-knit configuration of interests centred on particular elite women inside and outside of the state and (b) the ability to present this issue not only as a gender equality measure but as a corporate governance issue, thereby securing wider civil society support for the measure.

Conclusion

Rodan and Hughes's (2012) work on social accountability activism in the Southeast Asian region highlights the prominence of liberal and moral agendas that act to undermine the initial democratic impulses of these movements in ways that support existing (neoliberal and authoritarian) power hierarchies. Although their research is concerned with a rather different form of civil society engagement to the topic of this article, drawing attention to competing moral and liberal agendas within civil society in this manner is highly pertinent to the research presented here. For example, civil society engagement with gender and development policy-making in Malaysia has been framed around both a 'market feminist' agenda relating to women's labour market roles and a socially conservative (though arguably, equally neoliberal compatible) moral agenda relating to women's reproductive roles within the family.

Malaysian women have come to play important symbolic and material roles in a Malaysian modernity project currently preoccupied with the overriding pursuit of national economic competitiveness. The state's pursuit of economic competitiveness and 'modernity' more broadly, has, as Stivens (1998) points out, rested upon reworkings of public/private divides that reflect, not simply, the increased incorporation of women into the formal productive economy since the 1970s but also reconfiguration(s) of state–civil society relations. For example, competing conceptions of modern Malay womanhood exist within localised processes of Islamicisation of state and society that have developed alongside wider processes of Islamic globalisation(s). At the same time, a rising middle–class-oriented women's rights activism that has particular relationships with globalised forms of feminism has found a level of expression within the state—albeit one in which a market feminist agenda and corporate voices predominate (what Roberts (2014) terms 'transnational business feminism'). Thus the institutionalisation of specific social forces within the state occurs in dynamic interaction with the emergence of globalising social movements centred on both Islam and feminism. These complex gendered dynamics are productive of a state–civil society relationship that simply cannot be conceptualised in terms of the adversarial conceptualisation of state–civil society that dominates much of the Malaysian civil society literature.

The findings presented in this article can also be seen as bringing a specifically feminist lens to debates on civil society activism and social movements in Southeast Asia. First, one of the issues that emerges out of this study concerns how the continued subordination of the domestic, socially reproductive, realm intersects with other forms of social inequality in society and how these intersecting forms of inequality are reproduced within the associational world. How, for example, do the gendered, classed, and racialised practices of childcare and other forms of reproductive work impact on the agendas and practices of both women's movements and other NGOs mobilised around deeply gendered issues such as marriage, the family, or women's economic participation? Or why is it that the voices of migrant domestic workers or informal sector workers are largely missing in debates on women's economic participation? Second, and clearly related to the first point, is the need to look at how state–civil society coalitions formed around gender and competitiveness agendas are deeply classed—a reflection not only of the existence of an activist middle-class in Malaysia, but more significantly a reflection of the state's active role in subordinating class-based forms of political opposition since independence (Tajuddin, 2012). Notably, this issue is most obvious in relation to the case of women's representation on corporate boards whereby corporate interests have come to play an even more prominent role in state gender agendas. But we also see, in the case of family policy, how the state seeks to legitimate a particular policy direction through engagement with religious and ethnic-based organisations, thus shoring up the operation of a political system in which a politics of ethnicity performs an important role in maintaining the political hegemony of the ruling party (Nair, 2007a).

Finally, it is important to point out that the arguments articulated in this study are not meant to suggest that there is no scope for forms of civil society activism that seek to challenge the market logic of the current government's competitiveness agenda. Many Malaysian NGOs are engaged in activities that seek to challenge and ameliorate some of the ways in which the drive for economic competitiveness is accompanied by gendered and racialised processes and structures of economic marginalisation (e.g. elsewhere (Elias, 2010) I explore the activities of Malaysian pro-migrant worker NGOs). These struggles are important, but they are only part of the picture and we need to avoid characterisations of civil society solely as a space that can be simplistically equated with progressive and/or democratic politics. As the arguments articulated in this paper demonstrate, consent for the neoliberal compatible gender and competitiveness agenda in Malaysia takes shape within the context of state engagements with a civil society divided around intersecting issues of class, ethnicity, and religion. In this context, conservative religious values associated with Malaysia's new middle classes and corporate-aligned business interests win out.

Disclosure Statement

No potential conflict of interest was reported by the author.

Notes

1   The NEP was designed as an affirmative action strategy aimed, via systems of quotas and other policies, at raising the status of the county's Malay (or *bumiputera*) population. As a result of its colonial past, Malaysia is a multi-ethnic country. In 2010 of the three main ethnic groups, Malays made up 60.3% of the total population (Chinese 22.9% and Indian 6.8%).

2   It is important to note that Howell (2005) as well as Phillips (2002) suggest that feminist scholarship has tended to have an ambivalent relationship with the concept of civil society—not least because of the way in which a lot of the scholarship on civil society tends put forward a view of the associational word as an autonomous (and gender neutral) realm, analytically separate from not just the state but also the family and the household. By conceptualising civil society not as an autonomous 'neo-Tocquevillian' realm of politics but rather focusing on the permeability of the boundaries between state, market, civil society and household, this article seeks to demonstrate the utility of a focus on civil society for feminist political economy analysis.

3   Moreover, Malaysia has considerably lower female labour force participation rates in comparison to regional competitors such as Thailand (70.0%), Singapore (60.2%) and Indonesia (51.8%) (Malaysia, 2010, p. 178).

4   This issue was raised in an interview with officials from the National Institute of Human Development, Ministry of Human Resources (and a member of Pemandu's Human Capital SRI Lab), personal interview, 21 February 2012. However, the majority of the current work being undertaken on women's labour force participation involves the Ministry for Women Family and Community Development who have recently started work with UNDP Malaysia on a broad research project looked at how best to increase women's labour force participation. Personal interview with Principal Assistant Secretary, Planning and Research Unit, Policy Division, Ministry of Women, Family and Community Development. Putrajaya, 27 February 2012.

5   Hoffstaeder (2011, p. 14) notes the existence of a split between a secular (English-speaking, Western-educated) elite and an Islamic elite (Malay speaking, educated in the Middle East, Pakistan or Southeast Asia). While 'the secular elite is still (largely) congruous with the political elite', the Islamic elite 'operates both within and outside of the state apparatus'. Within this context, we can observe the rise of Islamic authorities (such as the courts) operating relatively autonomously from other state institutions (Hoffsteader, 2011, p. 72). JAKIM in particular, designed to incorporate non-orthodox Islamic groups into the state, plays a significant role in the state's (oftentimes overtly elitist) policing of Islamic identities, but also grants Islamic groups an access to state institutions that is often not available to other civil society actors.

6   These are issues that have had considerable media attention and were also all raised in interviews with members of the Social Services section of the state's Economic Planning Unit, Putrajaya 11 November 2011.

7   More secular organisations are involved but are few and far between. One such organisation is *Yayasan Strategik Social* the social development wing of the Malaysian Indian Congress (part of the ruling *Barisan Nasional* coalition).

8   This discussion draws upon personal interviews conducted with the head of Wanita ISMA and the director of the organisation's *konvensyen Keluarga,* Petailing Jaya, 10 February 2012.

9   See Hadiz and Teik (2011) on the forms of new Islamic populism in Southeast Asia. In the Malaysian case, it is important to point to the significant role of both class and state policies—notably the incubation of a Malay middle class under the NEP—that fostered forms of Islamic populism amongst the urbanising professional middle class. On the influence of groups such as ISMA and Perkasa in contemporary Malaysian politics, see Noor (2013, p. 97).

10 It should be noted that all Muslim couples in Malaysia are required to undertake a premarital training course administered by JAKIM the government's Islamic department as part of the marriage registration process.

11 Personal interview with the head of Wanita ISMA, Petailing Jaya, 10 February 2012.

12 Personal interview with the head of Wanita ISMA, Petailing Jaya, 10 February 2012.

13 See also work on Islamic Piety movements in Malaysia by Sylvia Frisk (2009) that points to women's agency, negotiating abilities, and their collective identities as pious Islamic women.

14 Personal interview with Empower director Maria Chin Abdullah, Petailing Jaya, 20 February 2011.

15 Personal interview with Marina Mahathir, Kuala Lumpur, 9 November 2011.

16 Personal interview with Senior Assistant Director NIEW, Kuala Lumpur, 31 October 2011.

17 Personal interview with Chief Executive Officer, Minority Shareholders Watchdog Group, Kuala Lumpur, 28 February 2012.

18 This issue was raised by the Chief Executive Officer, Minority Shareholders Watchdog Group, Kuala Lumpur, personal interview 28 February 2012. At the February 2012 Women in Leadership Forum Asia that I attended in Kuala Lumpur, prominent representatives from the Malaysian state and business community including NIEW

director Rafiah Salam, the director of the Malaysian Alliance of Corporate Directors, the chairman of the Malaysian Institute of Management and prominent Malaysian business women such as Raja Teh Maimunah the MD and CEO of Hong Leong Islamic Bank and the fund manager Shireen Ann Zaharah Muhideen also presented this issue in a similar manner (in relation to issues of both profitability and corporate governance as well as the role that women board members can play in promoting the interests of women further down the corporate ladder).

19   The WCI were unable to field a suitable candidate at the 2008 election and thus created the 'everywoman' character of Mak Bedah in order to highlight issues affecting women in Malaysia that were overlooked in mainstream political debate. See Lee (2011).

20   The Wanita Suara Perubahan protests took place on 18 March 2012 and involved many of the same women activists who had been involved in wider Bersih campaigns for clean government.

References

Abdullah, B. (2006). Foreword from the honourable Prime Minister of Malaysia. In LPPKN, *SMARTSTART: A guide for newly weds* (pp. 2–3). Kuala Lumpur: LPPKN.

Aspinall, E., & Weiss, M. L. (2012). The limits of civil society: Social movements and political parties in Southeast Asia. In R. Robison (Ed.), *Routledge handbook of Southeast Asian politics* (pp. 213–228). London: Routledge.

Bakker, I., & Gill, S. (2003). Ontology, method, hypothesis. In I. Bakker & S. Gill (Eds.), *Power, production and social reproduction* (pp. 17–41). Basingstoke: Palgrave Macmillan.

Bakker, I., & Gill, S. (2008). New constitutionalism and social reproduction. In I. Bakker & R. Silvey (Eds.), *Beyond states and markets: The challenges of social reproduction* (pp. 19–33). Abingdon: Routledge.

Cammack, P. (2006). Global governance, state agency and competitiveness: The political economy of the commission for Africa. *British Journal of Politics and International Relations, 8*(3), 331–350.

Carroll, T. (2012). Introduction: Neo-liberal development policy in Asia beyond the post-Washington consensus. *Journal of Contemporary Asia, 42*(3), 350–358.

Carroll, T., & Jarvis, D. S. L. (2015). The new politics of development: Citizens, civil society and the evolution of neo-liberal development policy. *Globalizations*, doi:10.1080/14747731.2015.1016301

CEDAW. (2006, May 24). *Malaysia needs new laws aimed specifically at ending discrimination on basis of sex, gender, say committee's expert members*. Committee on Elimination of Discrimination Against Women 731st & 732nd Meetings (AM & PM). Retrieved May 3, 2012, from http://www.un.org/News/Press/docs/2006/wom1562.doc.htm

Chin binti Abdullah, M. (2012). Women's rights to employment: The forgotten and invisible women workers. In *Equality under construction: Malaysian women's human rights Report 2010/11* (pp. 44–110). Petailing Jaya: Persatuan Kesedaran Komuniti Selangor (EMPOWER).

Connell, R. W. (1990). The state, gender and sexual politics: Theory and appraisal. *Theory and Society, 19*(5), 507–544.

Elias, J. (2009). Gendering liberalisation and labour reform in Malaysia: Fostering "competitiveness" in the productive and reproductive economies. *Third World Quarterly, 30*(3), 469–483.

Elias, J. (2010). Transnational migration, gender and rights: Advocacy and activism in the Malaysian context. *International Migration, 48*(6), 44–71.

Elias, J. (2011). The gender politics of economic competitiveness in Malaysia's transition to a knowledge-economy. *Pacific Review, 24*(5), 529–552.

Elias, J., & Gunawardana, S. J. (2013). The global political economy of the household in Asia: An introduction. In J. Elias & S. J. Gunawardana (Eds.), *The global political economy of the household in Asia* (pp. 1–13). London: Palgrave Macmillan.

Evans, M. (2011, April 13–15). *Single mothers in Malaysia: Social protection as an exercise of definition in search of solution*. Paper presented at the conference Social Protection for Social Justice, Institute of Development Studies, Sussex University.

Fatimah, S. (2007). Building healthy communities: The family is the basic group unit of society—the Malaysian experience. In A. Scott Loveless & T. B. Holman (Eds.), *The family in the new millennium: World voices supporting the 'Natural Clan': Volume 3 strengthening the family* (pp. 181–191). Westport, CT: Praeger.

Frisk, S. (2009). *Submitting to God: Women and Islam in urban Malaysia*. Copenhagen: NIAS Press.

Gerard, K. (2015). Explaining ASEAN's engagement of civil society in policymaking: Smoke and mirrors. *Globalizations*, doi:10.1080/14747731.2015.1016304

Hadiz, V. R., & Teik, K. B. (2011). Approaching Islam and politics from political economy: A comparative study of Indonesia and Malaysia. *The Pacific Review, 24*(4), 463–485.

Hall, S. (1986). Gramsci's relevance for the study of race and ethnicity. *Journal of Communication Inquiry, 10*(2), 5–27.

Hedman, E. (2006). *In the name of civil society: From free election movements to people power in the Philippines.* Honolulu: University of Hawaii Press.

Hilley, J. (2001). *Malaysia: Mahathirism, hegemony and the new opposition.* London: Zed Books.

Ho, Y. W. (2011, September 10). *Press statement: Launch of campaign Sexual Harassment Out (SHout).* Retrieved May 2, 2012, from http://www.awam.org.my/images/Press%20Statement%20SHout.pdf

Hoffstaedter, G. (2011). *Modern Muslim identities: Negotiating religion and ethnicity in Malaysia.* Copenhagen: NIAS Press.

Howell, J. (2005). Introduction. In J. Howell & D. Mulligan (Eds.), *Gender and civil society: Transcending boundaries* (pp. 1–22). London: Routledge.

Jones, G. (2012). Demographic and labour force dynamics. In H. Hill, S. Y. Tham, & H. M. Z. Ragayah (Eds.), *Malaysia's development challenges: Graduating from the middle* (pp. 255–275). Abingdon: Routledge.

Katz, C. (2001). Vagabond capitalism and the necessity of social reproduction. *Antipode, 33*(4), 709–728.

Koshy, S. (2010, April 11). The family must come first. *The Star Online.* Retrieved February 20, 2012, from http://thestar.com.my/news/story.asp?file=/2010/4/11/focus/6034704&sec=focus

Lall, S. (2001). Competitiveness indices and developing countries: An economic evaluation of the Global Competitiveness Report. *World Development, 29*(9), 1501–1525.

Lee, J. C. (2011). Mak Bedah goes shopping for a real candidate in Malaysia's 2008 general elections. *Indonesia and the Malay World, 39*(115), 357–372.

Loh-Ludher, L. L. (2009). From factories to telecentres: Journey of women in the Malaysian labour force. In A. Jamilah (Ed.), *Readings on women and development in Malaysia a sequel: Tracing four decades of change* (pp. 223–244). Selangor: MPH.

LPPKN. (2006). *SMARTSTART: A guide for newly weds.* Kuala Lumpur: LPPKN.

Mahathir, M. (1993). *Malaysia: The way forward.* Speech to the Malaysian Business Council. Retrieved September 14, 2010, from http://www.wawasan2020.com/vision/index.html

Malaysia. (2010). *Tenth Malaysia plan 2011–1015.* Putrajaya: Economic Planning Unit.

Maznah, M. (2004). Women's engagement with political Islam in Malaysia. *Global Change, Peace and Security, 16*(2), 133–149.

Nair, S. (2007a). The limits of protest and prospects for political reform in Malaysia. *Critical Asian Studies, 39*(3), 339–368.

Nair, S. (2007b). Challenging the Mullahs: Islam, politics and women's activism, interview with Zainah Anwar. *International Feminist Journal of Politics, 9*(2), 240–248.

Najib, T. R. (2010, June 10). *Tenth Malaysia plan 2011–1015.* Speech by the prime minister in the Dewan Rakyat.

Nevins, J., & Peluso, N. L. (2008). Introduction: Commoditization in Southeast Asia. In J. Nevins & N. L. Peluso (Eds.), *Taking Southeast Asia to market: Commodities, nature and people in a neoliberal age* (pp. 1–26). Ithaca, NY: Cornell University Press.

Ng, C., Maznah, M., & Hui, T. B. (2006). *Feminism and the women's movement in Malaysia: An unsung (r)evolution.* Abingdon: Routledge.

Noor, F. A. (2013). The Malaysian general election of 2013: The last attempt at secular-inclusive nation-building? *Journal of Current Southeast Asian Affairs, 32*(2), 89–104.

Pemandu. (2011). *Economic Transformation Programme annual report.* Retrieved May 3, 2012, from http://etp.pemandu.gov.my/annualreport

Phillips, A. (2002). Does feminism need a conception of civil society? In S. Chambers & W. Kymlika (Eds.), *Alternative conceptions of civil society* (pp. 71–89). Princeton, NJ: Princeton University Press.

Prügl, E., & True, J. (2014). Equality means business? Governing gender through transnational public–private partnerships. *Review of International Political Economy, 21*(6), 1137–1169.

Rai, S. (2002). *Gender and the political economy of development.* Oxford: Polity.

Rai, S. M., Hoskyns, C., & Thomas, D. (2014). Depletion: The cost of social reproduction. *International Feminist Journal of Politics, 16*(1), 86–105.

Ramasamy, P. (2004). Civil society in Malaysia: An arena of contestations? In L. H. Guan (Ed.), *Civil society in Southeast Asia* (pp. 198–216). Singapore: Institute for Southeast Asian Studies.

Roberts, A. (2014). The political economy of 'Transnational Business Feminism': Problematising the corporate-led gender equality agenda. *International Feminist Journal of Politics.* Advance online publication. doi:10.1080/14616742.2013.849968

Rodan, G., & Hughes, C. (2012). Ideological coalitions and the international promotion of social accountability: The Philippines and Cambodia compared. *International Studies Quarterly, 56*(2), 367–380.

Securities Commission Malaysia. (2011). *Corporate Governance Blueprint 2011: Towards excellence in corporate governance*. Kuala Lumpur: Securities Commission Malaysia.

Shields, S., & Wallin, S. (2015). The European bank for reconstruction and development's gender action plan and the gendered political economy of post-communist transition. *Globalizations*, doi:10.1080/14747731.2015.1016307

Sim, S. (2011, June 26). *Press: Quota is good but not enough—why federal government is pushing its duty on gender equality to the private sector* [Blog post]. Retrieved February 1, 2012, from http://stevensim.wordpress.com/2011/06/29/press-quota-is-good-but-not-enough-why-federal-government-is-pushing-its-duty-on-gender-equality-to-the-private-sector

Sim, S.-F. (2006). Hegemonic authoritarianism and Singapore: Economics, ideology and the Asian economic crisis. *Journal of Contemporary Asia, 36*(2), 143–159.

Stivens, M. (1998). Sex, class and the making of the new Malay middle class. In K. Sen & M. Stivens (Eds.), *Gender and power in affluent Asia* (pp. 87–126). London: Routledge.

Stivens, M. (2006). "Family values" and Islamic revival: Gender, rights and state moral projects in Malaysia. *Women's Studies International Forum, 29*, 354–367.

Tajuddin, A. (2012). *Malaysia in the world economy (1824–2011): Capitalism, ethnic divisions and 'managed' democracy*. Lanham: Lexington Books.

Tee, L. S., & Lee, L. (2011, November 19). Grooming more women for the board. *The Star Online*. Retrieved February 20, 2012, from http://biz.thestar.com.my/news/story.asp?file=%2F2011%2F11%2F19%2Fbusiness%2F9902529&sec=business

Thambiah, S. (2010). The productive and non-(re) productive women: Sites of economic growth in Malaysia. *Asian Women, 26*(2), 49–76.

Your 10 questions with Rita Benoy Bushon. (2011, September 3). *The Star Online*. Retrieved May 2, 2012, from http://biz.thestar.com.my/news/story.asp?file=/2011/9/3/business/9394544&sec=business

YouTube/undpmalaysia. (2011). *Business FM: Closing the gender gap in the Malaysian corporate sector and politics part 1*. Retrieved May 2, 2012, from http://www.youtube.com/watch?v=DpMItumn2tc&context=C3be138bADOEgsToP DskLPdg7_jTh4akJFVOrN6c1k

Explaining ASEAN's Engagement of Civil Society in Policy-making: Smoke and Mirrors

School of Social Sciences, University of Western Australia, Perth, WA, Australia

ABSTRACT   *Since the late 1990s, the Association of Southeast Asian Nations (ASEAN) has widened policy-making to include civil society organisations (CSOs), paralleling developments in other regional and global governance institutions where the inclusion of CSOs in policy-making is considered necessary to address these institutions' 'democracy deficit'. A rich empirical literature documents this trend, highlighting the range of participatory mechanisms and their challenges. However, theoretical explanations for why governance institutions engage CSOs and the limitations of these processes are lacking. This paper harnesses political economy analysis to explain this trend. Examining the form and function of civil society engagement in ASEAN, this article demonstrates that ASEAN's inclusion of civil society functions in legitimating its market-building reform programme, while its participatory mechanisms are structured to include amenable interests and marginalise non-compatible groups. Thus, ASEAN's engagement of CSOs and the broader trend of participatory policy-making should be considered as creating sites for contestation, rather than being implicitly democratising.*

A 'People-Oriented' ASEAN?

Following the regional financial crisis of 1997–1998, leaders of the Association of Southeast Asian Nations (ASEAN) began promoting the idea of a 'people-centred' community in Southeast Asia and, towards this end, widening policy-making to include civil society organisations (CSOs). ASEAN first signalled this shift with its *Vision 2020*, released in December 1997, that committed member states to creating a 'community of caring societies' where 'civil society is empowered' (ASEAN, 1997). This participatory agenda was restated in subsequent agreements, and with the decision to design the ASEAN Charter, the term 'people-centred' became even more 'en vogue' (Morada, 2008). Consulting with civil society thus became a consistent part of ASEAN rhetoric.

Accompanying this rhetorical shift was the emergence of two new forms of participation for CSOs in ASEAN. Since 1979 an affiliation system has operated where CSOs can apply for affiliation, which brings with it some participatory functions. However, since 2005 CSOs have been consulted by multiple ASEAN bodies, the most high-profile being the consultations conducted for the ASEAN Charter. Since 2006 CSOs have also participated in ASEAN through three annual sectoral forums on Migrant Labour, Social Welfare and Development, and Rural Development and Poverty Eradication, organised to facilitate dialogue between officials and CSOs. This widening of policy-making to include CSOs was an abrupt shift from ASEAN's previous style of regional governance, characterised by closed-door meetings and tacit agreements among leaders.

This shift was not a stand-alone endeavour, but emerged alongside the market-building reform programme that ASEAN embarked on after the regional financial crisis. ASEAN's conspicuous absence from the recovery process prompted criticisms, advanced by 'a bolder and better-educated middle class challenging the paternalistic order of the past' (Ahmad & Ghosal, 1999, p. 767), amidst a rising wave of populism and domestic political upheavals—most acutely in Indonesia with the collapse of the Suharto regime. In response to criticisms regarding its practices and purpose, ASEAN rapidly intensified regional economic integration through the creation of an integrated and liberal market—the ASEAN Economic Community—to facilitate states' efforts to compete for global capital flows. To further these market-building reforms,[1] regional governance was organised around a regulatory framework where state actors collaborate through regional networks to harmonise domestic policies (Gerard, 2014b). As noted by Jayasuriya, regulatory regionalism 'should not be viewed as a departure from the disciplines of the global economy, but as an attempt to instantiate the disciplines of neoliberalism within a regional framework' (2003, p. 206). This shift in regional governance mirrored regulatory transformations in statehood across members and their embedded 'politics of competitiveness', where 'the orientation of these regimes reflects national trajectories that have seen the outflanking or defeat of more radical class and developmental projects by enthusiastic proponents of capitalist development' (Cammack, 2009, p. 269; see introduction to this special issue by Carroll & Jarvis).

ASEAN is but one example of the broad trend of regional and global governance institutions widening policy-making to include CSOs. This trend emerged in the 1970s and increased in intensity from the 1990s. A rich empirical literature documents this trend and raises various questions such as why governance institutions have shifted to engage these disparate interests and how, and the limitations of this process. This article harnesses political economy analysis to explain the inclusion of CSOs in regional and global policy-making, and explores this trend through the lens of the ASEAN case, drawing on 54 interviews conducted with ASEAN officials and CSO representatives.

The first section outlines the limitations of mainstream International Relations (IR) approaches in accounting for this trend before describing the political economy approach used here, drawn from the framework of Jayasuriya and Rodan (2007) that considers modes of participation as the unit of analysis. The application of this framework—novel to the study of civil society participation in regional and global policy-making—acknowledges that different systems of structuring civil society participation produce varying opportunities for CSOs to influence policy. In the second section I apply this analytical framework to ASEAN's participatory channels.[2] Focusing on the questions of who can participate and how, and the struggles that have accompanied the establishment of these new modes of participation, I describe and explain the boundaries of civil society participation with reference to underlying political economy relationships. This article demonstrates that ASEAN's participatory mechanisms are structured to include particular interests amenable to its reform agenda and marginalise non-compatible groups. It asserts that ASEAN's 'people-centred' agenda is intended to address some of the social forces that have organised around issues arising from the rapid and predatory mode of capitalist development prevalent in the region, demonstrating that participatory policy-making is not implicitly democratising.

A Political Economy Approach to Understanding CSOs' Participation in Policy-making

ASEAN's shift to engage CSOs parallels the trend seen in many, if not most, regional and global governance institutions. This practice can be traced back to the founding of the United Nations; however, it has grown in intensity in recent decades. A rich empirical literature documents this trend and limitations of space do not warrant a comprehensive review. However, while describing the expanding presence of CSOs in regional and global policy-making, these studies also highlight the substantial differences that exist across institutions in the participatory mechanisms that have been established, and the forms of participation they subsequently enable. For example, the EU's Citizen's Initiative permits CSOs to propose agenda items for meetings of the European Commission (European Commission, 2010). However, CSOs seeking to lobby the WTO are limited to attending the Plenary Meetings of the Ministerial Council that are broadcast over the internet and participating in ad hoc public symposia where the agenda is set by the WTO (van den Bossche, 2010). Regional and global governance institutions regulate civil society access in a range of forms, creating varying opportunities for CSOs to influence policy-making.

Justifications for why these institutions open their political structures to include these disparate interests also vary across institutions. Empirically, claims of the benefits of civil society engagement are highly contested. Scholars and practitioners argue that civil society involvement in regional and global policy-making provides a partial solution to issues arising from the 'democracy deficit' that relevant institutions struggle with. Problematically, arguments for the accountability and legitimacy benefits of civil society participation assume that CSOs represent the interests of those that would otherwise be disenfranchised (cf. Verweij & Josling, 2003, p. 13), and that CSOs are, and remain, independent of the influence of states, donors, and private interests. The question of CSOs being consulted in policy-making is also distinct from whether CSOs shape political outcomes through such consultations, underscored by Betsill and Corell's (2008) assessment of the scholarship on civil society participation in environmental governance which highlights that while CSOs promote particular policy frameworks, little evidence exists demonstrating their influence on policy outcomes. Furthermore, CSOs and governance institutions are highly complex and diverse entities, creating significant logistical issues in establishing some form of collaborative relationship. Scholte (2011) highlights qualitative problems encountered during consultations, noting that CSOs may be consulted only towards the end of the policy cycle once the policy direction is decided; meetings may be convened at short notice, with little preparation or follow-up with participants; consultations may serve simply as public relations exercises during high-level meetings or 'tick-the-box' affairs; and finally, officials may consider consultations as a one-way rather than a two-way dialogue, disseminating information rather than hearing CSOs' views. Thus, institutions' inclusion of CSOs in policy-making has not been unproblematic or uncontested. These various issues raise questions regarding the overall impact of CSOs' inclusion on political outcomes.

Recognising the limitations of this process, scholars have called for caution in advancing civil society engagement in regional and global policy-making, recommending various prescriptions to advance this process in a manner that raises accountability, legitimacy, and representation in policy-making. For example, Scholte asserts: 'In a word, what is wanted in the period ahead is more, more inclusive, more competent, more coordinated, and more accountable civil society engagement at the heart of policy processes on the full range of global governance processes' (2007, p. 316). While these accounts highlight the limitations of this process, scholarly analysis should shift beyond recommending improvements to explaining how and why this process is constrained.

Theoretically, dominant IR approaches are limited in accounting for why and how regional and global institutions engage CSOs and the limitations of this process. The shortcomings of realist approaches in accounting for this trend require little elaboration: realists conceive of states as unitary actors in pursuit of their interests, making power the only mediating factor in international politics. Liberals consider the shift to include CSOs in policy-making as a means of increasing efficiency, needed to deal with the ever-growing complexity of regional and global policy-making (Florini & Simmons, 2000; Slaughter, 2004). However, it is not readily apparent that CSOs' participation increases the efficiency of policy-making, given that CSOs are another voice to be added to already crowded deliberations. Additionally, many institutions direct significant resources towards supporting CSOs' engagement, such as the UN's Non-Governmental Liaison Service. Beyond acknowledging CSOs as sources of information and conduits for publicising policy decisions, liberals also do not elaborate how CSOs participate. Slaughter posits that networks of non-state actors can support government networks in addressing the growing complexities of governance (2004, p. 33). However, the liberal framing of civil society consultations as directed towards problem-solving and consensus-building assumes that CSOs interact with officials in a non-conflictual manner. Liberals assume that these disparate actors are united by a common purpose that subsumes the politics that accompany this process, overlooking issues such as the unequal distribution of power that creates the potential for decisions to be imposed, rather than bargained (see Peters & Pierre, 2004).

While constructivists place greater emphasis on the role of CSOs in global politics, these accounts offer only a partial explanation for this trend. On the question of *why* these institutions widen policy-making to include CSOs, constructivists assert this can be explained through the concept of norm diffusion, as argued by Collins (2013) and Rüland (2014) in the ASEAN case and Saurugger (2010) in the EU case. However, constructivists acknowledge that this framework provides little in elaborating why actors that internalise a norm fail to exhibit the desired behaviour—what is termed 'partial norm socialisation' (Checkel, 2005; Risse, Ropp, & Sikkink, 1999; Saurugger, 2010). In her examination of the flawed implementation of the participatory norm in the EU, Saurugger (2010) observes that norms are rhetorically embraced when deemed necessary and later violated when doing so is feasible. However, this observation does not *explain* this trend according to the constructivist paradigm.

Constructivists have attempted to account for cases of partial norm by extending the norm diffusion logic to instances of institutional normative change, termed 'mimetic adoption' (Katsumata, 2011). In the ASEAN case constructivists have argued that officials sought to emulate regional integration processes in the EU or global norms as a legitimising tool; however, their embrace of these new ideas is superficial, directed only towards deflecting unwanted attention, which has created a gap between rhetoric and practice. These accounts explain ASEAN's participatory agenda and its limitations through interpretations of existing norms (Collins, 2013; Rüland, 2014), emphasising the role of extant ideas, known as an actor's 'cognitive prior' (Acharya, 2009), in shaping ASEAN's responses to new ideas. However, by explaining this process principally through ideational change, these accounts overlook the role of social conflict in this process, failing to systematically account for why some issues have been deemed suitable for civil society consultations in ASEAN (e.g. rural development and poverty eradication) and others have not (such as land evictions), nor why some CSOs are excluded and the rules governing how they can participate.

Constructivism does, in fact, account for instances of partial norm socialisation in constructivists' assertion that 'ideas matter'—to the extent that the shift to embrace a new idea will eventually produce the desired behaviour. Wheeler draws from Skinner in arguing this point:

> whether the actor is sincere or not is beside the point since what matters is that, once an agent has accepted the need to legitimate his behavior, he is committed to showing that his actions 'were in fact motivated by some accepted set of social and political principle'. (2000, p. 9; citing Skinner, 1988)

Similarly, Keck and Sikkink's (1998) 'boomerang effect' argues that in cases where actors embrace a norm for strategic reasons, they will be pressured to alter their behaviour accordingly and non-compliance will become increasingly difficult, leading to the norm being 'embedded'. Constructivists thus assert that an actor will alter their behaviour in accordance with a norm they embraced only for strategic reasons to demonstrate the authenticity of their shift to accept that idea. However, state actors frequently rhetorically embrace new ideas, while simultaneously seeking to reduce their commitments (Naidoo, 2010, p. 28). In the case of ASEAN's commitments to engage CSOs, officials have found it rather straightforward to rhetorically embrace civil society consultations while constraining participation in practice, described below. By considering norms as explanatory variables, where norms themselves are understood to generate the appropriate change in behaviour, constructivism is impoverished in explaining why an actor that adopts a norm does not alter its behaviour, and more so over time, as seen in the ASEAN case.

In light of the limitations of dominant IR theories in explaining how and why governance institutions consult CSOs, this study harnesses political economy analysis to explain this trend. Recognising that different systems of structuring civil society participation produce varying opportunities for CSOs to shape policy, this article applies the framework of Jayasuriya and Rodan (2007), where modes of participation serve as the unit of analysis. A mode of participation is the 'institutional structures and ideologies that shape the inclusion and exclusion of individuals and groups in the political process' (Jayasuriya & Rodan, 2007, p. 774). This framework recognises that institutions structure the form politics can take, making particular forms of participation acceptable. As such, modes of participation organise conflicts because they determine which conflicts are 'expressed, mediated or marginalized' (Jayasuriya & Rodan, 2007, p. 779). In analysing modes of participation, this approach is concerned with the questions of who is represented within these sites, what forms of participation are deemed permissible, the struggles that have taken place to establish these spaces, and whose interests are furthered through their creation. In examining who can participate and how, the key consideration is whether participation enables CSOs to contest policy, defined as the articulation of views that challenge institutional policy. This analytical focus is crucial because participation that entails representation but not contestation functions in legitimating prevailing interests, without providing a channel for CSOs to deliberate policy, thereby marginalising the conflicts CSOs have organised around.

The modes of participation framework is drawn from the work of social conflict theorists, considering institutions, markets, and states not as unitary, independent, and coherent entities but as social structures, meaning they are defined by conflicts among competing social forces.

Recognising that civil society consultations do not emerge independently but are shaped by struggles between competing social forces, this framework acknowledges these struggles as significant in determining how CSOs participate in policy-making. This framework thus enables analysis of the relationship between the structure of these spaces and the interests they privilege. Hence, this framework not only describes modes of participation as being more or less useful for activists' agendas, but explains why, with reference to underlying political economy relationships. This article extends the modes of participation framework from Jayasuriya and Rodan's (2007) application to domestic regimes to examine the relationship between CSOs and regional and global governance institutions. This extension of this framework is based on recognition that state borders do not constitute a boundary for political power, and actors will employ strategies to advance their interests across governance scales (Jessop, 1990). Each territorial scale, whether local, subnational, national, regional, or global, has a specific configuration of actors, resources, and political opportunities, and actors subsequently seek to rescale the governance of an issue in accordance with their interests (Hameiri & Jones, 2012). Consequently, the governance of a single territorial scale cannot be examined in isolation from others—domestic political projects are intricately bound up with the form and trajectory of regional and global governance institutions.

Jayasuriya and Rodan's interest in modes of participation was drawn from their examination of the emergence of a paradoxical trend in Southeast Asia where increasing political representation has been accompanied by a decline in opportunities for political contestation. They argue that the narrowing of opportunities for political contestation is linked to efforts to co-opt, marginalise, or exclude social forces that have emerged around issues associated with the rapid and predatory mode of capitalist development prevalent in the region, such as groups focusing on environmental conservation, social justice, and public sector reform.

The Southeast Asian civil society sector is one such social force. Activism has grown in response to governments' pursuit of a 'growth at all costs' agenda, carried out through authoritarian state behaviour. Issues that have been the consequence of this approach to state management, such as the commercialisation of endangered species, the mismanagement of shared resources, poor working conditions, child trafficking, and sex tourism, have increasingly been addressed by CSOs. Meanwhile, the common circumstances that these issues arose from across countries have provided fertile ground for CSOs to organise at the regional level. The regionalisation of activism is evident in the establishment of regional networks targeting ASEAN and the development of ASEAN-focused activities in existing networks (such as by having a staff member or 'desk' responsible for tracking ASEAN developments), seen in the Southeast Asian Committee for Advocacy (SEACA), the Southeast Asian Women's Caucus on ASEAN, FORUM-ASIA, and the Asian Partnership for the Development of Human Resources in Rural Asia (AsiaDHRRA), to name a few. Leaders of regional networks have come together to form the Solidarity for Asian People's Advocacy (SAPA) network that spearheads advocacy targeting ASEAN (Gerard, 2013).

CSOs' activities targeting ASEAN include SAPA's annual organisation of the ASEAN Civil Society Conference, held since 2005, as well as various issue-specific collaborations in the form of workshops, publications, and seminars. ASEAN's reform programme has prompted CSOs to pursue engagement and vocally criticise ASEAN's policies. CSOs have also targeted ASEAN in response to its claims that it is becoming more 'people-centred'. Prior to ASEAN's claims that it was widening participation to include CSOs, many activists did not seek to interact with ASEAN, instead '[paying] much more attention to the threats posed by international organizations' (Chandra, 2006, p. 74).

While some CSOs have increasingly made ASEAN a target of their advocacies, not all have embraced this change. A vast spectrum of views regarding the value of targeting ASEAN exists, from those that view engaging ASEAN as equivalent to their co-optation to those that consider engagement beneficial and devote resources to encouraging other CSOs to do the same. Many CSOs choose not to pursue their claims directly by participating in spaces established by ASEAN and instead seek to contest policy through activities outside of these spaces, such as through participation in the ASEAN Civil Society Conferences, the publication and dissemination of critical knowledge, or organising protests alongside ASEAN meetings (Gerard, 2013, 2014a).

In explaining the form and function of ASEAN's shift to include CSOs in policy-making, the following section examines who is represented within these sites, what forms of participation are deemed permissible, the struggles that have taken place in establishing these modes of participation, and their implications for relevant interests.

CSO Participation in ASEAN-Established Channels

CSO Affiliation

The system of affiliation dates back to 1979, when ASEAN first certified the Federation of ASEAN Public Relations Organizations and the ASEAN Bankers Association (ASEAN, 2009). The system operates by groups that meet particular criteria being granted affiliation, which brings with it the opportunity for some forms of participation. The guidelines governing the affiliation system were first agreed in 1979 and revised in 2006 and again in 2011, with the current version adopted by the Committee of Permanent Representatives (CPR) on 5 November 2012.

Affiliation is granted only to those organisations that meet stringent requirements. According to the 2012 guidelines, affiliated CSOs must be non-profit organisations committed to achieving the aims of ASEAN, with membership confined to member states. In their application for affiliation, CSOs must disclose their reasons for applying, details of their activities and membership, their constitution and registration papers, and background information on staff. All applications for affiliation must receive the approval of all member states, through the CPR. Additional to these formal criteria, officials noted that it is preferred if applicants conduct their activities across all member states, and do not operate outside of Southeast Asia or have extensive links (through funding and/or staff) with international organisations or non-ASEAN governments.[3]

These rigorous criteria are beyond the reach of many Southeast Asian CSOs, frequently lacking financial and decision-making reporting systems (Chong, 2011, p. 14). These criteria bias the affiliation system towards those organisations with formalised and legalised systems of operation, privileging middle-class organisations, and groups that are linked to states or other national (but not external) financiers. The additional informal criterion that organisations operate across all member states adds an extra tier to the hurdles of obtaining affiliation, given that some Southeast Asian states adopt a hostile approach to civil society operations, while the discretionary rejection of ties between accredited CSOs and international organisations or foreign governments further narrows the range of CSOs that fit this mould.

Despite the hurdles that must be passed for an organisation to gain affiliation, the forms of participation that are granted through this mechanism are not remarkable. Accredited CSOs can use the name 'ASEAN', display its flag and emblem, and play the ASEAN anthem; they can submit written statements to their nominated sectoral body; and the ASEAN Secretariat provides them with ASEAN publications each year. Affiliated CSOs can apply to receive Third Party funding for relevant projects, attend meetings of its sectoral body, initiate programmes of activities for consideration by its sectoral body, access relevant ASEAN documents for research, and use the ASEAN Secretariat facilities in Jakarta (ASEAN, 2012). The only form of participation that is *guaranteed* through affiliation is the ability to submit written statements to the CPR—all other forms of participation must be requested in writing, and there are no procedures to question a decision if an application is rejected. Furthermore, there are no processes to ensure the transparency of decision-making associated with affiliation applications or requests for particular forms of participation.

CSOs were hopeful that the most recent review would create a more participatory system.[4] However, officials indicated that the review was intended only to change the wording of the guidelines such that they align with the structural changes in ASEAN that were endorsed with the Charter, rather than marking an entirely new mode of engagement.[5] The 2012 guidelines do, however, include an additional obligation for affiliated CSOs, namely that their activities comply with the national laws of relevant countries (ASEAN, 2012, article 8). The 2012 guidelines also stipulate that the CPR conduct a review every three years of affiliated CSOs, and revoke affiliation for any organisation that does not meet their obligations or undertakes activities that are contrary to ASEAN and member states' aims (ASEAN, 2012, articles 10–11). CSOs can appeal the CPR's decision to revoke their affiliation; however, their appeal must be directed to the CPR, and 'upon appeal, the decision of the CPR shall be final and binding' (ASEAN, 2012, article 13), thereby aligning the appeals process with the interests of the CPR, rather than CSOs.

Affiliation may increase CSOs' access to ASEAN officials; however, this access continues only if CSOs do not challenge policy. This is because to maintain their affiliation CSOs must retain the favour of the CPR, as part of the review process conducted every three years. This can limit CSOs' range of possible responses to ASEAN policies, reducing the incentive for affiliated organisations to challenge policy. This was recognised by Land Watch Asia, in its pamphlet titled *Engaging the ASEAN: Towards a Regional Advocacy on Land Rights*. When describing the affiliation system this pamphlet advises, 'NGOs need to assess whether ASEAN views them as a partner or merely as a consultative body; that is, whether NGOs can define their own agenda or simply adopt ASEAN's own agenda' (Land Watch Asia, n.d.).

The limited scope for participation that is engendered through the affiliation system has meant that it includes only one CSO that is widely respected in the activist community, namely AsiaDHRRA. The list of affiliated CSOs is dominated by professional bodies, such as the ASEAN Bankers Association and the ASEAN Cosmetics Association, and the inclusion of the ASEAN Kite Council and the ASEAN Vegetable Oils Club has made it a source of ridicule for critics, such as Suryodiningrat (2009) who argues it displays 'the intent by which ASEAN perceives its subjects: with ridicule and condescension'.

Ad hoc Consultations

The ad hoc consultations with CSOs that have been conducted by some ASEAN bodies provide an insight into the limited forms of participation permitted in ASEAN policy-making and, importantly, the struggles between conflicting interests in defining how these consultations should be structured.

The inaugural occurrence of this mode of participation took place in July 2005, when the Secretary-General at the time, Ong Keng Yong, demonstrated an interest in holding a dialogue with CSOs. A meeting was subsequently held between Secretariat officials and representatives of three high-profile CSOs, namely AsiaDHRRA, SEACA, and FORUM-ASIA (Ramirez, 2008). At this meeting, officials encouraged the representatives of these three CSOs to jointly organise in seeking to engage ASEAN, and indicated that their contributions to regional policy-making would be welcomed. At this time, support among officials for the notion of consulting CSOs was at an all-time high, evident in the in-principle support officials granted to the holding of the first ASEAN Civil Society Conference alongside the Leaders' Summit in December 2005 in Kuala Lumpur (Gerard, 2013). Representatives of these three CSOs agreed to collaborate in their efforts to engage ASEAN. They subsequently held a meeting in October 2005 with other CSOs, where they agreed they would collaborate in organising the ASEAN Civil Society Conference. This first meeting between high-level Secretariat staff and representatives of three CSOs created an important precedent that was taken up by other ASEAN bodies.

The next ad hoc consultation was held during the drafting of the Charter in 2006, led by the Eminent Persons Group (EPG) on the ASEAN Charter. The EPG comprised one representative from each member state that was nominated by their respective governments, generally comprising ministers or diplomats, with some retired and others serving (ASEAN, 2006). They were given the task of '[putting] forth bold and visionary recommendations on the drafting of an ASEAN Charter' (ASEAN, 2005). This expansive mandate was reflected in the EPG's terms of reference, which noted the EPG could conduct 'region-wide consultations of all relevant stakeholders in ASEAN in the ASEAN Charter drafting process, especially representatives of the civil society' (ASEAN, 2005, section 4). This recommendation did not specify the extent of consultation to be undertaken, but it provided latitude for the EPG to meet with CSOs. Hence, alongside ASEAN's customary consultations with business groups and the ASEAN–ISIS think-tank network, the EPG also invited representatives of the SAPA network to a meeting from 27 to 29 June 2006 on the drafting of recommendations for the ASEAN Political-Security Community. While it was not invited to subsequent meetings, SAPA submitted its views on the Economic Community on 28 June in Singapore, and on the Socio-Cultural Community and Institutional Mechanisms on 10 November in Manila, and then submitted a final set of seven recommendations through the Philippine EPG representative that reiterated its previous submissions (Solidarity for Asian People's Advocacy, 2006). The SAPA submissions recommended incorporating environmental sustainability, human rights, and human security into the Charter, among other proposals regarding reforming institutional practices of consensus and non-interference. Chandra (2005) notes that only three EPG members were active in responding to SAPA's submissions, namely Tan Sri Musa Hitam of Malaysia, Ali Alatas of Indonesia, and Fidel Ramos of the Philippines—notably most of ASEAN's post-authoritarian members who faced a stronger imperative to respond to claims for reform from domestic CSOs. While the EPG report included some of SAPA's recommendations—importantly, its call for civil society consultation to be institutionalised—it emphasised CSOs' role as raising ASEAN's profile among Southeast Asian citizens, rather than in informing policy.[6]

The High-Level Task Force (HLTF) drafted the final version of the Charter and, like the EPG, comprised a representative from each member state, appointed by state leaders. However, while the EPG comprised a mix of retired and serving officials, 9 of the 10 HLTF representatives were serving officials, making them 'speak for their governments and related ministries and nobody else' (Chongkittavorn, 2007). The Terms of Reference of the HLTF did not specify any form of consultation to be undertaken, with the exception that the HLTF could consult members of the EPG if necessary (ASEAN, 2007c). However, the Philippines and Thai representatives pushed for a meeting with CSOs, which took place on 27 March 2007 in Manila, with 60 representatives of Southeast Asian CSOs (ASEAN, 2007b). At this meeting SAPA representatives again reiterated their three submissions on each of the proposed ASEAN communities, some of which had been included in the EPG report. However, these contributions were not included in the final version of the Charter.[7] The Charter mentions the term 'civil society' only once and in reference to the role of the ASEAN Foundation, which would collaborate with CSOs 'to support ASEAN community building' (ASEAN, 2007a). The ASEAN Foundation's interactions with CSOs, however, are limited to its provision of IT training courses—this interaction, therefore, not creating the opportunity for political participation.[8] The Charter did not expand civil society participation beyond the limits of the affiliation system: it specifies that entities that support the ASEAN Charter may engage with ASEAN; however, this same section then refers to an Appendix detailing the list of affiliated CSOs, thereby limiting participants to those with affiliation. The Charter thus codified civil society participation in ASEAN as being limited to the affiliation system.

The language of ASEAN's proclaimed 'people-focus' also changed with the Charter. The EPG used 'people-centred' in its report; however, the Charter used 'people-oriented', this being a weaker version of the first. The decision to include 'people-oriented' rather than 'people-centred' in the Charter signalled a subtle downgrading of ASEAN's participatory agenda from previous pronouncements, given reservations among officials regarding the latter term's greater inclusivity (Chandra, 2009, p. 10; Nesadurai, 2011, p. 173). Through the consultations conducted by the EPG and the HLTF on the Charter, opportunities were created for CSOs to contribute their views to this important document. However, the relevant ASEAN bodies set the terms of these consultations and created space for CSOs' views to be represented but not advanced through their inclusion in the Charter.

When Secretary-General Surin Pitsuwan commenced his appointment on 1 January 2008, he made known his support for civil society engagement from the outset by speaking at the SAPA Annual General Forum in Bangkok on 4 February 2008 where he 'showed an openness to civil society advocacies and stressed opportunities for cooperation' (Lopa, 2009). Pitsuwan held a meeting with CSOs and Secretariat officials on 5 March 2008 that 'explored windows of ASEAN engagement for civil society and laid down civil society plans for engaging the ASEAN' (Lopa, 2009). He then led the organisation of a conference, from 23 to 25 February 2009, to explore processes of stakeholder engagement in other regional organisations. It was attended by ASEAN and state officials, officials from other regional organisations, and representatives from 18 Southeast Asian CSOs.

Pitsuwan also pushed consultations with CSOs on the sensitive issue of human rights. Article 7.1 of the ASEAN Intergovernmental Commission on Human Rights' (AICHR) Terms of Reference states that the Secretary-General may 'bring relevant issues to the attention of the AICHR' (ASEAN Intergovernmental Commission on Human Rights, 2009). To inform his recommendations to the AICHR, Pitsuwan sought to meet with representatives of regional human rights organisations. He first proposed a meeting in 2009 and, anticipating that such a meeting would be opposed by some member states, he approached an ASEAN–ISIS think tank, the Centre for Strategic and International Studies (CSIS) in Jakarta, to ask for their assistance in facilitating the meeting. In the lead-up to the meeting, news of its occurrence reached the CPR and some responded with harsh criticisms.[9] Pitsuwan nonetheless went ahead with the meeting where CSOs presented him with a statement of their concerns that they wanted him to raise with the AICHR; however, he asked participants not to publicise the dialogue's occurrence.[10]

The following year, CSOs were informed that a similar meeting would not be possible because of the Secretary-General's hectic schedule; however, in 2011 Pitsuwan again approached the CSIS to assist in organising a meeting with regional human rights organisations. Again, in the lead-up to the meeting word of its occurrence spread among officials. However, this time some officials from ASEAN's post-authoritarian states indicated their desire to attend. Their attendance heightened the meeting's significance; however, classifying it as 'informal' meant that the consensus of member states was not necessary in order for it to proceed. These two meetings created space for human rights organisations to dialogue with officials on this highly sensitive topic. The struggles over its establishment highlight the opposition among officials to engaging CSOs in policy-making, particularly on the contentious issue of human rights—an issue that conflicts with the interests of some officials. These meetings did not, however, advance the claims of CSOs regarding ASEAN's human rights commitments, seen in the persistent ineffectuality of the AICHR (Solidarity for Asian People's Advocacy Working Group on ASEAN and Human Rights, 2012).

The other ASEAN body that has held consultations with CSOs is the ASEAN Committee on the Promotion and Protection of the Rights of Women and Children (ACWC). The ACWC was formed in 2010 following the birth of this idea in the Vientiane Action Programme in 2004 (article 1.1.4.7), as well as all member states ratifying the Convention on the Elimination of All Forms of Discrimination Against Women and the Convention on the Rights of the Child. It comprises two representatives from each ASEAN member state, one concerned with women's issues and the other with children's issues. There is some support among ACWC representatives for consulting CSOs regarding its policies, given that some of its representatives previously or currently are employed in the civil society sector.[11] The ACWC first held a consultation with CSOs on the drafting of its Terms of Reference on 29 April 2009 where a civil society representative spoke about relevant civil society activities and potential areas for collaboration with the ACWC (FORUM-ASIA, 2010). CSOs that had shown an interest in meeting with members of the ACWC, whether by having contacted the Chair or the Committee's national representatives, were invited to attend.

The ACWC has subsequently held a number of informal consultations with CSOs, with participation open to all organisations wishing to contribute. Some ACWC representatives were opposed to meeting with CSOs, so the preference has been to keep meetings informal so that discussions cannot be publicised and ACWC representatives' attendance remains optional. One ACWC representative reported that there has been increasing enthusiasm and willingness from representatives to meet with CSOs: 'At the beginning it was very informal ... those who felt like engaging did ... This time around, we were all there, and we all had to say something about what we did. I think that was very productive.'[12] ACWC representatives also reported that they regarded these informal meetings to be an improvement on their previous encounters with activists. One ACWC representative noted activists would

> hang around when we have formal meetings, they wait for you in the lobby or they follow you to the restroom. Always they would know where I'm staying, they are so good at spying on where I'm staying. In the middle of the night they are knocking on the door.[13]

Structured informal consultations with CSOs thus were attractive to ACWC representatives by overcoming such issues.

It is evident that the efficacy of the ad hoc consultations for CSOs depends on whether these interactions are classified as formal or informal. When regarded as formal, such as the consultations for the Charter, they require the approval of all member states, which functions in delimiting civil society participation. When classified as informal, a much freer dialogue has taken place. However, the informality of such interactions also limits their potential to shape ASEAN policy, as consensus among all member states is needed to endorse any proposed policy changes. Meanwhile, the personalities at the helm of ASEAN organs that have pursued consultations with CSOs have been instrumental in ensuring these interactions have taken place, and hence their continuation cannot be guaranteed. As such, these ad hoc consultations have functioned in creating spaces for dialogue between officials and CSOs, but they have not prompted changes to ASEAN policies in accordance with CSOs' agendas.

GO-NGO Forums

The third participatory mechanism established by ASEAN for CSOs are the annual GO-NGO forums that have been established by the ASEAN bodies for Migrant Labour, Social Welfare and Development, and Rural Development and Poverty Eradication ('GO-NGO' referring to government organisation/non-governmental organisation). These forums are held prior to the annual meeting of the relevant sectoral ministers' meeting and they are intended to create the opportunity for officials and CSOs to engage in a dialogue. These forums generally comprise a number of panels, after which participants divide into discussion groups that put forward recommendations based on their discussions. A drafting team made up of moderators, rapporteurs, and forum organisers then consolidates these recommendations, which are presented to participants in a plenary session for debate. Finally the recommendations are submitted to the relevant ministers for discussion at their annual meeting.

In the case of the Social Welfare and Development forum, it was first held from 7 to 9 September 2006 in Bangkok. The forum rotates annually among ASEAN states, and its organisation is shared between the Social Welfare Ministry of the host country, the ASEAN Secretariat and the International Council on Social Welfare, which is a global network of social welfare organisations. The organisation of the migrant labour forum is shared between the Labour Ministry of the host country, the ASEAN Secretariat, and the International Labour Organisation. It provides a forum for dialogue between government officials, workers' and employers' organisations, CSOs, and relevant international organisations such as the International Organisation on Migration. The first was held in Manila from 24 to 25 April 2008 and was organised as a follow-up meeting to the ASEAN Leaders Declaration on the Promotion and Protection of the Rights of Migrant Workers that was signed at the 12th ASEAN Summit in Cebu in January 2007. The Senior Officials' Meeting on Rural Development and Poverty Eradication then decided to hold an equivalent forum, with the first held in Da Nang on 12 June 2012. It was organised by the ASEAN Secretariat in collaboration with the state host, the Vietnamese Ministry of Agriculture and Rural Development, and attended by relevant ASEAN officials, CSOs, and representatives of the Food and Agricultural Organisation of the United Nations, the United Nations Development Programme, and the Asian Development Bank (AsiaDHRRA, 2012).

Across these GO-NGO forums, civil society participants are invited to attend rather than participation being open to those that wish to participate. While the list of invited participants extends beyond those that are affiliated with ASEAN, an informal system of selecting participants whose interests are deemed to align with ASEAN operates.[14] In this informal system of selecting participants, each country compiles a list of organisations they wish to invite. Each list is considered by members of the CPR and if any of the nominated invitees are deemed contentious by a member state, they will be removed from the list, as noted by an ASEAN official: 'We never know, some organisations are blacklisted in some countries. So as long as all 10 member states are agreeable to engage with certain organisations, although they are not affiliated, that should be fine.'[15] The invitees remaining on the list are subsequently asked to participate.

Given that all participants must receive the endorsement of all member states, ASEAN closely regulates which CSOs can participate in the GO-NGO forums. Many of the participants of these forums are GONGOs (government-organised non-governmental organisations), these being groups that are established and/or maintained by states. While the distinction between a GONGO and an independent CSO varies across countries, as does the extent of governmental control over their activities, organisations with a more contentious agenda and grassroots groups are generally not represented in the GO-NGO forums. Participation is largely restricted to nationally accredited CSOs, which, like the affiliation system, is biased towards organisations with formalised and legalised systems of operation and groups that do not contest national policies and maintain the favour of their governments. Through this system of regulating who can participate, these forums function in embedding prevailing institutional interests by creating a veneer of inclusiveness through dialogues between CSOs and officials, while ensuring that those groups that do not support these prevailing interests cannot attend.

Additionally, these forums provide a site for the representation of interests that are aligned with ASEAN's market-building reforms or particular state objectives. One example is the 192 recommendations that were put forward by the SAPA Task Force on ASEAN and Migrant Workers in May 2009, just prior to the 2nd ASEAN Forum on Migrant Labour in July (Southeast Asia Regional Cooperation in Human Development [SEARCH], 2010). A regional migrant workers advocacy organisation, SEARCH, noted that three out of the four government delegations that comprised the Drafting Committee of the ASEAN Committee on Migrant Workers used this document as their primary source of information (SEARCH, 2010). More significantly, however, of these three governments, the Indonesian and Philippine delegations adopted approximately 60 per cent of the recommendations into their initial bargaining positions (SEARCH, 2010). The alignment of the interests of the Indonesian and Philippine delegations with more than half of the recommendations put forward by the SAPA task force reflected the status of these two states as two of the three major intra-region sending countries for migrant workers, the third being Myanmar. These countries' views on the promotion and protection of the rights of migrant workers frequently conflict with those of recipient countries, the three largest in Southeast Asia being Malaysia, Thailand, and Singapore. This is because sending countries advocate for recipient countries to improve oversight of the working conditions of migrant workers employed in these states, and recipient states bear the cost of these regulations.

Thus, through participation, CSOs in this instance provided information; however, it was only adopted by those states whose interests it supported, while the conflicts between states over the regulations governing migrant workers meant that CSOs' views were not incorporated into regional policy. More generally, through the selection of which CSOs can participate and the limited influence their contribution has on regional policy, these participatory mechanisms function in legitimating ASEAN policy by sustaining its participatory rhetoric, while ensuring that groups cannot challenge policy or advance alternative ideas through these spaces.

Conclusion: Modes of Participation in Evaluating CSOs' Influence in Policy-making

Like many regional and global governance institutions, ASEAN has committed to widening policy-making to include CSOs. Through ad hoc consultations and the GO-NGO forums, ASEAN has established two new participatory mechanisms in support of its 'people-centred' approach to regional integration, alongside the existing affiliation system. Using the modes of participation framework to explain their form and function, this article has examined these participatory channels. These three modes of participation share three characteristics that function in preventing CSOs from using these channels to contest policy or advance policy alternatives.

First, regulations over who can participate in these spaces ensure that CSOs working on contentious issues and groups that vocally criticise policy are excluded. This is evident in two of these three opportunities, namely the affiliation system and the GO-NGO forums, being structurally biased towards the inclusion of organisations that are well-resourced, have formalised systems of operation, and do not vocally criticise ASEAN or state policy. Given that the CPR determines which CSOs can participate in these two spaces, dissenting voices are readily excluded. The ad hoc consultations conducted by various ASEAN bodies remain outside the control of the CPR, and consequently provide the opportunity for participation by groups seeking to contest policy. However, the informal status of the ad hoc consultations, which permits the inclusion of such groups, also ensures that these deliberations are unlikely to have any impact on policy, given that all policy decisions require the endorsement of all member states.

Second, strict controls over the nature of participation in these channels narrow the possible contributions by participants. The only form of participation guaranteed by the affiliation system is the ability to submit written statements to the CPR, restricting the potential for affiliated organisations to influence, or even deliberate, policy. The GO-NGO forums hold opportunities for participants to contest policy. However, the actual reform of policy relies on any recommendations gaining the full support of member states. As described in the case of the SAPA Task Force on ASEAN and Migrant Workers, while some of its recommendations for ASEAN's policy regulating the rights of migrant workers received the support of labour source countries, these were not supported by labour recipient countries, resulting in no substantive change to regional policy according to the agendas of CSOs. For the ad hoc consultations, the restrictions governing participation are shaped by whether a consultation is regarded as formal or informal. Formal gatherings remain tightly controlled affairs where opportunities for CSOs to deliberate policy are minimised, such as in the case of the Charter consultations. As informal meetings do not require the approval of the CPR, a more open and deliberative dialogue can take place, such as in the case of the meetings initiated by Pitsuwan on human rights. However, again, the informal nature of such consultations means they are unlikely to prompt policy reforms in accordance with CSOs' objectives. Meanwhile, their occurrence has also been heavily influenced by the personalities at the helm of the relevant ASEAN bodies and hence their continuation is not assured.

Third, the issue in question shapes the boundaries of all three participatory mechanisms, as outlined by one ASEAN official:

> If we are talking about poverty reduction or social welfare of vulnerable groups, I think those are soft issues, no hesitation from member states. But when we touch upon some sensitive issues, like for example human rights ... then the interaction with civil society is different.[16]

Those issues deemed 'sensitive' by officials are those where CSOs' advocacy challenges the interests and priorities of dominant social forces. These issues do not fall within the remit of concerns that are open for discussion between officials and CSOs, because doing so would create channels for the representation of dissenting views, supporting CSOs' claims for reform. However, consultations with CSOs on non-contentious issues permit officials to harness the contribution of organisations in support of its market-building reforms. The issue-specific nature of ASEAN's approach to engaging CSOs is evident in the GO-NGO forums, where ASEAN has designated specific sectoral concerns for dialogue between officials and civil society representatives, namely migrant labour, social welfare and development, and rural development and poverty eradication, all of which are relevant to ASEAN's programme for economic integration. However, effective regional human rights protections are one concern that does not align with this project, demonstrated in the opposition encountered by Pitsuwan in attempting to meet with human rights CSOs. Conspicuously absent from all opportunities for civil society participation are issues deemed even more contentious by officials, given that they directly oppose powerful interests, such as land evictions in Cambodia or political reform in Myanmar. These issues, and the relevant CSOs, are excluded from all spaces established by ASEAN for civil society participation.

These three features of ASEAN's approach to engaging civil society demonstrate how ASEAN's 'people-centred' shift functions in furthering prevailing institutional interests. Permitting some organisations to participate but limiting their ability to contest policy, these participatory mechanisms are structured to legitimise policy as testimony to ASEAN's 'people-centred' commitments while excluding dissenting social forces. ASEAN engages CSOs in this manner because its post-crisis engagement with civil society is directed towards boosting its legitimacy and furthering its narrow reform agenda, rather than creating opportunities for CSOs to contest this political project. As argued by Carroll in his examination of the World Bank's engagement practices, inclusive rhetoric is 'more than just spurious lingo or clever spin' (2010, p. 7, emphasis in original). Such rhetoric is designed to create legitimacy, in this instance, for ASEAN's political project. This inclusive rhetoric creates legitimacy because it is attached to the mechanisms that ASEAN has established to engage CSOs. However, these mechanisms are structured to include those groups that can advance ASEAN's set of narrow reforms, while circumscribing the participation of non-amenable interests. In doing so, ASEAN's approach to engagement functions in silencing its dissenters, who have become increasingly organised and vocal. The limited means for CSOs to assert their claims for reform through spaces established by ASEAN supports the decision of some CSOs to avoid engaging ASEAN altogether and pursue their agendas outside of such channels, where they contest the limited formal opportunities for their participation.

Applying the modes of political participation framework to the ASEAN case has permitted a systematic analysis of ASEAN's approach to engaging CSOs, and revealed how participatory channels are structured to support its market-building reforms. This framework draws into the analysis the conflicts that define relations between CSOs and governance institutions, and the role of prevailing institutional interests in structuring participatory channels. Claims that participatory policy-making addresses 'democracy deficits' must be considered in light of how participatory channels are structured—specifically, whether through participation CSOs access not only opportunities for representation, but also the means to contest policy or advance policy alternatives. As this article has demonstrated, the broader shift to engage CSOs in regional and global policy-making should be viewed as creating sites for contestation rather than being implicitly democratising.

Acknowledgements

The author wishes to thank Toby Carroll, Darryl Jarvis, and participants at the 'New Approaches to Building Markets in Asia' workshop for their feedback on an earlier draft as well as the journal's anonymous reviewers.

Disclosure Statement

No potential conflict of interest was reported by the author.

Notes

1   For a detailed discussion of market-building processes, see Carroll (2012, p. 354).
2   This article is concerned with those participatory channels established by ASEAN, and does not examine modes of participation outside of these spaces, such as protests at the biannual Leaders' Summits or the ASEAN Civil Society Conferences. For analysis of these modes of participation, see Gerard (2013, 2014a).
3   Interview with Malaysian Foreign Affairs Ministry official, Kuala Lumpur, 29 October 2011; interview with ASEAN Secretariat official, Jakarta, 20 October 2011.
4   Interview with Indonesian human rights activist, Jakarta, 19 October 2011.
5   Interview with ASEAN Secretariat official, 3 November 2011.
6   For a discussion of SAPA's responses to the EPG report and the Charter, see Collins (2008).
7   For examination of the differences between the EPG report and the Charter, see Igarashi (2011).
8   The ASEAN Foundation was established in 1997 with the aim of promoting people-to-people contacts; however, it remains primarily a grant-awarding body. All funding decisions of the ASEAN Foundation must receive the consensus of all member states through the ASEAN Foundation's managing body. This process of decision-making has seen the ASEAN Foundation twice reject applications for funding to support the ASEAN People's Assembly (Gerard, 2013).
9   Interview with Indonesian human rights activist, Jakarta, 19 October 2011.
10   Interview with Indonesian human rights activist, Jakarta, 19 October 2011.
11   For example, Indonesian representative, Ahmad Taufan Damanik, established the children's rights organisation, Yayasan KKSP.
12   Interview with ACWC representative, 11 November 2011.
13   Interview with ACWC representative, 11 November 2011.
14   Interview with ASEAN Secretariat official, Jakarta, 22 November 2011.
15   Interview with ASEAN Secretariat official, Jakarta, 22 November 2011.
16   Interview with ASEAN Secretariat official, Jakarta, 22 November 2011.

References

Acharya, A. (2009). *Whose ideas matter? Agency and power in Asian regionalism*. Ithaca, NY: Cornell University Press.
Ahmad, Z. H., & Ghosal, B. (1999). The political future of ASEAN after the Asian crisis. *International Affairs, 75*(4), 759–778.
ASEAN. (1997). *ASEAN vision 2020*. Jakarta: Author.
ASEAN. (2005). *Terms of reference of the Eminent Persons Group (EPG) of the ASEAN Charter*. Jakarta: Author.
ASEAN. (2006). *Biographies of the Eminent Persons Group on the ASEAN Charter*. Jakarta: Author.
ASEAN. (2007a). *Charter of the Association of Southeast Asian Nations*. Jakarta: Author.
ASEAN. (2007b). *Activities of the HLTF on the drafting of the ASEAN Charter (HLTF): January–October 2007*. Jakarta: Author.
ASEAN. (2007c). *Terms of reference: High Level Task Force on the drafting of the ASEAN charter (HLTF)*. Jakarta: Author.
ASEAN. (2009). *Register of ASEAN-affiliated CSOs*. Retrieved from http://www.aseansec.org/6070.pdf
ASEAN. (2012). *Guidelines on accreditation of civil society organisations (CSOs)*. Jakarta: Author.
ASEAN Intergovernmental Commission on Human Rights. (2009). *Terms of reference of the ASEAN Intergovernmental Commission on Human Rights*. Jakarta: Author.

AsiaDHRRA. (2012, June 25). 1st GO-NGO Forum RDPE affirms continued dialogue between governments and CSOs. *AsiaDHRRA*. Retrieved from http://asiadhrra.org/wordpress/2012/06/25/1st-go-ngo-forum-rdpe-affirms-continued-dialogue-between-governments-and-csos/

Betsill, M., & Corell, E. (2008). Introduction to NGO diplomacy. In M. Betsill & E. Corell (Eds.), *NGO diplomacy: The influence of nongovernmental organizations in international environmental negotiations* (pp. 1–19). Cambridge: MIT Press.

van den Bossche, P. (2010). Non-governmental organizations and the WTO: Limits to involvement? In D. P. Steger (Ed.), *Redesigning the World Trade Organization for the twenty-first century* (pp. 309–362). Waterloo, ON: Wilfrid Laurier University Press.

Cammack, P. (2009). The shape of capitalism to come. *Antipode, 41*, 262–280.

Carroll, T. (2010). *Delusions of development: The World Bank and the post-Washington consensus in Southeast Asia.* Basingstoke: Palgrave Macmillan.

Carroll, T. (2012). Introduction: Neo-liberal development policy in Asia: Beyond the Washington consensus. *Journal of Contemporary Asia, 42*(3), 350–358.

Carroll, T., & Jarvis, D. S. L. (2015). The new politics of development: Citizens, civil society and the evolution of neo-liberal development policy. *Globalisations*, doi:10.1080/14747731.2015.1016301

Chandra, A. (2005, October 12). ASEAN EPG, civil society and ASEAN Charter. *People's Agenda for Alternative Regionalisms.* Retrieved from http://www.alternative-regionalisms.org/?p=782

Chandra, A. (2006). The role of non-state actors in ASEAN. In Focus on the Global South (Ed.), *Revisiting Southeast Asian regionalism* (pp. 71–82). Bangkok: Editor.

Chandra, A. (2009). *Civil society in search for an alternative regionalism in ASEAN.* Winnipeg, MB: International Institute for Sustainable Development.

Checkel, J. T. (2005). International institutions and socialization in Europe: Introduction and framework. *International Organization, 59*(4), 801–826.

Chong, T. (2011). Executive summary. In T. Chong & S. Elies (Eds.), *An ASEAN community for all: Exploring the scope of civil society engagement* (pp. 9–20). Singapore: Frederich-Ebert-Stiftung.

Chongkittavorn, K. (2007, March 29). ASEAN drafters meet civil society groups. *The Nation.* Retrieved from http://www.nationmultimedia.com/2007/03/29/opinion/opinion_30030499.php

Collins, A. (2008). A people-oriented ASEAN: A door ajar or closed for civil society organisations? *Contemporary Southeast Asia, 30*(2), 313–331.

Collins, A. (2013). *Building a people-oriented security community the ASEAN way.* London: Routledge.

European Commission. (2010). *Proposal for a regulation of the European Parliament and of the Council on the Citizen's initiative.* Brussels: Author.

Florini, A., & Simmons, P. J. (2000). What the world needs now? In A. Florini (Ed.), *The third force: The rise of transnational civil society* (pp. 1–15). Washington, DC: Japan Center for International Exchange and the Carnegie Endowment for International Peace.

FORUM-ASIA. (2010). *Rights now: A training manual on ASEAN human rights mechanisms.* Bangkok: Author.

Gerard, K. (2013). From the ASEAN People's Assembly to the ASEAN civil society conference: The boundaries of civil society advocacy. *Contemporary Politics, 19*(4), 411–426.

Gerard, K. (2014a). ASEAN and civil society activities in 'created spaces': The limits of liberty. *The Pacific Review, 27*(2), 265–287.

Gerard, K. (2014b). *ASEAN's engagement of civil society: Regulating dissent.* Basingstoke: Palgrave Macmillan.

Hameiri, S., & Jones, L. (2012). The politics and governance of non-traditional security. *International Studies Quarterly, 57*(3), 462–473.

Igarashi, S. (2011). The new regional order and transnational civil society in Southeast Asia: Focusing on alternative regionalism from below in the process of building the ASEAN Community. *World Political Science Review, 7*(1), 1–31.

Jayasuriya, K. (2003). Governing the Asia Pacific: Beyond the 'new regionalism'. *Third World Quarterly, 24*(2), 199–215.

Jayasuriya, K., & Rodan, G. (2007). Beyond hybrid regimes: More participation, less contestation in Southeast Asia. *Democratization, 14*(5), 773–794.

Jessop, B. (1990). *State theory: Putting the capitalist state in its place.* Cambridge: Polity Press.

Katsumata, H. (2011). Mimetic adoption and norm diffusion: 'Western' security cooperation in Southeast Asia? *Review of International Studies, 37*(2), 557–576.

Keck, M. E., & Sikkink, K. (1998). *Activists beyond borders: Advocacy networks in transnational politics.* New York, NY: Cornell University Press.

Land Watch Asia. (n.d.). *Engaging the ASEAN: Towards a regional advocacy on land rights* (Issue Brief 2). Manila: Author.

Lopa, C. (2009). *The ASEAN People's Charter and the three pillars of ASEAN cooperation.* Paper presented at the 4th ASEAN Civil Society conference, Hua Hin.

Morada, N. M. (2008). ASEAN at 40: Prospects for community building in Southeast Asia. *Asia-Pacific Review, 15*(1), 36–55.

Naidoo, K. (2010). Boiling point: Can citizen action change the world? *Development Dialogue, 54,* 1–199.

Nesadurai, H. (2011). The ASEAN People's Forum (APF) as authentic social forum: Regional civil society networking for an alternative regionalism. In M. Beeson & R. Stubbs (Eds.), *Routledge handbook of Asian regionalism* (pp. 166–176). Oxford: Routledge.

Peters, G., & Pierre, J. (2004). A Faustian bargain? In I. Bache & M. Flinders (Eds.), *Multi-level governance* (pp. 76–91). Oxford: Oxford University Press.

Ramirez, M. (2008, February 8–9). AsiaDHRRA and ASEAN: A case study of the process of civil society engagement with a regional intergovernmental organisation. Paper presented at the FIM Forum, Montreal.

Risse, T., Ropp, S. C., & Sikkink, K. (Eds.). (1999). *The power of human rights: International norms and domestic change.* Cambridge: Cambridge University Press.

Rüland, J. (2014). The limits of democratizing interest representation: ASEAN's regional corporatism and normative challenges. *European Journal of International Relations, 20*(1), 237–261.

Saurugger, S. (2010). The social construction of the participatory turn: The emergence of a norm in the European Union. *European Journal of Political Research, 49,* 471–495.

Scholte, J. A. (2007). Global civil society – opportunity or obstacle for democracy? *Development Dialogue, 49,* 15–28.

Scholte, J. A. (2011). Global governance, accountability and civil society. In J. A. Scholte (Ed.), *Building global democracy? Civil society and accountable global governance* (pp. 8–42). Cambridge: Cambridge University Press.

Skinner, Q. (1988). Analysis of political thought and action. In J. Tully (Ed.), *Meaning and context: Quentin Skinner and his critics.* Cambridge: Polity Press.

Slaughter, A. (2004). *A new world order.* Princeton, NJ: Princeton University Press.

Solidarity for Asian People's Advocacy. (2006, November 24). SAPA letter to the EPG on the ASEAN Charter reiterating the key points of its submissions. *People's Agenda for Alternative Regionalisms.* Retrieved from http://www.alternative-regionalisms.org/?p=926

Solidarity for Asian People's Advocacy Working Group on ASEAN and Human Rights. (2012). *A commission shrouded in secrecy.* Bangkok: Asian Forum for Human Rights and Development.

Southeast Asia Regional Cooperation in Human Development. (2010). *Promoting a process of change: The Task Force on ASEAN Migrant Workers.* Retrieved from http://www.searchproject.ca/pubs/Task%20Force%20on%20ASEAN%20Migrant%20Workers.pdf

Suryodiningrat, M. (2009, March 5). Facing the people, ASEAN's strategic deficit. *The Jakarta Post.* Retrieved from http://www.thejakartapost.com/news/2009/03/05/news-analisys-facing-people-asean%E2%80%99s-strategic-deficit.html

Verweij, M., & Josling, T. E. (2003). Deliberately democratizing multilateral organizations. *Governance, 16*(1), 1–21.

Wheeler, N. J. (2000). *Saving strangers: Humanitarian intervention in international society.* Oxford: Oxford University Press.

The European Bank for Reconstruction and Development's Gender Action Plan and the Gendered Political Economy of Post-Communist Transition

STUART SHIELDS & SARA WALLIN

University of Manchester, Manchester, UK
University of Sheffield, Sheffield, UK

ABSTRACT *In this article, we explore the European Bank for Reconstruction and Development's (EBRD's) place in the gendered political economy of Eastern Central Europe's post-communist transition. We document the gendered modalities surrounding the EBRD's policy strategies for post-communist transition, suggesting that they help to naturalise certain gendered constructions of neoliberal development and market-building. To elaborate these claims we show first, how the EBRD largely ignored gender until the 'global financial crisis' when it discovered gender mainstreaming by mobilising the Gender Action Plan (GAP); and then second, how the 2013 revision of the GAP, the Strategic Gender Initiative extended the EBRD's gender aware activities. Both policies illustrate how the EBRD's understanding and application of gender fit firmly within a neoliberal framework promoting transition as a form of modernisation where gender inequality is always posited as external to the market and reproduces uneven and exploitative social relations.*

1. Introduction

In this article, we analyse the role played by the European Bank for Reconstruction and Development (EBRD) in advancing the policies and ideas of neoliberalisation in the post-communist space stretching from Eastern Central Europe (ECE) to Central Asia, and increasingly beyond. By drawing upon perspectives from critical and feminist International Political Economy (IPE) (see Shields, Bruff, & Macartney, 2011), we argue that the EBRD's recent incorporation of 'gender' corresponds to, and facilitates, the EBRD's enlarged role in propelling the further com-modification of (re)production in the region. As such, the EBRD plays a pivotal role in reorga-nising social relations into patterns more conducive to the construction of neoliberal hegemony.[1]

This becomes particularly evident through analysis of how the EBRD has become implicated in the construction and reconstruction of gender norms, identities, and relations in ECE since the so-called global financial crisis. As the extant transitions literature demonstrates (more often through its absence), ideas of gender, social construction, and historically specific norms of mas-culinity and femininity remain at the forefront of neoliberalisation in ECE. Debates on social, economic, and political reforms, alongside discourses of modernisation and nationalism, have centred upon the contestation of the meanings of gender roles and relations (Kuehnast & Nechemias, 2004).

The EBRD's 'discovery' of gender provides a robust illustration of the disciplinary aspects of neoliberalisation, especially how determining social reproduction is. Neoliberalisation constructs new forms of social relations wherein gender differences are both intensified and eroded as women increasingly enter the paid workforce and a rearrangement of the work involved in social reproduction across the state-labour market/family-household nexus (see Bakker, 2003, pp. 66–67; Bezanson, 2006). By representing and promoting an idea of women as individualistic consumers and entrepreneurs and promoting specific reforms in social policy, the EBRD influ-ences the negotiation of how social reproduction is mediated across state, market, and household scales to ensure the intensification of exploitation. We understand social reproduction as being constituted by three main elements: the biological reproduction of the species; the reproduction of the labour force; and the reproduction and provision of caring needs (Bakker, 2007, p. 541).

The argument unfolds in four stages. First, we engage critically with the existing deployment of neoliberalisation in the post-communist transitions literature. The starting point of our engagement is feminist and critical IPE which we utilise as a forceful heuristic to evaluate the discussion of post-communist transitions to dismiss the importance of gender relations in market-building, perpetuating our selective political and intellectual blindness to issues of social reproduction, consumption, and patriarchy in the context of transition. In Section 2, we utilise these insights to explore how the EBRD has managed to spend the first two decades of transition prior to 2008 deeply interred in gender blindness. This reading of EBRD activities communicates the part played by the EBRD in proffering three key policy discourses of neoli-beralisation in ECE absent of gender. Section 3 of the article shows how the EBRD arrived late to gender through analysis of the gender action plan (GAP) in the EBRD's wider market-build-ing activities. This constitutes a unique opportunity to analyse the EBRD's understanding of gender in its first explicit formulation. The GAP was first endorsed in 2008 coinciding with the 'global financial crisis' and published the year after. Its appurtenant documentation unveils how the EBRD has translated the wider turn to gender mainstreaming, such an emphatic component of the post-Washington Consensus (Bergeron, 2004). Section 4 offers further analy-sis of the EBRD's gender blindness by discussing the 2013 revision of the GAP: the Strategic Gender Initiative (SGI). This latter gender imperative demonstrates how the EBRD's under-standing and application of gender fit with its objective to promote transition as a form of mod-ernisation where gender inequality is always posited as external to the market.

2. Post-Communist Transition and Neoliberalisation

As an initial cut at the gendered dimensions of knowledge constructed by the EBRD within a broader framework of neoliberal development and post-communist transition, we want to reflect on the existing deployment of neoliberalisation in the post-communist transitions literature and, in particular, how this is articulated in the role of the 'international' in configuring successful transition. However, we also make a further theoretical move intimating that scholars have often been too quick to dismiss the importance of gender relations in reflecting on the role of global governance institutions in market-building, thus perpetuating our selective political and intellectual blindness to issues of social reproduction, consumption, and patriarchy.

Post-communist development is represented as a relatively straightforward division between internal/domestic factors and external/international factors; the latter especially driven by specific institutions (Dimitrova & Pridham, 2004; Linden, 2002). Following an initial focus on the International Monetary Fund (IMF) and World Bank (Stone, 2002), an ever-expanding literature has progressively directed its gaze to the EU, crowding out other institutions. The impact of external conditionalities and their associated norms on internal/domestic national polities (particularly those employed by the EU) feature often (O'Dwyer, 2005) amid ideas related to 'passive' forms of leverage (Vachudova, 2005). The seminal contribution here is Schimmelfennig and Sedelmeier's (2005) assessment of EU membership conditionalities. More explicit accounts situated within IR/IPE scholarship include Epstein's social constructivist account of international institutions driving Poland's liberalisation (2008), and Appel's (2004) meso-level focus on the external fiscal pressures driving privatisation. Despite some difference in explicating the balance between domestic/factors and external/international factors, the majority of approaches are informed by area studies predilections focused on how best to achieve the 'practical transformation' of antediluvian planned economies and the construction of functioning democracies. The EBRD remains a curious absence considering its activities in the region.

The relationship between domestic and international changes relies on an area studies methodological nationalism that conflates society with state and national territory as the unit of analysis (Pradella, 2014, p. 181). In one of the few developed critiques of methodological nationalism, Gore shows how the isolation involved in such an approach separates 'internal and external factors as determinants of national economic performance, with primacy being given to the former' (1996, p. 79). The analysis of transitology is disciplined via the construction of narratives which maintain the coherence of a field of study as it is already constituted: 'social amnesia should not be allowed to masquerade as scientific knowledge' (Hawkesworth, 2010, p. 285).

The key implication then for analysis of post-communist transition is how the relationship among the local, the national state, and regional and international institutions promulgates a particular closure around divergent paths to development. The rescaling of transition development is not merely to be understood as the benign influence of multilevel governance extended from the munificence of the EU. Instead this closure affects a new form of neoliberal authoritarianism where power is transferred to, and increasingly locked in to institutional and juridical arrangements (see Cammack, 2006; Carroll & Jarvis 2015; Gill, 1995; Jayasuriya, 2004; Swyngedouw, 2000). Neoliberalised institutions marshal the interests of capital to posit developmental beneficence in open, competitive markets, and the application of such strategies produces new institutional and regulatory landscapes supported by new functional logics and political imperatives (Peck & Tickell, 2002). Rather than any single monolithic form of policy, neoliberalisation should be interpreted as a:

> Hegemonic restructuring ethos, as a dominant pattern of (incomplete and contradictory) regulatory transformation, and not as a fully coherent system or typological state form. As such, it necessarily operates among its others, in environments of multiplex, heterogeneous, and contradictory governance. (Peck, Theodore, & Brenner, 2010, p. 104)

There are three main aspects: first, the economy, with scales from the global to the body; second, the state, the national scale; and third, the socio-cultural scale, from the home to the locality. This is where fundamental forms of class, gender, and racial oppression are configured (Mitchell, 2001, p. 149). We operationalise this at the nexus of social relations to expose gendered power relations in the social reproduction of a key institution of global governance and post-communist transition, reiterating Peterson's claim that patriarchy's enduring legacy is a binary construction of gender that casts women and femininity as essentially different from and inferior to men and masculinity.[2] Why does this matter? If as we claim, there must be a distinct gendered component to the reproduction of capitalist social relations, then the reproduction of gender must also be scalar. We therefore have a constructive template to reflect on the behaviours of sub-state actors, states, and international institutions that highlights the imbrication between the social relations of production and the gendered relations of reproduction (Marston, 2000, p. 219).

As scale is a social relation, there is a politics to its production which is related to the reconstitution of capital in general. Scale becomes a set of economic strategies for states but also bodies, localities, sub-state regions, and global cities, to follow. Different spaces of engagement translate specific policy interests into the general interest across a range of concrete gendered, social, and political processes, strategies, and struggles. By interrogating dominant conceptualisations of global/local relations in the theory and practice of neoliberalisation, feminist IPE demonstrates how gender operates at multiple scales across the global political economy from the level of ideology, representation, social relations, and to the body (Marchand and Runyan 2000, p. 8).

How then might this help us to reflect on the role played by the EBRD in advancing the policies and ideas of neoliberalisation in post-communist transition (beyond noting its absence from exiting academic debates)? The diffusion of gender equity concerns into global governance institutions constitutes one of the major trends of the post-Washington Consensus. Feminist IPE's critique of mainstream development thought has been essential in bringing about and enacting this transformation. To make gender more palatable to organisations operating within liberal conceptual frameworks, 'gender equity' has been framed as congruent with the objectives of economic growth, where equality between the sexes and women's empowerment are means to overcome macroeconomic inefficiency (Elson, 2009). Since this inclusion of gender in development is predicated upon an understanding of men and women as fundamentally different, with women seen as essentially reproductive and nurturing, 'gender equity' is reproducing rather than challenging gendered power relations:

> Contemporary development policy-making struggles to conceive of incorporating gender considerations beyond improving women's access to markets (local and global). Women should be educated to this purpose, receive better healthcare to be fit to do so, should be sufficiently Westernised and socially 'empowered' to prevent men impeding their access to market opportunities. Little work is done to encourage non-market based behaviours. (Elson, 2009, p. 115)

In contrast to much transitology literature, we consider gender as pivotal to any understanding of the relation between the international, neoliberalisation, and post-communist transition.[3] If one aim of the article is to highlight how neoliberal discourse and policy is a powerful, though contested, force in reconfiguring gender norms to fit the contemporary development project of market-building (on the latter point see Carroll, 2012), our focus on the EBRD offers a powerful interrogative of the variegated gendered practices of neoliberalisation that often appear contradictory and inconclusive (both in and beyond ECE) as the next section begins to explore.

As Ferguson (2010) argues, the study of social reproduction opens up the potential to analyse global processes as everyday processes, where local, domestic, and national actors are not passive recipients of top-down imperatives but are co-constitutive and reproduce its varied forms. Underpinning the allocation of both paid and unpaid work involved in social reproduction are gender norms, assigning different roles and responsibilities to men and women. By exposing the gender division of labour, where women are concentrated within low-pay, low-status sectors of the economy, and undertake a disproportionate share of unpaid work, feminist scholarship tenders a crucial challenge to the claims of universality and objectivity underpinning neoliberal development policy. The concomitant 'free' market populated by rational actors instead conceals and perpetuates inequalities (Rai, 2004, pp. 582–584). Neoliberal restructuring brings about a masculine bias by its tendency to assume that social reproduction accommodates macroeconomic changes. Gender norms that ascribe responsibility for reproductive work to women thus serve to facilitate a particular type of post-communist transition.

Given the commitment of the EBRD to neoliberalisation, in the next section we interrogate the role of the EBRD in the refinement of neoliberal strategies to maintain the disciplining power of capital. We do this by exploring the EBRD's participation in configuring three discursive shifts of transition. The first based on market construction from the early 1990s, the second based on reconfiguring institutional arrangements in ECE associated with EU accession, and third, the neoliberal promotion of competitiveness after EU membership.

3. Where Were the Women? EBRD: From Shock Therapy to Neoliberal Competitiveness[4]

In the preceding section we outlined a conceptual framing for engaging with post-communist transition. This involved locating our critical engagement with the existing literature in critical and feminist IPE. We take that heuristic in this section and utilise it to reflect on the apparent absence of gender in the EBRD's formulation of what constitutes appropriate policy choice during the post-communist period. Of course just because the EBRD does not acknowledge gendered aspects of its reform programme, it does not mean that the EBRD is not reproducing gendered knowledge. Gender equality may well now be considered one of the EBRD's integral activities; this was not always the case.

In the next section we will explore the EBRD's commitment to gender equality across its investment and donor-funded activities, unravelling how gender equality became a core component of advancing sound business management and sustainable economic development. For now though it is salient that the EBRD's gender commitment emerges most forcefully from 2003. Prior to 2003, however, various departments in the EBRD had shown some awareness of women within the broader process of transition. For example, the Financial Institutions Small Business Team promoted access to credit for women entrepreneurs but the silence on the matter from the 1990s onwards remains instructive.

Before proceeding further, it is important to detail three central shifts in the EBRD's policy discourse in order to expose the political and intellectual blindness to issues of social reproduction, consumption, and patriarchy in the context of transition. These discourses provide ideological coherence, legitimacy, and technical solutions to the problems of transition aimed at completing reform: first, the initial post-communist construction of the market; second, the configuration of the 'correct' institutional framework to facilitate transition; and third, the promotion of neoliberal competitiveness.

The initial discursive formation consolidated neoliberal thinking around a single legitimate route for transition. This is the pragmatic, stylised Washington Consensus 'toolkit' so familiar elsewhere in the global political economy from the 1970s. This Shock Therapy mapped out the parameters of the reform debate for the first half of the 1990s, embedding transition within an uncompromising anti-communist and pro-Western normative framework. The EBRD had three distinct undertakings: (1) an explicit commitment to political transformation; (2) a clearly defined emphasis on private sector development; and (3) a strategic role as the first pan-European institution linking the ECE states to the West (Smith, 2002). The EBRD blueprint for transition supplies a clear set of definitions and uncontroversial set of goals, while simultaneously offering expertise as a means of implementation (Shields, 2012, p. 24).[5] What is clear from this first period of transition is that women are absent. This contrasts with the IMF and World Bank who were already developing gender mainstreaming dimensions to their policies. As Siemienska (1996) relates, women might well have been involved in the movements that contributed to the collapse of state socialism but after 1989 the *construction of a whole new society* means that women's concerns are secondary, to be dealt with at an appropriate time (see also Einhorn, 1993).

The second major shift in EBRD policy discourse was from the market-building of the early 1990s and aimed to complete the transition process and open up institutional frameworks and practices that had been captured by oligarchic and exclusive interests. The EBRD was cognisant of this problem from as early as 1991:

> The countries of [ECE] have shown themselves determined to create new democratic market economies. The linkage between the political, economic and social components of the changes have become increasingly clear. A market economy requires an adequate legal and democratic political framework to foster the spirit of enterprise, individual rights and institutional stability necessary for sound investment. (EBRD, 1991, p. 26)

The harm done by rent seeking in the early stages of transition was further illustrated in the EBRD's key annual publication, the 1999 *Transition Report*: 'building institutions that support markets and private enterprise remains a fundamental challenge of transition, but establishing the appropriate laws and regulations is not sufficient' (EBRD, 1999, p. 9).

The need to open up key sectors of the economy to competition (especially the highly masculinised coal, ship building, and steel sectors) to promote entrepreneurship and remove existing distortions in the post-communist labour market, impeded the supply and development of quality human capital. The necessity to complement liberalisation and privatisation with the development of institutions and behaviour that support the functioning of markets and private enterprise was recognised. The policy shift from economic Shock Therapy to an *institutional* Shock Therapy was clear at the EBRD who averred,

> the next period of the transition must be led by high-quality investment ... with the right kind of institutions, leadership and partnership, the private markets in these countries can deliver the quality investment which is necessary for successful economic growth. (EBRD, 1995, p. 8)

No hint then of a critical assessment at the same time that indicated how women '[constituted] a significant proportion of the poorest, most disadvantaged sectors of society; they [formed] a majority of the unemployed and a minority of those being hired' (Molyneux, 1994, p. 293).

Progress in transition remained protracted (EBRD, 2004, p. 1; see also World Bank, 2004) and from the early 2000s a third shift occurred, emphasising the promotion of competitiveness. The 1999 *Transition Report* identified the first two shifts in policy discourse already noted above and foreshadowed the third: the centrality of competitiveness to transition. It claimed change must be:

embodied in the social norms, practices and behaviours of both government and the private sector – institutions need social capital and social foundations. The experiences of the first ten years of transition point to the ways in which both formal institutions can be built on firm foundations and social capital accumulated. Of particular importance are: (i) the experiences of liberalisation and privatisation, (ii) the demands for good governance from entrepreneurs and civil society, and (iii) the forces of competition. (EBRD, 1990, p. 9)

It is perhaps here, in the turn to competitiveness, where we can begin to see gender first explicitly emerging in the EBRD development discourse. If the juridical construction of the market and getting the correct institutions in place is insufficient for successful completion of transition then the alternative is to turn to the region's population and explore options to improve their entrepreneurial capacities.

Since the emergence of the competitiveness agenda, the EBRD has acted as a vehicle for what Carroll terms market-building, an 'all-encompassing technocratic agenda being operationalised in the name of development' (Carroll, 2012, p. 351) at the intersection of the financial sector and civil society. In effect the competitiveness shift is internalising Shock Therapy, a set of policies and ideas that guided the discursive construction of a neoliberal agenda for competitiveness. Labour market reform was an essential component of this strategy, and its principal objective, as elsewhere, was the creation of a 'flexible' labour force. It is perhaps not that surprising when the following discursive shift towards more gender aware development strategies explores how a whole segment of the population's entrepreneurs had been ignored.

Yet, the EBRD's shifts in discourse should not be interpreted as a progressive reorientation. It is instead another way for the EBRD to seek to reconstitute itself as a legitimate actor in the global political economy. Each permutation from the 1990s onwards should be understood in relation to the failure of the EBRD's neoliberal transition project to overcome recurrent crises of production and social reproduction. While the policy and rhetoric (on markets, institutions, competitiveness, and gender) signify important departures for the EBRD, all continue to be subsumed to the overarching objective to generate profit for the EBRD, as potential additional opportunities through which the EBRD might pursue the neoliberal project.

In asking where were the women, the EBRD has been too focused on an undifferentiated question of capitalist production. It has paid insufficient attention to social reproduction and consumption. It has therefore, rather like many critical IPE scholars, privileged the urban and regional scales and neglected the household as a key scale in capitalism (Steans & Tepe, 2010; Waylen, 2006). The next section of the article therefore communicates how the EBRD's recent policy and rhetoric on gender signify an important departure from its standard neoliberal prescriptions for post-communist transition. The turn to gender is situated in a wider process of macroeconomic review that gained impetus following the 2008 financial crisis.

4. How the EBRD Discovered Gender Matters: The 2009 Gender Action Plan

The shifts in the EBRD's discourse noted in the preceding section were primarily aimed at the consolidation of neoliberal strategies of accumulation. The post-communist state was at first rolled back, then later rolled out, and then further subjected to ever more vigorous exhortations to improve its competitiveness. The wide range of co-opted social forces had one silence: the absence of a self-conscious gendered dimension. In this section, the article explores how the EBRD began to take gender seriously in its policy advice. We explore how the GAP is focused on gender but simultaneously articulates a new discursive strategy of neoliberalisation. We do not suggest that the GAP fell fully formed from the sky in 2008: rather that there has been a set of internal policy shifts at the EBRD. The EBRD's first meaningful and formal engagement with the gendered dimensions of transition and development occurred when it declared support for gender equality as a signatory to the third Millennium Development Goal in 2003. The EBRD would later note how it had

> committed to launching and implementing a gender action plan in the Bank's countries of operations, to actively promote greater opportunities for women – increasing the economic participation of women in the private sector, including in decision-making roles, through EBRD projects, staff and clients – and to mitigate gender inequalities in the region. (EBRD, 2008a, p. 3)

Second, the EBRD's work on gender was set in motion through an internally driven revision process on the impact assessment criteria for EBRD funded projects. Initially redrafted from the Environmental Policy, the 2008 Environmental and Social Policy (E&SP) advocated the EBRD's initial efforts to integrate gender concerns. This was formulated at the level of impact mitigation, with the policy speaking to gender issues by highlighting women as one group made potentially more vulnerable to displacement following large scale EBRD projects (EBRD, 2008b, p. 36).

The E&SP forced social issues into the spotlight by compelling the EBRD to mainstream social and environmental concerns through all activities. This meant the reformulation of operational assessment criteria for funding. The bulk of the E&SP addresses labour standards, working conditions, and community impact, gender is only mentioned in relation to work place discrimination and the relocation of indigenous people (EBRD, 2008b). However, this shift concretely situates these policies within the EBRD investment mandate. In addition the E&SP also committed the EBRD to comply with EU standards for employment, including non-discrimination on the grounds of gender (EBRD, 2008b, p. 23). Since publishing the E&SP, the EBRD developed further guidelines on gender impact assessments and equal opportunities, and implemented or began the consolidation of 15 projects with a formal gender component (EBRD, 2013, p. 8). In 2010, the EBRD Board of Directors officially endorsed the GAP (EBRD, 2010a, p. 4). The GAP itself contained three parts: (1) the impact of economic transition for women; (2) the EBRD's efforts to promote gender equality; and (3) the EBRD's GAP. We consider each in turn.

4.1. *The Impact of Economic Transition for Women*

The initial stage of the GAP explored the divergence of women's and men's experiences of transition in terms of opportunities and access to resources including health, education, and political power. It also assessed the following areas: labour force participation, qualitative modifications in employment (i.e. types of jobs), wage equality, and access to finance. The GAP noted how women had been adversely impacted in labour force participation due to societal discrimination and increased caring duties following the neoliberalising roll-back of state provision. Discriminatory access to finance is particularly exaggerated in the Commonwealth of Independent States (CIS) where 'financial development and competition are less advanced' in comparison to ECE. Such discrimination stems from path dependent cultural, historical, and institutional starting points that can be stripped away through the increased participation of women in a 'more competitive financial market' (EBRD, 2010a, p. 7).

4.2. *The EBRD's Efforts to Promote Gender Equality*

The second component of the GAP indicates how, despite not having explicitly targeted gender concerns, the EBRD had already inadvertently managed to exert positive influence. The GAP offers a number of key illustrations of its accidental effectiveness. This is primarily through the existing influence of the E&SP, but the EBRD also had a track record in supporting women's access to finance and small business funding, offering technical assistance and advice to women, and through encouraging board-level appointments of women and even through the EBRD's Women in Business Awards.

4.3. *The EBRD's GAP*

The final component of the GAP then was the plan itself. This set out specific initiatives and policy priorities for the EBRD over the following two years. The main indicator of successful achievement of its aims would be the number of women in managerial positions in the private sector. Georgia, the Kyrgyz Republic, and Romania would pilot improving women's access to credit and business opportunities, while the EBRD would develop improved impact assessment tools inclusive of gender through further collaboration with civil society and other IFIs. The GAP's focus on women in Central Asia as drivers of economic growth formalised and embedded gender equality into the EBRD's policy discourse.[6]

It would be churlish not to partially welcome the benefits of the GAP as part of a move towards recognising the role of gender and women's unpaid labour in post-communist transition. As the GAP itself acknowledged:

> The Bank's mandate to support transition, economic growth and sustainable projects accompanied by the accelerated economic growth witnessed in the region has helped to improve the overall quality of life, improved the overall infrastructure, whether it be through increased communication, transport, clean water or access to energy. For women, who are often at home in the countries of operations, such improvements have a clear positive impact. (EBRD, 2009, p. 8)

However, we also sound a crucial note of caution that despite these proposals offering a form of gender mainstreaming at the EBRD, entirely absent from the GAP was any discussion of what gender might actually be. Rather than taking seriously issues of power relations, gender is ontologically flattened into the homogenous category of women.

The GAP made the case for gender equality in its first sentence: 'Gender equality is an important component of the development and transition processes in particular to better leverage the untapped potential of women in emerging markets' (EBRD, 2010a, p. 4). Later it suggested that women have positive impacts on market expansion through consumption and their contribution to better governance through less tolerance for corrupt practices. It is clear that gender sensitivity at the EBRD is ultimately to further proletarianise, commodify, and socialise the population of ECE:

> A key contribution of gender equality to growth is through labour productivity and the efficient allocation of human capital. When women have equal access to education, training and employment opportunities, companies are able to tap into a larger and more diversified workforce. (EBRD, 2010a, p. 11)

The GAP's continued focus on private sector participation and entrepreneurial activity continued to marginalise women's various productive and reproductive roles, hence the dearth of proposals concerning the imbalance of paid and unpaid labour. The individualising commodifying discourse of the Women in Business programme relaxes the familiar construction of *homo sovieticus* becoming *homo economicus* [sic], women need to 'change their mind set in order to become more entrepreneurial' (Greenberg, 2010, p. 18).

Given the EBRD's previous discounting of the role of gender as part of its mandate this change perhaps indicates a crucial shift in emphasis. The unfolding of the 2008 'global financial crisis' opened up policy space for the EBRD to begin to incorporate more advocacy for gendered understandings of transition. At first blush this might appear to be a positive step forwards. Certainly in liberal terms it might. Under the varying titles of 'transnational business feminism' (Roberts, 2014), 'post-feminism', and 'market feminism' (Kantola & Squires, 2012), the growth of a business-oriented, pro-capitalist form of feminism is endemic to this current formulation of gendered global governance. Discourses on women and gender equality have played an important role in the response to the global financial crisis. By invoking a series of assumptions on women's biological and social characteristics, women have been portrayed as better financial managers and a key group of consumers who in turn may increase corporate profitability. Yet the translation of such an instrumental understanding of formal gender equity inserted into policies promoting female entrepreneurship exhibits a tension with social reproduction (Elson, 2009, pp. 38–42). This instrumentalist reading of gender continues to subjugate gender analysis within the broader over-determination of neoclassical understandings of the economy. The EBRD's 'discovery' of gender is thus predicated on equality of opportunity, premised upon foundations of the individual's responsibility to seize economic opportunity, and fails to consider how women's social reproductive work can be accommodated.

This resonates with Penny Griffin's pioneering work on the World Bank (2009, p. 113) that reveals how gender is a part of discourse in two ways. As this section illustrated there is, first, the official formulation of gender policy, which is articulated in EBRD documentation. Second, gender is an unacknowledged part of the EBRD's conceptual framing of the problems of post-communism and is implicated deep within EBRD praxis. Put simply, it is not that prior to 2008 the EBRD failed to have an implicit understanding of gender. Rather that the EBRD offered its social policy prescriptions and investments with no sensibility of the effects of policy on gender relations and social reproduction (see Bacheva, Kochladze, & Dennis, 2006). Since the GAP, the EBRD may well be more gender aware but that gender analysis is utilised as an investment tool replete with ideas on women's natural role in the economy (EBRD, 2010b, p. 5). Such concerns were unimportant for the reconstruction and development of post-communist societies. In the next section we bring the investigation up to date, exploring how the EBRD has engaged with gender issues since the GAP.

5. Reproducing Neoliberalisation at the EBRD after the GAP: The 2013 Strategic Gender Initiative

From the preceding sections it should be clear that the EBRD is committed to neoliberal forms of market-building and development strategies. This may not be so remarkable, but in contrast to many other regional development institutions the EBRD is fully committed to economic *and also political change*. Just after its establishment the EBRD acknowledged this, accepting that,

> this poses a major challenge: to create a new economic framework, while simultaneously changing the political system, behaviour, and even the attitudes of the people involved, without creating intolerable social conditions which could seriously endanger their societies and threaten those nearby. (EBRD, 1991, p. 23)

The EBRD has a specific mandate to 'foster transition to market-based economies and to promote private entrepreneurship, while also promoting sustainable development' (EBRD 2012, p. 13). Therefore EBRD activities in the realm of gender are necessarily located within a liberal feminist framing. As with other institutions of global governance, gender equality is articulated in terms of 'Business Cases' or 'Smart Economics'. As Chant notes, the 'adoption of gender equality as a strategy for development effectiveness' (2012, pp. 199–200) gains increasing momentum, endorsed and promulgated by a wide range of international institutions, non-governmental organisations, and government bodies especially in the wake of the 2008 global financial crisis (Bedford, 2009; Elias, 2013; Roberts, 2014; Roberts and Soederberg, 2014). How has this been evident at the EBRD?

The impact of the 'global financial crisis' should not be understated. As the then Chief Economist of the EBRD, Erik Berglof, noted in the 2010 *Transition Report*, the crisis was not a moment for ECE to lose its collective nerve: 'complacency would threaten not only recovery, but also long-term economic growth. There can be no return to the region's pre-crisis dynamism without new reform' (EBRD, 2010c, p. iv). From 2008 resources directed at gender-related work were expanded to enable further opportunities for reform. The establishment of a dedicated Gender Team illustrates this well given that coordination of the GAP had fallen on EBRD staff with little experience of working on gender. Additional support for developing and disseminating the GAP was to be provided by a Gender Steering Group that consisted of senior members of departmental staff as well as volunteers. Though the overriding concern for selection to the Gender Team, overshadowing expertise and experience of working on gender, was candidates' knowledge and understanding of how the EBRD goes about its business (Wallin, 2012). Since then the EBRD has developed more institutional infrastructure for its work on gender culminating in the 2013 SGI.

The SGI emerged as a significant internal response to problems experienced with the GAP. Internal responsibility for the GAP was located in the Stakeholder Department, a non-operational department of an institution primarily focused on project work. This meant that despite the institutional pressure to find an approach to gender that would 'fit' the EBRD's transition mandate, internal operational procedure sidelined gender. The SGI has become the EBRD's main policy on gender. The Gender Team now has three employees with experience of working on gender in other international institutions. It has also shifted into the Environmental Department that operates directly at project level. This provides opportunities to integrate gender at earlier stages of the project cycle.

To illustrate this point further, the EBRD had argued in the GAP that gender equality was linked to a specific notion of post-communist development in the following ways:

> Gender equality leads to market expansion through the creation of products and services that appeal to women consumers. It leads to the strengthening of market-based institutions and policies designed to improve labour conditions, favour social inclusion and reduce discriminatory practices. It also leads to a transfer of skills and behaviours that enhance existing human resources. It further contributes to the adoption of the latest management best practices, including policies related to corporate social responsibility. (EBRD, 2009, p. 11)

The SGI continues to align gender within the EBRD's wider neoliberal framework of transition. This enables the EBRD to demonstrate how gender does not stretch its mandate. The SGI repeatedly stresses the EBRD's limited resources and seeks to outline an approach where 'the Bank can best add value given its mandate and business model' (EBRD, 2012, p. 5).

Where the GAP claimed that it would embed gender mainstreaming in the EBRD (2009, p. 4, 11–12), it contained no systematised approach to operationalising this beyond extant opportunities in the appraisal and risk mitigation stages of project development (EBRD, 2009, p. 12). In comparison the SGI introduced a much more detailed and robust approach to including gender to support the operations and objectives of the EBRD. However, the SGI discarded gender main-streaming in favour of a more targeted approach. The SGI continued to support a range of initiat-ives such as development of guidance tools, policy dialogue, and women in management and director positions, easily redolent of the GAP. Yet it also introduced a new method for identify-ing appropriate locations for the EBRD to work on gender issues.

This more targeted method in the SGI set out to identify the 'gender gap' to achieve a greater impact on 'women's economic opportunities' (EBRD, 2012, p. 10). The SGI is based on assess-ment of the gender gap across legal and social regulation, health, education, labour policy, labour practices, employment, firm ownership, and access to finance. As with the GAP, this is translated in the SGI into *a focus on women and their potential contribution to growth and efficiency*. Gender is described in terms of an attribute that 'can both determine or impede a person's econ-omic opportunities' (EBRD, 2012, p. 14). The main authority this is derived from is the manage-ment consulting firm McKinsey. McKinsey's encouragement of 'gender diversity' stems from their commitment to competitiveness, the skills available to a company, and better targeting of women as consumers (McKinsey & Company, 2007, pp. 10–11). Such an instrumentalised view of gender equality is connected to wider objectives, particularly securing greater labour market deregulation. Gender inequality can be remedied by including women in the market. In an uncanny echo of Chant's argument (2012), McKinsey, quoted fulsomely in the SGI, rec-ommended a set of 'best practices' to increase the number of women in managerial positions by promoting workplace options such as flexible working and the encouragement of women to 'master the dominant codes' via networking (McKinsey & Company, 2007, pp. 20–21).

There is therefore a profound absence in the GAP and then recapitulated in the SGI: neither addresses the social reproductive content in the type of work they promote. This is strongly indicative of how gender has been subsumed to the EBRD's wider objectives. The GAP con-tained some recognition of how women's opportunities in the labour market are limited by their reproductive responsibilities:

> Indeed, many women had to choose between participating in the formal labour market and under-taking 'caring' jobs. The shrinking of public expenditures allocated to childcare or care for the elderly shifted the burden of child and elder care from the public sector onto the individual. These caring tasks mostly fell to women. Further, in the emerging private sector, employers engaged in discrimination against women with children far more than state employers did. Private sector employers have also been less willing to accommodate maternity leave. (EBRD, 2009, pp. 5–6)

Compare this with the SGI, where social reproduction is briefly mentioned but, again, markets have been assigned a key role in negotiating women's double burden,

> Reducing the amount of time women spend on unpaid work via improved infrastructure can free women's time and help them spend it more productively and efficiently, such as engaging in econ-omic activities that will eventually contribute to women's empowerment and closing of gender gaps in the labour market. (EBRD, 2012, p. 13)

In effect, gender is only relevant to the EBRD to the extent it can 'aid the purpose of the Bank' (EBRD, 2012, p. 7). The Bank's rationale for addressing gender inequality derives from a view of gender inequality as a form of market inefficiency where the exclusion of 50% of the popu-lation *is first and foremost a waste of resources*. EBRD President Suma Chakrabati summarises this appositely: 'The Bank recognises that gender equality is a fundamental aspect of a modern, well-functioning market in as much as it contributes to the efficient use of all resources' (EBRD, 2012, p. 5).

6. Conclusions

This article offers an examination of gender in relation to the EBRD within a wider schema of a neoliberal politics of market-building and development. Our particular focus was on post-communist transition, and while these issues discussed here have certain features unique to the ECE experience of development under the EBRD, we have also located our critique within a wider global framing of the gendered dimensions of neoliberalisation. The article proposes that analysis of the EBRD opens up multiple opportunities to engage the gendered reconfigurations affected by the relationship between neoliberalisation and social reproduction. Central to the article then is an understanding of neoliberalisation as a highly gendered, variegated, and socialised uneven process of capital expansion and circulation, simultaneously contriving mechanisms of development and underdevelopment. The discursive formation of post-communist transition reifies neoliberal institutions (especially the market) so as to close down the categories of political economy and deny their contradictory social and gendered constitution. The article is a first step in due consideration of the historicity, gendered composition, and contingency of reform.

A threefold series of strategies was employed by the EBRD case that led to the closure of policy flexibility: first, the initial construction of the market; second, institutional reforms necessitated by market failures; and third, the promotion of neoliberal competitiveness. From 2003 onwards the EBRD became increasingly cognisant of the importance of gender and acknowledges that it can and should work on gender. Stimulated by the opportunities presented by the global financial crisis, in 2008 the EBRD introduced the GAP and then the SGI in 2013. Both framed gender as a 'business case' that adds value to the EBRD's transition mandate. By representing and promoting an idea of women as individualistic consumers and entrepreneurs, while promoting reforms in social policy, the EBRD influenced the negotiation of how socially reproductive work is distributed among the state, market, and household scales to ensure social reproduction and the intensification of exploitation. The EBRD's gender equality agenda thus both disciplines workers to support the market and removes alternative options configuring a clear tension with social reproduction.

Acknowledgements

An earlier version of this article was presented at the Citizens, Civil Society and the Politics of 'Market Building' in Asia workshop, Lee Kuan Yew School of Public Policy, National University of Singapore, 23–24 February 2012. We are grateful to the workshop participants for their remarks. Huw Macartney and Bill Paterson offered thoughtful comments on earlier drafts. In addition we extend our appreciation to the editors of this special issue whose patience we have sorely tested. Finally, we would also like to thank the three referees for the journal. Their comments, advice, and critical (and in one case extensive) engagement with the initial submission have proved invaluable in helping us to revise the article.

Disclosure Statement

No potential conflict of interest was reported by the authors.

Funding

Sara Wallin acknowledges the support of the Economic and Social Research Council [grant number NE/J500215/I].

Notes

1   To achieve this we situate the article at the intersection of dialogue between feminist and critical IPE. In no way do we intend to suggest that feminist IPE is not critical. This is more a comment on the disciplinary constructions of particular forms of knowledge. We do this mindful that the restructuring of relations of production under neoliberalisation requires an examination of the changing relations of social reproduction and consumption, taking core concepts of gender seriously. We develop this further in the next section but for now see for example Waylen, 2006; Steans and Tepe, 2010; Murphy, 1996, Macartney and Shields, 2011.

2   Peterson enlarges on this:

> Corollary stereotypes of (devalued) femininity and (valued) masculinity map onto the gendered dichotomy of public and private that locates women and feminized work/activities in the family/household as unpaid, unskilled, reproductive and 'natural' – in contrast to (over)valorized masculine activities in the public sphere, cast as paid, skilled, productive and 'political'. (2003, p. 9)

3   For notable exceptions see Pollert (1999); Stenning and Hardy (2005); Kuehnast and Nechemias (2004); and Gal and Kligman (2000), but we would note that many of these interventions remain on the margins of the transitological orthodoxy.

4   This section draws on material from Shields (2015) which outlines the shifting internal discourse of policy at the EBRD in more depth than the necessarily truncated version here.

5   The outcome was that it was considered better to undertake all the changes concurrently and as rapidly as possible, because of the threat that the 'losers' would feel the social costs and uncertainties pushed through by the shocks of change a lot quicker than the 'winners' would experience success—a message that persists to this day (on ECE compare World Bank 2004; and EBRD 2007; and for contemporary developments in the Middle East/North Africa [MENA] see EBRD 2012).

6   This occurred roughly concurrently with the EBRD's burgeoning interest in Central Asia and the CIS. In an effort to remedy the 'poor investment climate and underdeveloped market economies', the EBRD had launched the 'Early Transition Countries Initiative' in 2004. This included advice and finance provided to SMEs while the EBRD 'engage[d] in policy dialogue to the purpose of institutional reform' (EBRD, 2004). The Women in Business programme constitutes an integral part of this, clearly indicating that governments need 'better realise the potential of women's contribution to economic development in emerging markets' (Greenberg, 2010, p. 2). The programme targets women-led enterprises and has executed 86 projects involving consultancy, guidance and subsidies for female entrepreneurs, 36 focus groups and workshops to develop business skills, alongside study tours and networking activities in Azerbaijan, Armenia, Georgia, Serbia, and the Southern Caucuses. (Greenberg, 2010, p. 3).

References

Appel, H. (2004). *A new capitalist order: Privatization and ideology in Russia and Eastern Europe*. Pittsburgh, PA: University of Pittsburgh Press.

Bacheva, F., Kochladze, M., & Dennis, S. (2006). *Boom time blues: Big oil's gender impact in Azerbajan, Georgia and Sakhalin*. Prague: CEE Bankwatch Network & Gender Action.

Bakker, I. (2003). Neoliberal governance and the reprivatisation of social reproduction: Social provisioning and shifting gender orders. In I. Bakker & S. Gill (Eds.), *Power, production and social reproduction* (pp. 66–82). Basingstoke: Palgrave Macmillan.

Bakker, I. (2007). Social reproduction and the constitution of a gendered political economy. *New Political Economy*, *12*(4), 541–556.

Bedford, K. (2009). Gender and institutional strengthening: The World Bank's policy record in Latin America. *Contemporary Politics*, *15*(2), 197–214.

Bergeron, S. (2004). The post-Washington consensus and economic representations of women in development at the World Bank. *International Feminist Journal of Politics*, *5*(3), 397–419.

Bezanson, K. (2006). *Gender, the state, and social reproduction: Household insecurity in neo-liberal times*. Toronto: University of Toronto Press.

Cammack, P. (2006). *The Politics of Global Competitiveness*. Institute for Global Studies, Manchester Metropolitan University, e-space Open Access Repository Papers in the Politics of Global Competitiveness No. 1.

Carroll, T. (2012). Working on, through and around the state: The deep marketisation of development in the Asia-Pacific. *Journal of Contemporary Asia*, *42*(3), 378–404.

Carroll, T., & Jarvis, D. S. L. (2015). The new politics of development: Citizens, civil society and the evolution of neo-liberal development policy. *Globalizations*, doi:10.1080/14747731.2015.1016301

Chant, S. (2012). The disappearing of "smart economics"? The world development report 2012 on gender equality: Some concerns about the preparatory process and the prospects for paradigm change. *Global Social Policy*, *12*(2), 198–218.

Dimitrova, A., & Pridham, G. (2004). International actors and democracy promotion in Central and Eastern Europe: The integration model and its limits. *Democratization*, *11*(5), 91–112.

EBRD. (1990). *Agreement establishing the European Bank for Reconstruction and Development*. London: Author.

EBRD. (1991). *A changing Europe: Annual review and financial report*. London: Author.

EBRD. (1995). *Transition report 1995: Investment and enterprise development*. London: Author.

EBRD. (1999). *Transition report 1999: Ten years of transition*. London: Author.

EBRD. (2004). *Early transition countries initiative*. Retrieved from http://www.ebrd.com/pages/about/where/

EBRD. (2007). *Annual report 2007*. London: Author.

EBRD. (2008a). *EBRD-NGO Newsletter*. September 2008. Retrieved from http://www.ebrd.com/downloads/cso/newsletter/0908.pdf

EBRD. (2008b). *Environmental and social policy 2008*. Retrieved from http://www.ebrd.com/pages/research/publications/policies/environmental.shtml

EBRD. (2009). *Annual report 2009*. London: Author.

EBRD. (2010a). *Gender Action Plan*. Retrieved from http://www.ebrd.com/pages/about/principles/gender/plan.shtml

EBRD. (2010b). *Gender toolkit: Matrix 1 issues relevant to performance requirements*. Available at www.ebrd.com/downloads/sector/gender/Gender_Toolkit_Matrix1.pdf.

EBRD. (2010c). *Transition report 2010: Recovery and reform*. London: Author.

EBRD. (2012). *EBRD launches first investments in emerging Arab democracies*. Retrieved from http://www.ebrd.com/english/pages/news/press/2012/120918.shtml.

EBRD. (2013). *Strategic gender initiative*. EBRD. Retrieved from http://www.ebrd.com/downloads/sector/gender/strategic-gender-initiative.pdf

Einhorn, B. (1993). *Cinderella goes to market: Citizenship, gender and women's movements in east Central Europe*. Oxford: Verso.

Elias, J. (2013). Davos woman to the rescue of global capitalism: Postfeminist politics and competitiveness promotion at the World Economic Forum. *International Political Sociology*, *7*(2), 152–169.

Elson, D. (2009). Gender equality and economic growth in the World Bank world development report 2006. *Feminist Economics*, *15*(3), 35–59.

Ferguson, L. (2010). Interrogating 'gender' in development policy and practice: The World Bank, tourism and microenterprise in Honduras. *International Feminist Journal of Politics*, *12*(1), 3–24.

Gal, S., & Kligman, G. (2000). *The politics of gender after socialism: A comparative-historical essay*. Princeton, NJ: Princeton University Press.

Gill, S. (1995). Globalisation, market civilisation, and disciplinary neoliberalism. *Millennium - Journal of International Studies*, *24*(3), 399–423.

Gore, C. (1996). Methodological nationalism and the misunderstanding of East Asian industrialisation. *European Journal of Development Research*, *8*(1), 77–122.

Greenberg, I. (2010). Women in business: BAS programme Armenia and Georgia, London: EBRD. Retrieved January 12, 2011, from http://www.ebrd.com/pages/research/publications/brochures/women.shtml

Griffin, P. (2009). *Gendering the World Bank*. Basingstoke: Palgrave.

Hawkesworth, M. (2010). Policy discourse as sanctioned ignorance: Theorizing the erasure of feminist knowledge. *Critical Policy Studies*, *3*(3–4), 268–289.

Jayasuriya, K. (2004). The new regulatory state and relational capacity. *Policy & Politics*, *32*(4), 487–501.

Kantola, J., & Squires, J. (2012). From state feminism to market feminism? *International Political Science Review*, *33*(4), 382–400.

Kuehnast, K., & Nechemias, C. (2004). *Post-soviet women encountering transition: Nation building, economic survival and civic activism*. Washington, DC: Woodrow Wilson Center Press.

Linden, R. H. (ed.) (2002). *Norms and nannies: The impact of international organizations on the Central and East European States*. Lanham, MD: Rowman & Littlefield.

Macartney, H., & Shields, S. (2011). Finding space in critical IPE: A scalar-relational approach. *Journal of International Relations and Development*, *14*(4), 375–383.

Marchand, M. H., & Runyan, A. (2000). *Gender and global restructuring: Sightings, sites and resistances*. Oxon: Routledge.

Marston, S. A. (2000). The social construction of scale. *Progress in Human Geography*, *24*(2), 219–242.

McKinsey & Company. (2007). Women matter: Gender diversity, a corporate performance driver. Retrieved from http://www.asx.com.au/documents/media/women_matter_english.pdf

Mitchell, D. (2001). The geography of injustice: Borders and the continuing immiseration of California agricultural labor in an era of 'free trade'. *Richmond Journal of Global Law and Business*, *2*, 145–166.

Molyneux, M. (1994). Women's rights and the international context: Some reflections on the post-communist states. *Millennium: Journal of International Studies*, *23*(2), 287–313.

Murphy, C. (1996). Seeing women, recognizing gender, recasting international relations. *International Organization*, *50*(3), 513–538.

O'Dwyer, C. (2005). Reforming regional governance in East Central Europe: Europeanization or domestic politics as usual? *East European Politics and Societies*, *19*(4), 219–243.

Peck, J., Theodore, N., & Brenner, N. (2010). Postneoliberalism and its malcontents. *Antipode*, *41*(S1), 94–116.

Peck, J., & Tickell, A. (2002). Neoliberalizing space. *Antipode*, *34*(3), 380–404.

Peterson, V. S. (2003). *A critical rewriting of global political economy: Integrating reproductive, productive and virtual economies*. London: Routledge.

Pollert, A. (1999). *Transformation at work in the new market economies of central Eastern Europe*. London: Sage.

Pradella, L. (2014). New developmentalism and the origins of methodological nationalism. *Competition & Change*, *18*(2), 180–193.

Rai, S. (2004). Gendering global governance. *International Feminist Journal of Politics*, *6*(4), 579–601.

Roberts, A. (2014). The political economy of 'Transnational Business Feminism': Problematizing the corporate-led gender equality agenda. *International Feminist Journal of Politics*. doi:10.1080/14616742.2013.849968

Roberts, A., & Soederberg, S. (2014). Politicizing debt and denaturalizing the 'New Normal'. *Critical Sociology*. doi:10.1177/0896920514528820

Schimmelfennig, F., & Sedelmeier, U. (2005). *The Europeanization of Central and Eastern Europe, Cornell studies in political economy*. Ithaca, NY: Cornell University Press.

Shields, S. (2012). *The international political economy of transition: Neoliberal social forces and Eastern Central Europe's transformation*. London: Routledge.

Shields, S. (2015). The European Bank for Reconstruction & Development (EBRD) as organic intellectual of neoliberal transition. In S. Park & J. Strand (Eds.), *Global Economic Governance and the Development Practices of the 'Other' Multilateral Development Banks*. London: Routledge.

Shields, S., Bruff, I., & Macartney, H. (2011). *Critical international political economy: Dialogue, debate and dissensus*. Basingstoke: Palgrave Macmillan.

Siemienska, R. (1996). Gendered perceptions: Women in the labour market in Poland. *Women's History Review*, *5*(4), 553–566.

Smith, A. (2002). Imagining geographies of the "new Europe": Geo-economic power and the new European architecture of integration. *Political Geography*, *21*(3), 647–670.

Steans, J., & Tepe, D. (2010). Introduction – Social reproduction in International Political Economy: Theoretical insights and international, transnational and local sitings. *Review of Interntaional Political Economy*, *17*(5), 807–815.

Stenning, A., & Hardy, J. (2005). Public sector reform and women's work in Poland: "Working for juice, coffee and cheap cosmetics!" *Gender, Work & Organization*, *12*(6), 503–526.

Stone, R. W. (2002). *Lending credibility: The International Monetary Fund and the post-communist transition*. Princeton, NJ: Princeton University Press.

Swyngedouw, E. (2000). Authoritarian governance, power, and the politics of rescaling. *Environment and Planning D: Society & Space*, *18*(1), 63–76.

Vachudova, M. A. (2005). *Europe undivided: Democracy, leverage, and integration after communism*. Oxford: Oxford University Press.

Wallin, S. (2012, September). *Gender and the EBRD's response to the global financial crisis*. Paper presented at the 8th Pan-European Conference on International Relations, Warsaw.

Waylen, G. (2006). You still don't understand: Why troubled engagements continue between feminists and (Critical) IPE. *Review of International Studies*, *32*(1), 145–164.

World Bank. (2004). *World Development Report 2005: A Better investment climate for everyone*. Washington, DC: World Bank and Oxford University Press.

Neoliberalising Cambodia: The Production of Capacity in Southeast Asia

JONATHON LOUTH

University of Adelaide, Adelaide, Australia

ABSTRACT   *The current Cambodian experience of re-integration into the regional and global economies reveals a process of violent neoliberal accumulation. Under the guise of clean, frictionless neoclassical economics, neoliberalism has reformulated the role of state and society. This article examines how notions of 'capacity' or 'capacity-building' reflect a commitment to this understanding of economic systems. Market building and deepening, which involve the expansion and regulation of 'capacities', are intrinsically tied to this commitment. It is argued that technocratic, administrative, and pseudo-scientific discursive acts are central to the production and reproduction of neoliberal agendas. This is evidenced by the complicit role of international financial institutions, the Cambodian state, civil society groups, and governance structures more generally. Yet the ever-deepening roll-out of neoliberalism in Cambodia is far from complete. What is evident is that this unique proto-regulatory environment reveals the poverty that surrounds the call to increase or develop 'capacity'. Importantly, the article concludes that the whole process of producing space and capacity is not a neat and linear set of affairs. The world of abstractions and dominant discursive acts cannot completely subsume the lived experience of the everyday.*

UNTAC, the United Nations Transitional Authority in Cambodia, made the point that its main goal in the post-conflict phase of the early 1990s was to 'build a new country' because of the absence of capacity (Hughes, 2011, p. 1503). This is an admirable aim, but one that is loaded with political sentiment: it alludes to a space of nothingness, so empty that capacity cannot even be conceived. Capacity, as this article will show, is about the realisable potential. The example above illustrates how predominately Western powers and organisations cannot conceive that some differing form of capacity might be realisable. Why? Because it does not align with dominant notions of space and what might usefully occur within it. Looking forward, this article is concerned with Cambodia's reintegration into the wider economy and the role that regional and international institutions play in helping Cambodia to 'realise' its potential. The current Cambodian experience reveals a process of violent neoliberal accumulation under the guise of clean and order-inducing economic presuppositions. Yet the whole process of producing space and capacity is not a neat and linear set of affairs—there is a roughness to everyday experience that is either ignored or made to fit, violently if need be. The article argues that capacity is not an *a priori* condition, but that it is a political and ideological construct that is produced as part of an expansionary capitalist logic. Stretching a Lefebvrian analysis beyond the dynamics of urbanisation, processes like market building, market deepening, and regional integration are shown to reproduce and reshape the 'realisable potential' of not just the emerging Cambodian market economy, but an emerging Cambodian market *society* (see Carroll & Jarvis, 2013, 2015).

What is highlighted is that the *naturalness* and legitimacy attached to this brave new regulated and surveillanced economic world is underpinned by an implicit neoclassical economic ontology. Moreover, it is a worldview that is premised on a frictionless and closed system understanding of the global political economy. These ideas inform practices that can be ascribed to the notion of the regulatory state. However, in the Cambodian context the attempt to apply regulatory frameworks, cloaked in the language of 'capacity', is in its infancy. The situation is one of a *proto-regulatory state*, within which the application of emerging administrative and bureaucratic procedures encounters a number of challenges. This includes the 'papering over' of difficulties and non-conforming practices, the overreliance upon the (international) non-government organisations (INGOs) sector as a proxy civil society, through to elite interests appropriating regulatory and managerial processes to continue and justify traditional power bases and to support regimes of accumulation (see Carroll & Jarvis, 2015). Of course, these endogenous challenges, while specific to the Cambodia setting, are shaped by exogenous factors; a list of influences that includes International Financial Institutions (IFIs), INGOs, foreign interests, and multinational corporations. The importance of the Cambodian case study is that it reveals the poverty of neoclassical economic underpinnings, particularly those elements that have been absorbed into neoliberal ideology and regulatory practices. The space, and the capacity to act within it, is clearly identifiable as a construct to suit particular interests.

The article proceeds in four stages. First, the concept of building capacity and state capacity is examined. The regulatory state is posited as a means to appreciate how 'capacity' is the realisable potential or a desired outcome within this emerging regulatory space. Second, Henri Lefebvre's work on the production of space is introduced. By augmenting his ideas, it is argued that capacity, as something that is thought to be realisable and desirable within space, is a *social* product. This makes clear how political and ideological imperatives drive our understanding of space. The important point is how a Newtonian-inspired Western scientific economic ontology drives technocratic, administrative, and pseudo-scientific discursive acts that define the dominant space. Third, the article shows how these neoliberal constructions of space and capacity are replicated and reproduced in Cambodia by IFIs, the state, civil society groups, right down to local communes. This incorporates market building and deepening agendas, but within this there lies spaces and possibilities (albeit limited) to resist. This feeds into the final point, with some (cautious) concluding remarks about the separation between the lived experience of daily life and the abstraction of 'capacity.' It is the sentiment that while space and concepts of capacity are dominated by neoclassical abstractions (and neoliberal applications), the moments of separation between the 'smooth' of the abstract and the 'rough' of the lived offer emancipatory potential.

Capacity as a Project

In a 2003 paper, Hang Chuon Naron, now the Cambodian Secretary of State at the Ministry of Economics and Finance, gave a glowing assessment of the country's gradual integration and financial reforms. In the paper, he plots Cambodia's move towards a market economy from the 1980s, which included reforms in the latter half of the decade that removed state domination of foreign trade and loosened laws around foreign investment. He highlighted how the post-Paris peace accords era of the 1990s was accompanied by a period of greater trade liberalisation and Cambodia's 'impressive strides in re-establishing political and economic stability and re-integrating itself into the international community' (Naron, 2003, p. 3). With respect to Cambodia's 1999 admission into the Association of Southeast Asian Nations (ASEAN), Naron (2003) continues the line of argument stressing the lengths to which the Government has gone to fulfil the requirements of membership. This has included the reduction in tariffs through to the aligning of laws governing trade, commerce, investment, and finance sectors. This is very much a tale that is still being told, with *The Wall Street Journal* recently reporting that the commencement of trading on Cambodia's Securities Exchange in 2012 should be seen as 'a symbol of Southeast Asia's emergence on global stage [*sic*]' (Hookway & Bellman, 2012). A decade after his original paper, Naron has continued his narrative of an economic revival, stating recently that economic growth is the solution to poverty (Heng, 2013). Yet the ideas behind the 'global stage' and the 'successful' liberalisation process speak to a wider programme of regional integration that lionises productive capacity and the financialisation of capitalist expansion. Post-conflict Cambodia is simply being absorbed and integrated into widening global markets and production networks. It is seen as a 'frontier market' (Chiou, 2012) that provides 'cheap labor and [a] strategic geographic location' (Murray, 2012, p. 80), with its attractiveness also highlighted due to the absence of capital controls, with foreign companies permitted to own 100% of enterprises within the country (Chiou, 2012; Murray, 2012). This is the context (and the boundaries) in which capacity is routinely referred to, conjuring notions of potential and, in many instances, a preferred and optimal space.

This raises a number of important questions: How is capacity 'created'? How is capacity recognised? And to what extent is capacity political? Current debates on Cambodia and poverty alleviation, to take one example, are centred on projects that claim to develop 'institutional and human capacity building in all sectors' (IMF, 2006, p. X) and are often linked to government-supported market solutions. The latter, in particular, looks to the capacity within markets to reduce poverty and improve living standards. This has seen the rapid development of sectors like garment manufacturing through to the explicit emphasis on earnings from foreign remittances (Elias & Louth, in press; Cross, 2015; Carroll & Jarvis, 2015). Elsewhere, NGOs spend inordinate amounts of time developing their 'capacity', particularly in relation to financial and development capacity, pursuing training and assessment in 'financial management capacity,' extending to notions around 'organisational structure, management and government capacity' (Pearson, 2011, p. 1039).[1] For IFIs capacity building is seen as much more than simply providing additional training. There is an emphasis on the improvement of governance with a focus on institutional and organisational structures. In the Cambodian case this has included recognition by the Asian Development Bank (ADB) that subnational entities need to address 'attitudinal and governance issues' (Niazi, 2011, p. 76);[2] an acknowledgment that IFIs are complicit in the scaling of capacity as a project 'all the way down'. In short, as Hameiri (2009) has argued, to 'build' capacity is a political project; it is about achieving particular criterion. This is true of INGOs as much as it is of IFIs: the Country Director of a large development agency noted that 'organisational capacity is the ability to be able to achieve what you've set out to do' (Action Aid Cambodia, Country Director, interviewed by author, Phnom Penh, Cambodia, 3 March 2014). The capacity project, if it could be deemed such a thing, impacts not only who are the winners and losers, who does or does not achieve, but the very 'conception of the political community and the status of the state that represents and governs it' (Hughes, 2011, p. 1503). This last point captures how capacity—the imagined and desired space of possibility and potentialities—is not just an objective measure or a level of attainment, but a product of particular practices that both frame and shape state and institutional structures that are themselves locked into the reproduction of those very spaces.

The place of the state in all of this is fundamental; developing state capacity is seen as a solution. For some, as Caroline Hughes has pointed out, the (neoliberal) concept of capacity and 'capacity building' was thought to be a means to overcome the post-Cold War 'New Barbarism' argument that particular societies and cultures were ill equipped to deal with the challenges of globalisation (Hughes, 2011, p. 1495). Yet even within this jaundiced view, the realising of capacity, as global markets and production networks expand, is intrinsically linked to the role of the state as a central if not compromised regulatory structure. Jayasuria (2005) pushes the concept of the regulatory state where 'the function of the state' moves 'from the direct allocation of social and material goods and resources to the provision of regulatory frameworks within the economic order' (p. 384). In this conception, state capacity is linked to an instrumental process of facilitating markets, while attempting to locate or emphasise a state's comparative advantage (and allows the move from 'state building' to 'capacity building') (see Jayasuria, 2004). The rise of the regulatory state has displaced the 'interventionist' state (Jarvis, 2012, p. 465), encouraging regimes of 'competitive benchmarking' where, in this case outlined here, developing states are assessed by their 'progress towards establishing conditions thought to be most conducive to the private sector' (Carroll, 2012b, pp. 384, 391).

The regulatory state represents a transformation; 'stateness' and the 'arena of society' (Nettl, 1968, p. 564) has become managerial and de-politicised. The focus becomes one of measures and attainment. To do poorly is due to a lack of capacity or weak capacity. To do well and to achieve or be able to achieve within the prescribed space is to have strong capacity (more often described in terms of 'good governance'). It is within this de-politicised environment that the shift to technocratic, procedural, and administrative oversight gives the appearance of the clean, legitimate, smooth, sustainable, and policy-driven focus on 'market operation, efficiency, and development' (Jarvis, 2012, p. 471). In this context, the state is, as Nettl (1968) proposed, a conceptual variable and not a fixed entity or vessel. It is a process of (social) production where capacity is abstracted in accordance with political and ideological imperatives. What is not acknowledged is the manner in which such abstractions represent an *intrinsic violence*. These abstractions, to turn to the work of Lefebvre (1991/1974), are not 'empty'; they speak to dominant ontological assumptions that inform how space and order are imagined. Lefebvre did not write with either neoliberalism or abstracted concepts of capacity in mind. His interests were specifically on urbanisation, cities, and spatial practice. However, his work on space and its production speak to it being constituted by and through particular social relations (Springer, 2010). Capacity, in this context, can be understood as part of a spatial project that is proceduralised and that belongs to a wider political economy debate of the role of constitutive actors, structures, and processes that are central to its production.

The Production of Capacity

The idea that capacity can be 'built' is a curious concept; there is an enthusiasm that if individuals are properly trained or institutions appropriately organised then good things will come. What must be recognised, however, is that those who seek to build capacity 'are not merely imparting knowledge, but intervening politically' (Hughes, 2011, p. 1499). Moreover, the whole process is tinged by ideological and pseudo-scientific assumptions; a process that largely encourages a more effective penetration of capital, supported by technocratic and bureaucratic procedural imperatives. This proceduralising of regulation results in prioritising the 'implementation of regulation rather than with the values that are pursued' (Black, 2000, p. 598; see also Jarvis, 2012). However, importantly, the 'technicization' of procedure is beholden to a worldview of neoliberal market logic, which, in turn, is beholden to a powerful abstract scientific understanding of 'how things work'. Black (2000), while critiquing a fairly rigid and closed account of autopoiesis, notes that '[p]rocedural law requires only(!) that the state understands the strategic structures of systems, "what makes them tick"'—regulative functions appeal to an objective idea of action and agency within space. This is the implicit ideological impetus: the space within which social, political, and economic systems reside and the potential capacity within that space can be harnessed, marketised, and regulated according to clear sets of rational, reductionist, and axiomatic principles. The following section debunks the meta-theoretical commitment that contributes to these foundational assumptions. It is argued that capacity is the *perceived* realisable potential within a *socially* produced space. This draws directly on the work of Lefebvre and the role neoclassical economics has played in the production of how space and what occurs within it is imagined. Important to this analysis is the role and centrality of 'traditional' science. From this reworking of Lefebvre's ideas, capacity, as applied to the rolling out and deepening of neoliberalism, is a spatial project that is intrinsic to determining the (often future) parameters within which social relations are reproduced.

The production of capacity is a reworking of Lefebvre's argument that space is produced and that it is not something we just fill up or that it exists independent of us (Lefebvre, 1991/1974). The concept that space is an objective and scientifically determinable notion is due to the absorption of Newtonian thought. It is through these influences that linear notions of determinacy have translated into the dimensionality of place that are often associated with fixed ideas of the state (or city, etc.). As 'substantive items' states can be understood as simply possessing a geometric and locatable dimensionality (Agnew, 2011; Harvey, 2003). Lefebvre (1976) overturned these notions, arguing that space 'has always been political and strategic' and that it is 'filled with ideologies' (pp. 30–31). Central to this process is the impact of science and the scientific method on how space is imagined. In pursuing this line of thought Lefebvre does not simply reproduce a Marxist orthodoxy of 'ontological prioritization of materiality over representations' (Wilson, 2011, p. 376). The 'veil of ideology' (Lefebvre, 1991/1974, p. 106) is implicit to the production of space and the consequent imagining of capacity. Any concept of 'stateness' (regulatory or otherwise) is immediately contingent upon the ontological claims that underpin it.

Lefebvre (1991/1974) created a conceptual triad to justify his claim that '(social) space is a (social) product' (p. 26); a dialectical construct that consists of three distinct notions of space. First is that of 'spatial practice' which is the *perceived space* where production (hierarchical organisation of the division of labour, society, etc.) and reproduction (bio-physiological relations—sexual relations, family, etc.) occur. It is here where the day-to-day of everyday lives takes place in the process producing and maintaining a level of cohesiveness (Lefebvre, 1991/1974). The second and crucial element to the triad is the notion of 'representations of space'. This is the *conceived space* where order and ideology are tied to discursive practices. This is the 'conceptualized space' of technocrats, professionals, scientists, and the techno-bureaucracy (Lefebvre, 1991/1974, 1976; Merrifield, 1993). Capacity—what is deemed poss-ible—is primarily produced within the confines of these discursive practices. Finally, there is 'representational space', which is the *lived space* of images and symbols (Lefebvre, 1991/ 1974, pp. 33, 39). This is the realm of culture, art, writing, and philosophy, an important yet dominated space that is distinguishable from, but, at the same time, a part of physical and social space (Merrifield, 1993). It is within this space that an emancipatory or politics of resist-ance might be realised, but the lived is too often dominated by the conceived.

The domination of the 'conceived' over the 'lived' relates to how capital dominates the pro-duction of space (Merrifield, 1993). Yet it is not just a case of the power of capital to create and sustain favourable production networks or to exert control over national economies, it relates to the representation and the production of an ontological position of a 'pure', scientific, and objec-tive space. In the same manner in which the town planner or architect appropriates scientific knowledge (Lefebvre, 1976, p. 30), so too do the planners and architects of government and inter-governmental institutions. Neoclassical economics has occupied, absorbed, and trans-mitted this scientific space. The policy process, as a matter of routine, appropriates and absorbs the resultant technocratic and scientific language. Moreover, 'the polycentric and multi-scaler' (Brenner & Theodore, 2002, p. 351) merging of neoliberalism to this process informs the wider appropriation through governance structures and civil society. It is the power of a scien-tific way of thinking, drawn from the triumph of Newtonianism, that has continued to restrict how space and knowledge are produced (see Urry, 2001). More on this is touched upon later in the article, both in terms of the historical root of the paradigm and in relation to particular economic assumptions, notably the use of gravity as an analogy. However, it is worth noting that the production of a 'pure' space and the interactions that occur within in it has not resulted in a universal or a singular notion of what neoliberalism is. What neoliberalism takes from econ-omic neoclassicism is not 'accuracy', but merely the (selective) *reassurances* of a scientific para-digm that parades the 'certainty' of 'abstract quasi-mathematical modelling' (Hay, 2004, p. 520). In essence, neoliberalism is a political ideology that adheres to (an often convenient) mix of con-victions of which a stated belief in the fundamentals of neoclassical economics forms the bedrock (see Brenner & Theodore, 2002). On the development of these foundational assump-tions it is the Chicago School that is routinely acknowledged, not just for its well-documented role in the development of neoliberalism, but also for its celebration of neoclassical economics as a 'core scientific theory' (Van Horn & Mirowski, 2009, p. 139). Yet contradictions, assump-tions, and variation are evident in the application of neoclassical economics, which has led some to claim that: 'Neoliberalism is to neoclassical economics as astrology is to astronomy. In both cases, it takes a lot of blind faith to go from one to the other' (Marangos, 2008, p. 238; Rodrik, 2002). Indeed, there is a convenient fiction at play, within which a closer inspection reveals a double movement. First, there are the ontological assumptions of a 'pure' scientific space within the neoclassical position and, second, the 'roll-out' of neoliberalism. Wider processes of marketisation and capacity building seek the authority of the first movement to provide legiti-macy to the ideological position of the second.

The expansion of this 'authoritative' ideological framework is what underpins *deep* market-isation and the building of markets. The rapid advance of neoliberalism since the 1970s, which has been accompanied by an 'exteriorization of economic flows and capacities' (Peck & Tickell, 2007, p. 30) and the move to a world market (see Cammack, 2012; Carroll & Jarvis, 2015), makes overtures to 'a universal and ahistorical conception of market primacy' (Tickell &

Peck, 2003, p. 168). This is despite the fact that neoliberalism is routinely 'enmeshed, blended, and imbricated with other forms of governance' (Peck & Tickell, 2007, p. 31). In essence, what has been normalised is the 'sanctity of the market' where technocratic discourse has displaced the political. This rigorous insertion and belief in instrumental rationality (Hay, 2004, p. 523) as belonging to the 'pure' conceived space is easily evidenced by examining the continual 'roll-out of new rounds of institutional and discursive practice' (Peck & Tickell, 2007, p. 35). The implications are far-reaching whereby 'regimes of compliance' set out the boundary conditions and the nature of the space within 'which market participants must conform' (Carroll & Jarvis, 2013, p.121; Carroll & Jarvis, 2015). The regulatory role of the state and society-at-large is further complicated as the public and the private become fused through ever-deepening and 'locked-in' patterns of consumption, production, regulation, and financialisation. This is a process that Carroll (2012b) refers to as 'deep marketization', which extends to current experiences of market building, and is the arena in which supposedly apolitical and instrumental market processes, functions, and expansion occurs 'on, through and around the state' (p. 384). The state becomes 'insulated from politics' (Carroll, 2012a, p. 355), while the proliferation of 'private authority to set standards, rules and construct rule based regimes' (Carroll & Jarvis, 2013, p.119; see also Carroll & Jarvis, 2015), represents the neoliberal appropriation of the conceived through a breadth of 'pure' (and discursive) practices that incorporate:

> transparency and accountability regimes governing various industry sectors, reciprocity and non-discrimination regimes in cross border investments, procurement standards, traceability and reporting regimes, customs and trade practices, regulatory shifts in modes of corporate governance (including corporate social responsibility), risk management and mitigation codes, and regimes of financialisation in relation to performance, reporting and accounting standards. (Carroll & Jarvis, 2013, p. 121)

The space within which we all act and live out our everyday lives is constrained by the discursive practices mentioned above, but a closer investigation of the historical and scientific roots of the *conceived space* is warranted. Understanding the 'first movement' of neoclassicism as 'pure' and scientific reveals the poverty and reliance that much of the social sciences places on an out-dated yet still influential scientific paradigm.

Space as an abstract notion is, more or less, assumed to be Newtonian. The predictive power that had been unleashed by Newton informed the development of the social sciences, the newly created fields of sociology, political *science,* and economics were particularly enamoured with the scientific and the magisterial influence of Newton (Louth, 2011). In more recent times, it is at the abstracted and conceived level where sway continues to hold; concepts from natural equilibrium, reductionism, gravitational attraction, and linear cause and effect continue to permeate across the social sciences. The boundaries of capacity are determined and produced in accordance with these abstractions. Within this there lies the much-documented path connecting positivism and economics. Beginning with Smithian analogies of a self-regulating and equilibrium finding 'invisible hand', an 'economic' understanding of social systems has developed over time (Louth, 2011). This has shaped how interactions are imagined to take place within abstract capitalist space, giving 'life' to the 'economic man' and the 'rational individual' (Grant, 2002, p. 125) as core constituents of economic systems. This *is* the inescapable meta-theoretical root of market rationalism and with it the consequent conceptualisation of market building. Constrained by paradigmatic parameters, space—and concepts of order and capacity within it—is enshrined by notions of universalism, linearity, and predictability. Conceptually, this provides the clean, homogeneous plane for the expansion of capitalist interests, shaping the domination of the *lived* and the (re)production of the perceived.

It is this reductionist and Newtonian-inspired economic thinking that provides the ballast to concepts of a 'weightless' economy, where financialisation and neoclassical frictionless notions of comparative markets drive adjustments in the global economy (Dunn, 2004). These *representations of space* produce an implicit acceptance that the economic world is akin to a natural process; what becomes evident is that the trail from neoclassical to neoliberal economic approaches stems from these Newtonian ideas. Turning to the work of Lefebvre (irrespective of his primary focus on urbanisation) not only renders this process visible, but also it helps to unpack the consequences of accepting an abstract closed system mentality as a means to explain the movement and domination of capital. As Charnock (2010) recognises, the work of Lefebvre speaks to an open Marxist perspective that is not restricted by a reductionist and closed system understanding of capitalism. Indeed, evident are explicit notions of emergent behaviour and self-organisation in the self-creation and self-production of humankind's involvement in the unrealised domination of the market. It is not a closed system of simple domination, but a scaled penetration into 'every aspect of everyday life' (Charnock, 2010, p. 1296). The regulatory state becomes an amorphous concept of bounded potentiality. These potentialities are influenced and shaped by political and ideological constraints; in essence the spatial practices and lived experiences are restricted according to an expansionary capitalist logic. However, there always remains a (limited) *capacity* for novel and emergent behaviour by those who constitute the state and civil society.

The shift to an open and nonlinear appreciation of how systems and the co-constituting referents within them interact provides not only an interesting understanding of elite and state practices, but also voice to the politics of everyday lives, whether in reference to complicit involvement or points of resistance.[3] Here there is a connection to Lefebvre's position that social space is a product of the 'dynamism' of '*all* matter and reality' (Merrifield, 1993, p. 517). Yet this self-organising dynamism does not equate to all spatial possibilities being explored. In actuality, the dynamism within any complex and open systems can be restrictive in that dominant social patterns and the discursive acts push out and make alternatives unviable or even 'unthinkable'.[4] The development of a (proto) regulatory state can be imagined in this context. As it reaches into the arena of society, the stateness it appeals to incorporates civil society as a part of the social relations that constitute the state (Jessop & Sum, 2006). For Lefebvre, this reflects how civil society is sandwiched between political and economic realms; filling the gaps created by the rolling out of neoliberalism, the consequence being that civil society simply becomes a part of the 'domain of the state' (Merrifield, 2006, p. 125). Likewise, it is not difficult to turn to Gramscian ideas that civil society is central to the 'production of hegemony' (Jessop & Sum, 2006, p. 161). In either instance, whether appealing to Gramsci or Lefebvre, civil society simply becomes one of the 'mechanisms of neoliberal localization' (Brenner & Theodore, 2002, pp. 368–372). All the various subsystems and microsystems constituted by the day-to-day interactions of everyday life normalise these power dynamics (see Jessop & Sum, 2006). As Springer (2010) argues in his excellent volume on Cambodia and its emerging neoliberal order, 'civil societies are simultaneously enmeshed in processes of capitalist usurpation and notions of statehood' (p. 37).

Operationalising Capacity and the Capacity to Resist

Quite simply, this dynamism and domination within civil society belongs to the same market-building processes that underscore the constant 're-making [of] social relations' in Southeast Asia (Cammack, 2012, p. 375). Civil society groups have emerged in this market building space as actors who facilitate a range of capacities. Consider the manner in which Cambodian NGOs seek to integrate into the 'capacity project'. Many indigenous NGOs have prioritised the development of 'book-keeping, English, computer skills, and organisational development' capacities at the expense of 'actually engaging in political activities on behalf of the poor' (Hughes, 2011, p. 1510), but the more significant point relates to how capacity projects are operationalised. Managerialism under the guise of new public management (Un & Hughes, 2011) is the vehicle for transferring bureaucratic and administrative forms of domination. However, no system, or state, or local experience is ever exactly the same. A 'friction' within each unique environment will come into play, illustrating the emergence of novelty and alternative niches. Managerialism in the Cambodian context 'is made to fit into existing patron client relationships' (Un & Hughes, 2011, p. 202), illustrating how the nature of interactions within the capitalist space has been altered and not completely dominated or homogenised. This gives a roughness to any attempt to build capacity, as the lived experiences of everyday lives, although dominated, can potentially play a self-determining role. Unfortunately, it largely plays to the advantage of more powerful groups who are seeking to secure or cement their domination, which means that, although cultural differences between sites of capitalist production show differentiation, cultural practices are often absorbed and then regurgitated via administrative, coercive, and discursive acts. To some extent tradition becomes bureaucratised and can be utilised as a form of domination and control (Hughes, 2006). Compounding the Cambodian situation and the possibility of resistance is the general weakness of civil society, as it is not easily differentiated from state interests and is dominated by (often) pre-existing patron–client relationships (Paling, 2012; Un, 2006). Indeed, NGOs have emerged as a proxy (and regulated) civil society within Cambodia (Springer, 2010; Un, 2006). This 'enmeshment' basically suits the interests of Cambodia's emerging transnational class. It is less an encroachment on or a redistributing of responsibilities to civil society, than it is the convenient development of a civil society that suits the interests of elites who are responding to the wider spatial practices of regional and international political economic regimes.

Immediately, the space within which any notion of capacity can be articulated is revealed as manifold in its dimensionality. The Cambodian state, for instance, remains important to assisting the expansion of capital. The state, while hollowed out (Su, 2012), provides not only a regulatory framework and the environment within which civil society operates, but it remains a site or a location for capital to be fixed. Garment manufacturing, rice production, and tourism, while radically altering geographies and space, rely upon the state to provide *an* order. Yet there is a tension in that the regulatory frameworks that support local industries are similarly tied to a long list of regional and global production and financial networks. The impact of this can be seen in the accommodations that are made to facilitate the expansion and building of markets—this is where deep marketisation and financialisation shift patterns of accumulation away from purely productive forms to the more abstract realm of finance (Carroll, 2012b). This is evident, for instance, with the aligning of laws and regulations to meet ASEAN integration and co-operative framework aims (see Hing, 2013). Overall, the process is emblematic of the neoliberal project of *rebuilding* the state as an entity that is transaction cost-focused, efficiency-minded, de-politicised with the aim of 'rolling out' and embedding 'market institutionalising processes' (Carroll, 2012a, pp. 354–355; see also Roberts, 2010). Yet, as has been argued, the development of a Cambodian market society that is watched over by the 'regulatory state' is far from complete and, at best, reference could be made to a proto-regulatory state. Traditional Khmer patronage systems remain influential (see Un, 2013; Un & Hughes, 2011), yet this emerging regulatory stateness, far from being a simple instrumental description, is an example of a spatial fix. Harvey (2003) captures the sentiment of how a scaling up of space replicates local, national, and regional fixes and fluidity whereby 'regional economies ... achieve a certain degree of structured coherence to production, distribution, exchange and consumption' (p. 102) but with the important implication that this breadth of scale incorporates 'the totality of productive forces and social relations' (Harvey, 2001, pp. 328–329). This coherence in the Southeast Asian environment is achieved via (the often violent) integration and transformation of local communities that encourage day-to-day spatial practices that conform to the new geographies of regionalism and regulatory states.

Of course, this process never remains fixed or determined (despite Newtonian assumptions). Harvey's (2003) focus on the tension between 'fixity and motion' (p. 101) recognises the tension between territorial configuration and the de-territorialisation tendencies of capital. The spatial fix is linked to capital accumulation and the consequent insatiable and expansive production of space. The 'fix' comes from the absorption and then the limitation of the productive space (Wilson, 2011). For instance, in post-conflict Cambodia the control of roads was a means to reconfigure and dominate space (Hughes, 2006). However, as the capacity within the space is exploited to its full potential a new 'crisis' emerges that must be overcome, leading to new forms of spatial transformation (Wilson, 2011). However, Wilson (2011) highlights, in his example of a regional development programme in southern Mexico, that contradictory spatial transformations can occur. Quoting Lefebvre, Wilson points out:

> ... that abstract representations of space cannot succeed in 'papering over all differences' (Lefebvre, 1991/1974, p. 55), as through the process of their implementation they are confronted by the materiality of the spatial practices and representational spaces that they have discursively erased, which constitute the grounds for resistance and transformative possibilities.

In Cambodia the reorganisation of geographic and economic space has produced resistance. Communities, civil society, and human rights organisations have attempted varying forms of resistance, ranging from land grabbing protests (LICADHO, 2010), anger at hydro-electric developments (Win, 2013) through to civil society groups and trade unions coming together to push for a living wage for garment manufacturing workers (People's Tribunal, 2012).[5] Indeed, public protest is on the increase in Cambodia with some 850 protest in the first half of 2014 (Titthara, 2014), giving the appearance that the 'papering over' is starting to become unstuck. Expanding on the examples above, garment manufactures have repeatedly gone on strike for better working conditions and opposition groups have protested the recent election results. The state has cracked down on these movements with the shooting of protesters and the gaoling of union and opposition leaders (see Sochua, 2014; Wight, 2014). Moreover, public protests are representative of a reclaiming of space; indeed, the emergence of social movements can be considered to be 'manifest expressions of deeper, broader, latent dissatisfactions' (Willner quoted in Springer, 2011, p. 46). Yet despite these important and intensifying movements there remains a relentlessness to neoliberal and spatial transformation. Solving these 'problems' has centred on the economic imperative of 'returning to business'. One of the first headlines to appear after the resolution between government and opposition parliamentarians declared: 'Deadlock end lifts business spirits' (Morton & de Carteret, 2014). The accompanying picture was of the front desk of the Cambodian Securities Exchange. This is indicative of not only the rapid—if sometimes problematic—integration into the emerging regional neoliberal order, but also of the further abstraction of this process and its separation from the everyday.

The recent announcements to list both the Sihanoukville Autonomous Port (Marks, 2011) and the Phnom Penh Autonomous Port (Kunmakara, 2012) on the Cambodian stock market is an example of the constant production of additional capacity that reshapes the everyday lives of people; and, in this case, the new capacity to be exploited is particularly abstracted from the reality of the day-to-day. Yet what needs to be remembered is that any 'fix', while a continuous and iterative process, is geographic and locatable, in addition to this, it refers to a 'fix' as release or a solution for any crises via 'a fresh round of accumulation' (Wilson, 2011, p. 376). This means that even as capital accumulation becomes increasingly financialised and is defined by a move to abstract immateriality, materiality remains: production has a location, labour has a location, financial centres have a location, and states remain as (or, in the case of Cambodia, are becoming) regulatory gatekeepers. What there is, however, is a constant spatial and temporal reorganisation according to the needs of growth and productive forces. Within all of this there is an intersection of regimes of accumulation and the endemic drive of capital to reconfigure and (re)produce the broader neoliberal project 'within geographically localized production systems' (Brenner, 1998, p. 463). To return to an earlier theme, both the state and civil society are central to producing the appropriate regulatory environment, whether it be the expansion of 'hard legal disciplines' (Cutler, 2006, p. 539), through to seemingly innocuous training manuals of civil society groups that seek to develop human or stakeholder capacities (see Network for Sustainable Hydropower Development in the Mekong Countries, 2013). The issue with this expansionary logic is that it either ignores, or attempts to smooth over, or is simply unable to recognise that contradictions and schisms arise through the subjugation of conformity in line with the *conceived* and abstract notion of how the world *is*, even if it produces conflicts with or exacerbates the lives of others elsewhere (i.e. the exploitation of labour or environmental degradation).

Unfortunately, as philosopher of science Kuhn (1962) pointed out, paradigms are defended even in the face of quite dramatic contradictions. The same is to be said of the conceived correctness of clean, simple, and linear spaces of abstracted economic models. Errors or contradictions are often ignored, with the simple frictionless model of capital flows and competitive equilibrium adapted and manipulated to effectively explain and justify spatial transformation (see Wilson, 2011). This is where pressure is brought to bear on each nested subsystem to conform and to help 'close the circuit' as part of the 'self-destructive twist, at the level of everyday life' (Lefebvre, 1984, p. 108). The state in both Gramscian and Lefebvrian constructions remains the predominant site (and product) of hegemonic struggle. Hegemony and the domination of the everyday is managed, consented to and, in some instances, coerced by the state (Lefebvre) and civil society (Gramsci) (Kipfer, 2008). Everyday life becomes regimented and dominated by a bureaucratic rationality. Indeed, life in Cambodia is increasingly showing signs of 'voluntary programmed self-regulation' so that it might fit into an imagined neoclassical 'closed circuit'; a process where everyday life becomes 'one perfect system obscured by the other systems that aim at systematizing thought and structuralizing action' (Lefebvre, 1984, p. 72). While this level of domination is some way off in Cambodia, coupled by the fact that emergence and novelty can *never* be completely subsumed, the weight (and violence) of the state, regional actors and the integration into the global political economy are central forces behind the drive to 'close the circuit'. Capacity has become the mantra of this spatial reckoning.

Scales of Influence: IFIs and Facilitating Capacity

Considering how space and capacity is produced allows for an ontological shift to occur. Space can be appreciated as a contested concept within which global spatialities are scaled and historicised (Amin, 2002). However, although multiple scales are evident and important to our understanding, capitalist space produces a discourse of simplistic geographic dimensionality. Place is absorbed and occurs within neoliberal space; these places, whether states, global cities, or industrial zones, are conceptualised as occupying or simply existing as important nodes within this space. The international economic system is articulated through our understanding and lived experience of global cities, financial centres, and bureaucratic practices (Lefebvre, 1991/ 1974). Our urban spaces and their interconnections are defined by business networks and they have become the loci for centralised neoliberal decision-making (see Lefebvre, 1976). Of course, for the Cambodian example it is not just about easy-to-describe de-politicised business networks. The 'papering over' of the roughness is far from complete. Elite practices ensure that traditional patron–client relationships continue to dominate everyday politics. Indeed, patron–clientelism is pervasive through an alternative complex system of intersecting, nested, competitive, and multiple networks (see Un, 2006). Further to this, patron–clientelism has become embedded and sustained post-1993 via the development of political institutions and so-called democratic consolidation (Un, 2006). Add to this a weak civil society, elites 'have co-opted, transformed, and rearticulated neoliberal reforms' to produce a 'distinctly Cambodian' blended form of neoliberalism (Springer, 2010, p. 144). However, the radical transformation of everyday life in Cambodia has commenced apace; the *lived* and *perceived* is being transformed in accordance with these new amalgamated dominant *representations of space*, revealing how abstract neoliberal logic becomes the basis for ordering and understanding the world around. Space is colonised under the guise of (Newtonian) neoclassical economics and it is performed through the application of policy (Wilson, 2011). IFIs seek to enhance, enable, and create capacity in accordance with contestable yet often quite irrepressible *representations of space*. What could be, 'financial *potential*,' for instance, is 'an ideologico-scientific name for the possible' (Lefebvre, 2009/1975, p. 113).

Returning to the Cambodian example, in February 2012, I interviewed the in-country resident representative of the IMF. The resident representative was quick to point out that the IMF's role in Cambodia is to act as an advocate for 'macroeconomic and financial stability' and is there to simply offer 'technical assistance to the central bank'. This is inclusive of 'how to develop monetary policy' and appropriate reporting and accountancy methods (IMF resident representative, interviewed by author, Phnom Penh, Cambodia, 8 February 2012). The resident representative was firm in his position that the IMF in Cambodia acts 'purely in an advisory role'. He was very clear that 'there is no programme ... there are no conditions' and what exists in Cambodia is a 'very open dialogue', which is all about 'good surveillance' guided by 'pleasant interaction'. The answers were wholly consistent with what one would expect from an in-country IMF resident representative, but it is illustrative of an imagined 'natural' order. Effective surveillance and technical assistance is attached to a *conceived* and appropriate way of managing an economy. This assistance is tied to concepts and language like 'best practice', 'comparative advantage', 'competitiveness', and 'capacity building'. The IMF is simply helping Cambodia to do the best it can to create and support a robust and competitive economy. The IMF is simply there, as was confirmed by the most senior in-country officer, to help improve the 'capacity' of the Cambodian economy (IMF resident representative, interviewed by author, Phnom Penh, Cambodia, 8 February 2012). However, as has been clearly articulated, the concept of capacity—particularly when applied as an instrumental term—reveals the nature of *conceived representations of space* that are produced via scientific and technocratic discursive acts. Capacity conjures the potential and, in many instances, an optimal space. Capacity, then, is about the unrealised, the untapped, or the inefficiently explored or exploited within a socially produced neoliberal space.

The fixation with 'capacity' as a term and, by implication, a discursive pseudo-scientific act is significant. In a 61-page glossy ADB report celebrating 20 years of ADB involvement in

Cambodia, the word capacity appears on 37 occasions; and nearly always alongside words like: building, institutional, development, community, and 'public financial management' (ADB, 2012). The World Bank (2012) is also enthusiastic when it comes to 'building', 'enhancing', 'strengthening', and 'developing' capacity in a similarly glossy report (32 mentions over 40 pages) entitled 'Matching Aspirations: Skills for Implementing Cambodia's Growth Strategy'. The IMF and the World Bank are in step and focused on 'strengthening of capacity' (IMF, 2011). The IMF (2012, 2013) in recent reports has placed an emphasis on 'supervisory capacity'. Moreover, space is a concept continually alluded to by the IMF. The same reports noted a number of key issues, two of which are 'fiscal space' and 'financial deepening', arguing fiscal space needs to be 'rebuilt' and 'safeguarded' (IMF, 2012, p. 9, 2013, pp. 11, 14). In a not too dissimilar fashion to the claim that Cambodia needed to be rebuilt during the 1990s post-conflict phase, it is about 'restoring and expanding fiscal space' (World Bank, 2011, p. 1). The IMF (2012)—in its cooperative capacity—has sought to encourage trade liberalisation, reformed revenue collection, and the development of 'new institutional arrangements' to monitor public–private partnerships to allow, in part, for transparent 'comparative bidding and dispute resolution mechanisms' (pp. 9–10). Financial deepening has been encouraged for a number of reasons, including increasing the 'supervisory capacity' of the National Bank of Cambodia (IMF, 2012, 12). This is considered especially important for the successful maintenance of the recently launched Cambodian Securities Exchange—a future space that is currently being produced and colonised simultaneously, and a space that radically abstracts the 'frictionless' economy from the real and the lived (especially as it will be a means to access 'domestic capital markets' for the first time (World Bank, 2011, p. 13)).

The discursive acts go further. It is not simply just a reference to the word 'capacity,' but the idea of what is possible and the forces that govern relations within the (frictionless) space. The nature of this spatiality is encapsulated in a 2012 ADB report on deepening ASEAN. The report appealed to and promoted a 'gravity effect' as a means to understand the interconnections among emerging financial markets (Gochoco-Bautista & Remolona, 2012). The 'gravity effect' is a Newtonian economics *metaphor* that represents the intensity of trade, particularly when looking at trade liberalisation regimes. Expectations of intensity—whether lower or higher— are explained in *relation* to the effect of gravitational pull (Curtis, 2002). Within the ADB metaphor the already quite abstract notion of 'cross border equity flows' are claimed to occur in the same manner as goods transactions, with distance acting as a 'proxy for information costs' (Gochoco-Bautista & Remolona, 2012, p. 30). This sits comfortably with IMF (2012) arguments that 'real' trade in Cambodia will benefit from its geographic closeness 'to the world's fastest growing markets, and economic rebalancing in Asia' will inform its integration 'into the Asian supply chain' (p. 15). Home biases are seen to exist, and are *explicitly* explained by the gravitational pull argument. The ADB identifies other points of gravitational attraction: bank lending, for instance (Gochoco-Bautista & Remolona, 2012). However, a gravity effect could not be a more Newtonian reference point. It can be visualised as a mechanistic model of the solar system where the authority of celestial mechanics of an out-dated scientific paradigm is transmitted and the movement of the sun, planets, and moons is equated to interrelations among emerging regional economies. Within this clean and neat system the relation between each atomised entity can be spaced according to their 'mass' and then put into motion according to the conditions found in a precise and absolute Newtonian space. As a metaphor it goes further referring to 'frictionless trade' (there is no friction in space) and attempts to establish a relationship between a notion of equilibrium and mass (mass being volume of trade) (Deardorff, 1998, p. 12).

Yet, friction—the messy world of politics—is always and forever inescapable, and the 'production, realization and distribution of surplus value' will always be located in very real *places* (Merrifield, 1993, pp. 521–522). Take as an example land grabbing and the general selling-off of land in Cambodia. The full extent is unclear, but the figure is somewhere between 22% and 40% of the country now being held in foreign hands, with much of the land has been sold off to Chinese and Vietnamese investors (Levy & Scott-Clark, 2008; Murray, 2012; Sovachana, 2013). In the Chinese case, largely led by Yunnan province, this is reflective of emerging accumulation and regionalisation regimes into the greater Mekong sub-region (Su, 2012). In the case of the Vietnamese it represents links to wider processes of capitalist expansion, particularly in relation to assistance received from the International Finance Corporation (Hodal & Kelly, 2013). In both cases they are processes that have been facilitated through neopatrimonial linkages (see Un & So, 2011) that have taken advantage of Cambodia's 2001 Land Law; a law that has been utilised to evict poor people from their land (Sochua & Wikström, 2012). In both instances the emerging neoliberal framework legitimises dispossession. Indeed, it is accumulation via a distinctive Cambodian neoliberalism (Springer, 2011)—a proto-regulatory environment with Cambodian characteristics. This is a capitalist 'spatial reckoning' that normalises and *produces* a real estate market (Lefebvre, 1976); geographical space can be designated, bought and sold. This is neither a frictionless process nor is it a metaphorical world of gravitational attraction; it is an arena of *intrinsic violence* where space and capacity are realised and constructed in very real terms. The coercive practices of land grabbing through to the instituting of development practices and reform packages by IFIs are an expression of violent accumulation that should not be seen as localised practices that simply sit 'within' wider patterns of hegemonic consent (Grovogui & Leonard, 2008). Points of resistance can and do occur, but unfortunately such groups are often seen to be standing in the way of the natural and unstoppable forces of a capitalist 'order of things'. The worlds of global production networks, regionalism, state capacity, local government and everyday lives exist in a dynamic tension, but, ultimately, capacities of what can be or should be done exude an economic ontology that acts as the bedrock for the neoliberal reconfiguration of Cambodian communities. Importantly, this is not simply a hierarchical top-down process, certainly the domination is driven by downward pressure, but the production and acceptance of the *nature* of the spaces is constituted and reinforced by all levels. But there remains significant differentiation—scale and dimensionality allow for niche spaces and novelty to emerge. This means that despite commonalities the Cambodian experience will be different from that being experienced in other emerging economies and the place of everyday political economy is where, for academic disciplines, hierarchical divisions of scale can be subsumed and, for the lived, a politics of resistance can be imagined.

Concluding Remarks: Everyday Lives and the Repressive Confines of Capacity

The recent turn towards the study of the international political economy of the everyday has sought to illustrate how everyday lives do not merely exist within states, but are participants (willing or not) in wider economic practices. Everyday lives co-constitute the multi-scaler dimensionality of the global political economy. As forms of spatial practices the '[h]ow, what, and with whom we spend, save, invest, buy and produce in our ordinary lives shapes markets and the manner in which states intervene' (Hobson & Seabrooke, 2006, pp. 3–4, 16). We are all a part of this process and contribute to the spatial practices of day-to-day activity, but this domain of *perceived* space, as has been shown, has been constrained and disciplined by the '*abstract* and conceived space' of capitalist domination (Merrifield, 1993, p. 525). It is within this socially produced space that daily life is transformed so as to meet the imperatives and patterns derived from a capitalist logic (Davies, 2006). However, this article has argued that this process is far from complete in Cambodia. Indeed, the transformation occurring in Cambodia offers an insight into the messy application of a neoliberal regulatory environment. It illustrates the scaled and spatial complicity from a range of actors: IFIs, the Cambodian state, NGOs, civil society, right down to the commune level. Cambodia's experience of neoliberal transformation via 'microregulatory interventions', from forced evictions to union crackdowns (Springer, 2009, p. 142), is evidence of how space is (violently) reshaped, constraining, and altering the lives of Cambodians, to meet the needs of penetrative neoliberal agendas. As Lefebvre notes, there is a 'violence that is intrinsic to abstraction' (Lefebvre, 1991/1974, p. 289). Quite evidently, the capacity for individuals to act becomes relational to the 'repressive "confines"' (Hobson & Seabrooke, 2006, p. 15) of the dominant social space.

The process if far from neat and simple: a frictionless Newtonian concept of space may well inform regulatory frameworks or the nature of land ownership, but the outcomes of this process are neither clear nor entirely predictable. Open and nonlinear intersecting systems will rarely conform to reductionist logic. Yet despite the fact that most examples illustrate how the lived is subsumed or forced to adapt, it offers the glimmer of potential and of alternative spaces and capacities. So long as it is realisable that the rough of the lived can never entirely conform to the smooth of the abstract, the space in-between is where points of resistance can emerge. To find reprieve or to consider alternatives then the *lived space* of culture, art, and ideas needs to exploit the schism and unevenness that the confines of the technocratic *representations of space* cannot smooth over. Lifeworlds can be reformulated and reshaped, but the uniformity of a frictionless Newtonian environment cannot subsume everything: contradictions and schism will arise that will need to be dealt with. The lived is very much a dominated space, but within it, because of the separation between the abstract and the lived, there lies this alternative capacity for novelty and emancipatory ideas. Lefebvre (1991/1974) argued that this is the space of symbols and images and that it 'conceals more than it reveals' (p. 32), but he also maintained 'that there are no new ideas without a utopia' (Lefebvre, 1976, p. 35), a thought that indicates that the socially produced 'reality', the expansion and grind of capitalist domination could be overcome or, at the very least, mediated. As Davies (2006) eloquently expressed, '[t]he everyday is misery and power, a burden and a resource, the programming of social demands and the possibility for social command'. (p. 232). The emergence of genuine indigenous counter-capitalist political and moral common-sense (Grovogui & Leonard, 2008) may well be a long way off, but for any counter-hegemonic movement to occur there must be a capacity to produce knowledge and ideas that can inform the development of an alternative common-sense (Gill & Law, 1989). It is these points above that require further exploration and research; the Cambodian proto-regulatory environment—an incomplete and often compromised form—is a contestable representation of space within which the capacity for a meaningful politics of resistance might lie.

This article has shown that the siren call of capacity is a discursive act that is (often unknowingly) underpinned by a Newtonian mindset of abstracted neoclassical frictionless movement and spatial transformations. The resultant economic ontology is central to the justification of the neoliberal agenda of IFIs, regulatory states, civil society groups, and the majority of governance structures that seek to reshape or integrate communities, economies, institutions, and political and social behaviour across multiple scales. The current Cambodian experience reveals the process of violent neoliberal accumulation in accordance with these sanitised and orderly principles from a range of international organisations and IFIs; principles that are readily adopted by the Cambodian state, operating in a more opportunistic as opposed to an abstracted regulatory function. Importantly, what has also been shown is that this whole process of producing space and capacity is not a neat and linear set of affairs. It is a multi-scaler process, where the international, national, local, and individual worlds overlap and interact to co-constitute the production of space. Within that the limitations of the Newtonian-inspired economic ontology is revealed. The abstract cannot completely subsume the lived experience. Even within the most repressive confines there is an opportunity to resist and to consider alternatives.

Acknowledgement

I express my thanks to Darryl Jarvis and Toby Carroll for their patience and insightful comments. Earlier versions of article also benefited from comments from Stuart Shields and Steven C. Hobden. I am also indebted to the helpful comments from two anonymous referees. I am also grateful for the keen proof-editing skills of Mary Hajistassi and Katherine Harrison. Usual caveat applies and responsibility for any errors or misinformation is mine alone.

Disclosure Statement

No potential conflict of interest was reported by the author.

Notes

1   In an interview with the author (a Cambodian-based former NGO director and now a learning facilitator consultant) expanded upon this definition describing it in instrumental terms as a range of context specific competencies include 'a combination of some really hard abilities and skills and ... soft skills [like] communications, relationships, negotiation skills, problem solving skills, analytical skills, learning skills, all of those things that are very, very hard to pin down' (Jenny Pearson, interviewed by author, Phnom Penh, Cambodia, 27 February 2014).
2   The decentralisation and deconcentration programme outlined in this document is the embodiment of the reproduction and cascaded effects of neoliberal regulatory processes. The document outlines governance and managerial process and procedure right down to the commune level (see Niazi, 2011). For an excellent account on the historical development of communes and local governance in Cambodia, see Sedara and Öjendal (2009).
3   An overlooked area of resistance within Cambodia—occurring within *representational space*—is the growth of artists' collectives and organisations. These emerging and critical groups run counter to the dominant discourse of a lack of indigenous capacity or critical ability. The Bophana center (http://bophana.org/en/) is a notable example, although it receives considerable support from Western NGOs and governments. More impressive are the growing movements within the White Building. The White Building was constructed as part of a modernisation and public housing programme in the 1960s (pre-Khmer Rouge) to deal with the rapid urbanisation of Phnom Penh. The building is located in a central and much desired location and is receiving attention from the Government (and developers). It is perceived (and is represented) as a slum, yet 'the White Building is one of the city's most vibrant communities, housing more than 2500 residents, including classical dancers, master musicians, skilled craftspeople, cultural workers, civil servants, and street vendors.' (http://www. whitebuilding.org/en). There are multiple arts and community-based movements emerging from within the building (field notes, 2014).
4   The references to nonlinearity, self-organisation, open systems, and emergence refer to lessons drawn from complexity theory. This area of study challenges the meta-theoretical dominance of traditional Newtonian (and Cartesian) thought (See Louth, 2011 and, in reference to Cambodia, Louth, 2014).
5   From 5–8 February 2012 the People's Tribunal on Living Wage as a fundamental right of Cambodian Garment Manufacturers organised by Asia Floor Wage—Cambodia (AFW-C) took place. I attended the press conference in Phnom Penh, Cambodia where the petition of the first People's Tribunal was released. The AFW-C consists of the following civil society organisations: Cambodia Confederation of Trade Unions; Cambodia Labour Confederation, Community Legal Education Center, Cambodia National Confederation, Cambodia Women

Movement Organization, National Union Alliance Chamber of Cambodia, Cambodian Confederation Unions, Cambodia Worker Center for Development, and the American Center for International Labor Solidarity.

References

Asian Development Bank. (2012). 20 year anniversary 1992–2012. *The Asian Development Bank in Cambodia: From rehabilitation to inclusive growth*. Phnom Penh: Author.

Agnew, J. A. (2011). Space and place. In J. A. Agnew & D. N. Livingstone (Eds.), *The SAGE handbook of geographical knowledge* (pp. 316–330). London: Sage.

Amin, A. (2002). Spatialities of globalisation. *Environment and Planning A, 34*, 385–399.

Black, J. (2000). Proceduralizing regulation: Part 1. *Oxford Journal of Legal Studies, 20*(4), 597–614.

Brenner, N. (1998). Between fixity and motion: Accumulation, territorial organization, and the historical geography of spatial scales. *Environment and Planning D: Society and Space, 16*(4), 459–481.

Brenner, N., & Theodore, N. (2002). Cities and geographies of "actually existing neoliberalism." *Antipode, 34*(3), 349–379.

Cammack, P. (2012). Risk, social protection and the world market. *Journal of Contemporary Asia, 42*(3), 359–377.

Carroll, T. (2012a). Neo-liberal development policy in Asia beyond the post-Washington consensus. *Journal of Contemporary Asia, 42*(3), 350–358.

Carroll, T. (2012b). Working on, through and around the state: The deep marketisation of development in the Asia-Pacific. *Journal of Contemporary Asia, 42*(3), 378–404.

Carroll, T., & Jarvis, D. S. L. (2013). Market building in Asia: Standards setting, policy diffusion, and the globalization of market norms. *Journal of Asian Public Policy, 6*(2), 117–118.

Carroll, T., & Jarvis, D. S. L. (2015). The new politics of development: Citizens, civil society and the evolution of neo-liberal development policy. *Globalisations*, doi:10.1080/14747731.2015.1016301

Charnock, G. (2010). Challenging new state spatialities: The open Marxism of Henri Lefebvre. *Antipode, 42*(5), 1279–1303.

Chiou, P. (2012, May 11). *Challenges of new Cambodia stock exchange*. CNN. Retrieved from http://edition.cnn.com/2012/05/10/business/cambodia-stock-exchange/index.html

Cross, H. (2015). Finance, development and remittances: The extending scale of accumulation in migrant labour regimes. *Globalizations*, doi:10.1080/14747731.2015.1016302

Curtis, J. (2002, November 11–12). *Multilateralism in a regionalizing world: NAFTA, FTAA, APEC and all that*. Paper presented to developing patterns of regional trading arrangements in the Asia-Pacific region: Issues and implications workshop, Vancouver.

Cutler, A. C. (2006). Gramsci, law and the culture of global capitalism. *Critical Review of International and Social Political Philosophy, 8*(4), 527–542.

Davies, M. (2006). Everyday life in the global political economy. In M. de Goede (Ed.), *International political economy and poststructural politics* (pp. 219–237). Houndsmill: Palgrave Macmillan.

Deardorff, A.V. (1998). Determinants of bilateral trade: Does gravity work in a neoclassical world? In J. A. Frankel (Ed.) *The regionalization of the world economy* (pp. 7–22). Chicago, IL: University of Chicago Press.

Dunn, B. (2004). *Global restructuring and the power of labour*. Houndsmill: Palgrave Macmillan.

Elias, J., & Louth, J. (in press). Regional disputes over the transnationalisation of domestic labour: Malaysia's 'maid shortage' and foreign relations with Indonesia and Cambodia. In J. Elias & L. Rethel (Eds.), *The everyday political economy of Southeast Asia: economic cultures and global flows*.

Gill, S. R., & Law, D. (1989). Global hegemony and the structural power of capital. *International Studies Quarterly, 33*(4), 475–499.

Gochoco-Bautista, M. S., & Remolona, E. M. (2012). *Going regional: How to deepen ASEAN's financial markets* (ADB Economics Working Paper Series Report No. 300). Manila: Asian Development Bank.

Grant, R. W. (2002). The ethics of incentives: Historical origins and contemporary understandings. *Economics and Philosophy, 18*(1), 111–139.

Grovogui, S. N., & Leonard, L. (2008). Uncivil society: Interrogations at the margins of neo-Gramscian theory. In A. J. Ayers (Ed.), *Gramsci, political economy, and international relations theory: Modern princes and naked emperors* (pp. 169–188). Houndsmill: Palgrave Macmillan.

Hameiri, S. (2009). Capacity and its fallacies: International state building as state transformation. *Millennium: Journal of International Studies, 38*(1), 55–81.

Harvey, D. (2001). *Spaces of capital: Toward a critical geography*. New York: Routledge.

Harvey, D. (2003). *The new imperialism*. Oxford: Oxford University Press.

Hay, C. (2004). The normalalizing role of rationalist assumptions in the institutional embedding of neoliberalism. *Economy and Society*, *33*(4), 500–527.

Heng, C. L. (2013, April 10). Cambodia's economic growth will help poverty reduction. *The Southeast Asia Weekly*. Retrieved from http://www.thesoutheastasiaweekly.com/?p=5978

Hing, V. (2013). *Leveraging trade for economic growth in Cambodia* (CDRI working paper series no. 81). Phnom Penh, Cambodia: Cambodian development resource institute (CDRI).

Hobson, J. M., & Seabrooke, L. (2006). *The case for an everyday international political economy* (Working paper no. 26). Copenhagen: International center for business and politics, Copenhagen Business School.

Hodal, K., & Kelly, C. (2013, May 13). Deutsche bank and IFC accused of bankrolling Vietnam firms' land grabs. *The Guardian*. Retrieved from http://www.theguardian.com/world/2013/may/13/deutsche-bank-ifc-bankroll-vietnam-cambodia-laos

Hookway, J., & Bellman, E. (2012, April 18). Cambodia joins stocks party. *Wall Street Journal*. Retrieved from http://online.wsj.com/article/SB10001424052702304331204577351551608365784.html#articleTabs%3Darticle

Hughes, C. (2006). The politics of gifts: Traditions and regimentation in contemporary Cambodia. *Journal of South East Asian Studies*, *37*(3), 469–489.

Hughes, C. (2011). The politics of knowledge: Ethnicity, capacity and return in post-conflict reconstruction policy. *Review of International Studies*, *37*(4), 1493–1514.

IMF. (2006). *Cambodia: poverty reduction strategy paper* (IMF Country Report. No. 06/266). Washington, DC: Author.

IMF. (2011) *IMF mission concludes the 2011 article IV consultation discussions with Cambodia*. Press Release No. 11/447, December 7.

IMF. (2012). *Cambodia 2011 article IV consultation* (IMF Country Report. No. 12/46). Washington, DC: Author.

IMF. (2013). *Cambodia 2012 article IV consultation* (IMF Country Report. No. 13/2). Washington, DC: Author.

Jarvis, D. S. L. (2012). The regulatory state in developing countries: Can it exist and do we want it? The case of the Indonesian power sector. *Journal of Contemporary Asia*, *42*(3), 464–492.

Jayasuria, K. (2004). The new regulatory state and relational capacity. *Policy & Politics*, *32*(4), 487–501.

Jayasuria, K. (2005). Beyond institutional fetishism: From the developmental to the regulatory state. *New Political Economy*, *10*(3), 381–387.

Jessop, B., & Sum, N. (2006). Towards a cultural international political economy: Poststructualism and the Italian school. In M. de Goede (Ed.), *International political economy and poststructural politics* (pp. 157–176). Houndsmill: Palgrave Macmillan.

Kipfer, S. (2008). How Lefebvre urbanized Gramsci: Hegemony, everyday life, and difference. In K. Goonewardena, S. Kipfer, R. Milgram, & C. Schmid (Eds.), *Space, difference, everyday life: Reading Henri Lefebvre* (pp. 193–211). New York: Routledge.

Kuhn, T. (1962). *The structure of scientific revolutions. International encyclopaedia of unified science*, Vol. 2(2). Chicago, IL: University of Chicago Press.

Kunmakara, M. (2012, July 31). Phnom Penh autonomous port pushes for IPO. *Phnom Penh Post*.

Lefebvre, H. (1976). Reflections on the politics of space. *Antipode*, *8*(2), 30–37.

Lefebvre, H. (1984). *Everyday life in the modern world*. London: Continuum.

Lefebvre, H. (1991/1974). *The production of space* (D. Nicholson-Smith, trans.). Maldon: Blackwell.

Lefebvre, H. (2009/1975). The state in the modern world. In N. Brenner & S. Elden (Eds.), *State, space, world: Selected essays* (pp. 124–137). Minneapolis: University of Minnesota Press.

Levy, S., & Scott Clark, C. (2008, April 26). Country for sale. *The Guardian*. Retrieved from http://www.guardian.co.uk/world/2008/apr/26/cambodia

LICADHO (Cambodian League for the Promotion and Defense of Human Rights). (2010). *Eviction and land grabbing surges across Cambodia*. Retrieved from http://www.licadho-cambodia.org/printnews.php?id=109

Louth, J. (2011). From Newton to Newtonianism: Reductionism and the development of the social sciences. *Emergence: Complexity and Organization*, *13*(4), 63–83.

Louth, J. (2014). Complexity, capacity and Cambodia: The neoliberalisation of space and scale. In P. Taylor & P. Wagg (Eds.), *Work and society* (pp. 196–218). Chester: University of Chester Press.

Marangos, J. (2008). The evolution of the anti-Washington consensus debate: From 'post-Washington consensus' to 'after the Washington consensus'. *Competition and Change*, *12*(3), 227–244.

Marks, S. (2011, July 10). Shares needed as Cambodia gets a stock exchange. *New York Times*. Retrieved from http://www.nytimes.com/2011/07/11/business/global/shares-needed-as-cambodia-gets-a-stock-exchange.html?pagewanted=all

Merrifield, A. (1993). Place and space: A Lefebvrian reconciliation. *Transactions of the Institute of British Geographers*, *18*(4), 516–531.

Merrifield, A. (2006). *Henri Lefebvre: A critical introduction*. New York: Routledge.

Morton, E., & de Carteret, D. (2014, July 23). Deadlock end lifts business spirits. *Phnom Penh Post*.

Murray, L. R. (2012). Target Cambodia. *World Policy Journal*, *29*, 79–87.

Naron, H. C. (2003). *Trade liberalisation: A Cambodian perspective* (Asia pacific school of economics and government working papers). Australian national university, 3–8.

Nettl, J. P. (1968). The state as a conceptual variable. *World Politics*, *20*(4), 559–592.

Niazi, N. H. (2011). *Deconcentration and decentralization reforms in Cambodia: Recommendations for an institutional framework*. Philippines: Asian Development Bank.

Network for Sustainable Hydropower Development in the Mekong Countries. (2013, October 8–11). *Regional training workshop for civil society on 'dealing with social aspects.'* Siem Reap, Cambodia.

Paling, W. (2012). Planning a future for Phnom Penh: Mega projects, aid dependence and disjointed governance. *Urban Studies*, *49*(13), 2889–2912.

Pearson, J. (2011). Integrating learning into organizational capacity development of Cambodian NGOs. *Development in Practice*, *21*(8), 1037–1049.

Peck, J., & Tickell, A. (2007). Conceptualizing neoliberalism, thinking Thatcherism. In H. Leitner, J. Peck, & E. S. Sheppard (Eds.), *Contesting neoliberalisms: Urban frontiers* (pp. 26–50). New York: Guilford Press.

People's Tribunal. (2012, February 5–8). *Living wage as a fundamental right of Cambodian garment workers.* – Phnom Penh: Cambodia-Japan Co-Operation Centre.

Roberts, J. (2010). The state, empire and imperialism. *Current Sociology*, *58*(6), 833–858.

Rodrik, D. (2002, May 23–24). *After neoliberalism, what?* Paper presented at the alternatives to neoliberalism conference, sponsored by the new rules for global finance coalition.

Sedara, K., & Öjendal, J. (2009). Decentalization as a strategy for state reconstruction in Cambodia. In J. Öjendal & M. Lilja (Eds), *Beyond democracy in Cambodia: Political reconstruction in a post-conflict society* (pp. 101–135). Copenhagen: NiAs Press.

Sochua, M. (2014, January 13). Another dark day in our history. *Phnom Penh Post*.

Sochua, M., & Wikström, C. (2012, July 18). Land grabs in Cambodia, *International Herald Tribune*. Retrieved from http://www.nytimes.com/2012/07/19/opinion/land-grabs-in-cambodia.html?_r=0

Sovachana, P. (2013, June 26). Cambodia is ingrained with corruption, political patronage. *The Cambodia Daily*. Retrieved from http://www.cambodiadaily.com/opinion/cambodia-is-ingrained-with-corruption-political-patronage-32120/

Springer, S. (2009). Violence, democracy, and the neoliberal "order": The contestation of public space in posttransitional Cambodia. *Annals of the Association of American Geographers*, *99*(1), 138–162.

Springer, S. (2010). *Cambodia's neoliberal order: Violence's, authoritarianism, and the contestation of public space*. Abingdon: Routledge.

Springer, S. (2011). Articulated neoliberalism: The specificity of patronage, kleptocracy, and violence in Cambodia's neoliberalization. *Environment and Planning A*, *43*, 2554–2570.

Su, X. (2012). Rescaling the Chinese state and regionalization in the great Mekong subregion. *Review of International Political Economy*, *19*(3), 501–527.

Tickell, A., & Peck, J. (2003). Making global rules: Globalization or neoliberlization? In J. Peck & H. Wai-chung Yeung (Eds.), *Remaking the global economy* (pp. 163–181). London: Sage.

Titthara, M. (2014, July 15). Nearly 850 protests this year: Police. *Phnom Penh Post*.

Un, K. (2006). State, society and democratic consolidation: The case of Cambodia. *Pacific Affairs*, *79*(2), 225–245.

Un, K. (2013, August 9). The Cambodian people have spoken. *New York Times*.

Un, K., & Hughes, C. (2011). The political economy of good governance. In C. Hughes & K. Un (Eds.), *Cambodia's economic transformation* (pp. 199–218). Copenhagen: NiAS Press.

Un, K., & So, S. (2011). Land rights in Cambodia: How neopatrimonial politics restricts land policy reform. *Pacific Affairs*, *84*(2), 289–308.

Urry, J. (2001). Sociology of space and place. In J. R. Blau (Ed.), *The Blackwell companion to sociology* (pp. 1–16). Malden: Blackwell.

Van Horn, R., & Mirowski, P. (2009). The rise of the Chicago school of economics and the birth of neoliberalism. In P. Mirowski & D. Plehwe (Eds.), *The road from Mont Pelerin: The making of the neoliberal thought collective* (pp. 139–180). Cambridge, MA: Harvard University Press.

Wight, E. (2014, February 28). Free the 23: Meet the global campaigners supporting Cambodia's garment workers. *Phnom Penh Post*.

Wilson, J. (2011). Colonising space: The new economic geography in theory and practice. *New Political Economy 16*(1), 373–397.

Win, T. L. (2013, October 27). Cambodian fury over proposed dam. Al Jazeera. Retrieved from http://www.aljazeera.com/indepth/features/2013/10/cambodian-fury-over-proposed-dam-201310249856459998.html

World Bank. (2011). *Cambodia: More efficient government spending for strong and inclusive growth*. Integrated fiduciary assessment and public expenditure review (IFAPER), poverty reduction and economic management unit East Asia and pacific region (Report No. 61694-KH)

World Bank. (2012). *Matching aspirations: Skills for implementing Cambodia's growth strategy* (Report No. 67349-KH). Phnom Penh, Cambodia.

Index

accumulation: crisis in 8; and illegal (migrant) labour 36–7; primitive and migrant labour 34–5; re-legitimising efforts 8

activism *see* civil society activism

Afghanistan 18

Africa: civil society and working around the state 40; remittances and increased inequality 39–40; Senegal 35–6, 38–9; sub-Saharan Africa 13–14, 32

agriculture: agricultural sector, Asia 10; dominance in emerging economies 10; subsistence agriculture and impact of mining, Laos 62

ASEAN (Association of Southeast Asian Nations): ad hoc consultations with CSOs 95–9; Cambodia's admission to 124, 130; Charter drafting process, 2006 96–7; civil society inclusion 88–9; Committee on the Promotion of the Rights of Women and Children (ACWC) 98; consultations on Rights of Women and Children (informal) 98–9; contentious/non-contentious issues and CSO participation 101–2; CSO affiliation system 89, 94–5, 101; CSO engagement with 93–4; Eminent Persons Group (EPG) 96; GO-NGO forums 99–100, 101; High-Level Task Force (HLTF) 96–7; human rights consultations (informal) 97–8; market-building agenda 89, 102; migrant labour forums 99, 100; and mimetic adoption of participatory agenda for CSOs 91–2; people-orientated, term 97; promotion of people-centred agenda 88–9, 102

Asia: agricultural sector 10; political contestation, declining opportunities for 93; pursuit of

economic competitiveness 73, 82, 89, 93; regionalisation of activism 93; as site for global financial capital 8–9

Asian Development Bank (ADB): capacity, use of term 133–4; on gravitational pull effect, emerging markets 134; marketisation, risks of 11; stance on NGOs, Laos 58; and threats to marketisation 21

autocratic regimes 9

Betsill, M. 90

Brenner, N. 13

Cambodia: capacity building 131–2; capacity building and NGOs 130; capacity building and role of the state 130; civil society resistance 131; IMF's role in 133; land grabbing 135; market economy agenda 124; operationalising capacity 129–31; patron-clientelism 133; as proto-regulatory state 123, 130; regional integration programme (ASEAN membership) 124, 130; reorganisation of geographic and economic spaces 131

Cammack, P. 6, 7, 35, 89

capacity building: Cambodia 129–31; and discursive practices of conceived space 127, 133–4, 135–6; as key term, global financial institutions 133–4; and neoclassical economic ontology 123; overview of 124; as a political and ideological construct 123, 124–5; and regulatory framework, 129; and the regulatory state 125–6; as social product 126; and state capacity 125

capitalism *see* global capitalism

For Product Safety Concerns and Information please contact our EU
representative GPSR@taylorandfrancis.com Taylor & Francis Verlag GmbH,
Kaufingerstraße 24, 80331 München, Germany

Printed and bound by CPI Group (UK) Ltd, Croydon, CR0 4YY
08/05/2025
01864321-0001